RxJS Cookbook for Reactive Programming

Discover 40+ real-world solutions for building async, event-driven web apps

Nikola Mitrović

RxJS Cookbook for Reactive Programming

Portfolio Director: Ashwin Nair
Relationship Lead: Bhavya Rao
Project Manager: Aparna Nair
Content Engineer: Adrija Mitra
Technical Editor: Sweety Pagaria
Copy Editor: Safis Editing
Indexer: Pratik Shirodkar
Production Designer: Jyoti Kadam
Growth Lead: Anamika Singh

First published: March 2025

Production reference: 2301025

Published by Packt Publishing Ltd.
Grosvenor House
11 St Paul's Square
Birmingham
B3 1RB, UK.

ISBN 978-1-78862-405-3

www.packtpub.com

*To my mom for her tireless dedication and sacrifices that paved the way for everything I have today.
Thank you for believing in me and supporting my dreams, even when it meant
putting my needs before your own. There are no words to describe how grateful
I am for your love and everything you have done for me. You are the real MVP.*

- Nikola Mitrović

Foreword

I met Nikola in 2023 during my visit to Belgrade for a conference, where we both shared the stage for the first time. Nikola was talking about browser web APIs and gave an amazing talk. He is a well-known person in the community for sharing knowledge on web technologies and their ecosystem. Nikola is the best person to write this book as he has great knowledge of working on web APIs, Angular, and NestJS.

This is a great guide if you want to get comfortable with reactive concepts using RxJS. The first two chapters cover the real-time usage of various RxJS operators, and then we learn about animation, testing, and how you can improve performance using RxJS.

I really like how the state management topic was covered. NgRx is a widely adopted solution for state management, but it's important to understand how we can do it using RxJS, and the book covers that part really well.

Toward the end, the book covers real-time communication using RxJS, where RxJS really shines. It also demonstrates how to effectively use RxJS with NestJS by building microservices.

Santosh Yadav

Google Developer Expert for Angular | GitHub Star | Nx Champion | Developer Advocate

Contributors

About the author

Nikola Mitrović is a seasoned software engineer and consultant with experience that spans nearly a decade, with technical expertise in micro-frontend architecture and web performance, as well as technologies such as Angular, React, Next.js, Node.js, NestJS, NX, and AWS. He is an enthusiastic public speaker and has presented at some of the world's largest tech conferences, sharing his passion for crafting exceptional web experiences. He has business domain expertise in EdTech, HealthTech, and Digital Identity.

For the last couple of years, Nikola has been in leadership roles, inspiring a culture of technical excellence, continuous learning, collaboration, and psychological safety within the organization. He strongly believes in leading with empathy, honesty, and passion, empowering teams with trust and autonomy.

Prior to this, Nikola was a partner, technical architect, and development lead at Vega IT, where he was recognized as the company's MVP for three consecutive years (2022-2024).

About the reviewers

Aleksandar Makarić is a passionate, self-taught developer with a strong focus on performance optimization and accessibility. Proactive and detail-oriented, he excels in UI/UX, SEO, and refining team processes. Aleksandar believes in the power of knowledge-sharing and values soft skills, which foster team cohesion and productivity. More than just a coder, he thrives as a problem solver, always aiming to create meaningful impact through his work. And when it comes to RxJS, he relishes the challenge of picking the perfect operator—why settle for `throttleTime` when a well-timed `auditTime` could be the secret to optimal throttling in high-frequency streams?

I extend my heartfelt gratitude to my family and colleagues for their unwavering support during my transition to software engineering. Your encouragement has been invaluable. Special thanks to the author of this book, whose work has inspired and guided my growth in both my career and my life. His insights have profoundly shaped my approach to programming – thank you for being a mentor and role model.

Sunil Raj Thota is a seasoned software engineer with extensive experience in web development and AI applications. Currently working in the Amazon QuickSight team, Sunil has previously contributed to significant projects at Yahoo Inc., enhancing user engagement and satisfaction through innovative features at Yahoo and AOL Mail. He has also worked at Northeastern University as a research assistant and at MOURI Tech as a senior software engineer, optimizing multiple websites and leading successful project deployments. Sunil co-founded ISF Technologies, where he has championed user-centric design and agile methodologies. He has also contributed to the books *AI Strategies for Web Development* and *The Art of Micro Frontends*. His academic background includes a master's in analytics from Northeastern University and a bachelor's in electronics and communications engineering from Andhra University.

Learn more on Discord

To join the Discord community for this book – where you can share feedback, ask questions to the author, and learn about new releases – follow the QR code below:

https://packt.link/RxJSCookbook

Table of Contents

Chapter 2: Building User Interfaces with RxJS   35

Chapter 3: Understanding Reactive Animation Systems with RxJS   79

Chapter 5: Performance Optimizations with RxJS   123

Chapter 9: Going Real-Time with RxJS   211

Chapter 10: Building Reactive NestJS Microservices with RxJS   243

Preface

RxJS or **Reactive Extensions for JavaScript** is a JavaScript library designed to simplify working with asynchronous data flows, orchestrating events and sequences of data over time.

However, there is a belief in the community that RxJS has a steep learning curve, despite its amazing capabilities. One reason why RxJS has this reputation is that most tutorials, books, and online materials focus heavily on RxJS operators. These resources explain how each operator works in depth, with accompanying visuals. While these resources are really helpful and essential when starting to learn RxJS, developers may still face challenges such as debugging and optimizing RxJS streams, testing RxJS streams effectively, managing reactive state, fully adopting a reactive paradigm, and identifying the correct RxJS operator for real-world scenarios.

RxJS Cookbook for Reactive Programming takes a slightly different approach. This is a full stack book that emphasizes building modern web applications using RxJS techniques, patterns, and operators that naturally fit specific scenarios. Each chapter is composed of practical recipes that offer solutions to a wide range of challenges, spanning from handling side effects and error resiliency patterns in client apps to creating real-time chat applications and event-driven backend microservices.

As you progress through the book, you will develop a profound understanding of the potential of reactive programming in complex real-life scenarios. This book empowers developers to seamlessly integrate RxJS with popular web development frameworks and libraries such as Angular and NestJS, serving as an invaluable guide for developing web applications that are modern, progressive, resilient, responsive, performant, and interactive.

By the end of the book, you will have mastered the art of reactive programming principles, the RxJS library, and working with Observables, while crafting code that reacts to changes in data and events in a declarative and asynchronous manner.

Who this book is for

This book is ideal for intermediate-to-advanced JavaScript developers who want to adopt reactive programming principles using RxJS. Whether you're working with Angular or NestJS, you'll find recipes and real-world examples that help you leverage RxJS for managing asynchronous operations and reactive data flows across both your frontend and backend.

What this book covers

Chapter 1, Handling Errors and Side Effects in RxJS, equips you with essential techniques to gracefully handle errors and maintain stream integrity, including implementing powerful resiliency patterns such as exponential backoff and circuit breaker, ensuring your application remains responsive and resilient.

You'll also delve into the art of side effect management, learning how to seamlessly perform tasks such as logging, API calls, and DOM updates without disrupting your data flows. Finally, you'll explore the fascinating world of WebSockets as side effects and discover how to implement heartbeat techniques to ensure connection integrity in a truly reactive way.

Chapter 2, Building User Interfaces with RxJS, shows you how to craft components such as reactive audio players, infinite scroll experiences that captivate users, intuitive drag-and-drop interfaces, responsive phone swipe components, and many more.

By harnessing RxJS to handle user input, create event streams, and connect to asynchronous data, you'll unlock the full potential of reactive UI components, enabling you to create seamless user experiences.

Chapter 3, Understanding Reactive Animation Systems with RxJS, teaches you how RxJS can be used to craft dynamic and interactive animations that captivate users.

You will learn how to model animation logic as streams of values, transforming and combining them to achieve fluid, performant animations that run at 60 fps. You'll explore techniques for creating smooth transitions, choreographing complex sequences, and synchronizing animations with other application events. You'll also build engaging animation components, such as a bouncing ball animation, animate loading button state transitions, and recreate the mesmerizing effects of `particles.js`.

Chapter 4, Testing RxJS Applications, guides you through various techniques for testing your reactive code effectively, including a deep dive into using **Mock Service Worker (MSW)** for seamless integration testing and exploring NgRx state unit testing.

You will discover how to handle asynchronous data streams in your tests, master marble testing for complex scenarios to confidently verify complex scenarios and prevent regressions, and learn how to simulate time-based operations with ease. You'll also explore practical examples of using MSW to mock API responses and streamline your integration testing workflow, delve into the intricacies of NgRx state management, and learn how to write effective unit tests for your state management logic. By the end of this chapter, you'll be equipped to create a reliable and maintainable RxJS code base.

Chapter 5, Performance Optimizations with RxJS, delves into managing data flow and strategically using operators to streamline asynchronous operations. You will discover how to choose the right operators to minimize redundant calculations and reduce rendering overhead.

This chapter also explores building a custom performance monitoring system to track Core Web Vitals, gaining valuable insights into an application's performance, and identifying areas for improvement. You will learn how to leverage Web Workers alongside RxJS streams to offload heavy calculations from the browser's main thread, further enhancing performance. You will also discover how to transform performance bottlenecks into optimized, efficient streams.

Chapter 6, Building Reactive State Management Systems with RxJS, explores how RxJS provides a reactive approach to managing application state, promoting predictability, testability, and reactive updates. This foundation will then enable you to build custom reactive state management solutions from scratch.

You will learn how to navigate the complexities of state management in Angular applications using powerful libraries such as NgRx, mastering even the most intricate state interactions.

You will learn about TanStack Query by building your own custom version of it, gaining deep insights into asynchronous state management, and discovering how the async nature of Observables fits perfectly into this paradigm.

Chapter 7, Building Progressive Web Apps with RxJS, explores how RxJS can be leveraged to enhance your Angular apps with key **progressive web app (PWA)** features, including push notifications, background synchronization, and offline capabilities.

You will learn how to use RxJS to manage push notifications effectively, delivering timely and relevant updates to your users. You will implement background synchronization with Dexie.js and RxJS to keep data up to date without interrupting the user's workflow. Finally, you will learn how to leverage RxDB and RxJS to provide a seamless user experience even when the network is unavailable, ensuring your application remains accessible and functional at all times.

Chapter 8, Building Offline-First Applications with RxJS, delves into the crucial world of offline-first applications and demonstrates how RxJS empowers you to achieve seamless offline experiences.

You will gain fine-grained control over offline data synchronization by mastering various strategies, including cache-first, network-first, stale-while-revalidate, and cache-network race, and learn how each strategy impacts user experience and data reliability and choose the best approach for your specific needs.

Beyond basic synchronization, you will explore advanced techniques for handling data updates with the optimistic update pattern. You will also learn how to provide an immediate response to user actions, even before confirming with the server, while ensuring data integrity and a smooth transition when the connection is restored.

Chapter 9, Going Real-Time with RxJS, dives into the world of WebSockets and demonstrates how RxJS empowers you to create seamless real-time features in your Angular and NestJS applications.

You will learn how to use WebSockets to establish persistent client-server connections for bidirectional communication and instant data updates, and explore practical examples such as crafting a real-time dashboard that dynamically tracks and visualizes data updates. Then, you will dive into building smooth gameplay for a multiplayer tic-tac-toe game. Finally, you will craft a chat application with voice messaging capabilities for a truly immersive chat experience.

Chapter 10, Building Reactive NestJS Microservices with RxJS, explores how RxJS can bring reactive programming elegance to building NestJS APIs.

You will learn how to model real-time data flows and build fault-tolerant microservices with RxJS's sophisticated error handling and resiliency patterns. You will expand your toolkit by integrating asynchronous messaging platforms such as Kafka, enabling event-driven architectures and handling high-volume data streams for seamless communication between services.

Finally, you will delve into gRPC, leveraging its efficiency for high-performance remote procedure calls in your microservices architecture.

To get the most out of this book

You should be experienced with JavaScript and web concepts in general. It would be good to have experience with frameworks and libraries such as Angular and NestJS on the server side. It would be an advantage to have strong fundamentals in the asynchronous programming area, functional programming, and reactive programming basics. You will get the most out of this book if you are already familiar with core RxJS concepts such as Observer and Iterator patterns, Observables, Subscriptions, operators, Subjects, and Schedulers.

Software/hardware covered in the book	Operating system requirements
RxJS v7	Windows, macOS, or Linux
Angular v19+	
Node.js v22+	
npm v11+	
pnpm v10+	
NestJS v11+	

In *Chapter 10*, you will need to run a local Kafka server for one of the recipes. You can find detailed information on this in the Kafka documentation `https://kafka.apache.org/quickstart`.

Note

This book does not use Angular's Resource API, as it was still in the experimental phase at the time of publication.

If you are using the digital version of this book, we advise you to type the code yourself or access the code from the book's GitHub repository (a link is available in the next section). Doing so will help you avoid any potential errors related to the copying and pasting of code.

Download the example code files

You can download the example code files for this book from GitHub at `https://github.com/PacktPublishing/RxJS-Cookbook-for-Reactive-Programming/tree/main`. If there's an update to the code, it will be updated in the GitHub repository.

We also have other code bundles from our rich catalog of books and videos available at `https://github.com/PacktPublishing/`. Check them out!

Conventions used

There are a number of text conventions used throughout this book.

`Code in text`: Indicates code words in text, database table names, folder names, filenames, file extensions, pathnames, dummy URLs, user input, and X/Twitter handles. Here is an example: "Notice one more important change from the previous example with `distinctUntilChange`."

A block of code is set as follows:

```
combineLatest({
    searchName: searchNameInputValue$,
    searchIngredient: searchIngredientInputValue$
}
```

Any command-line input or output is written as follows:

```
npm run build && http-server ${build-location} -c-1 -o
```

Bold: Indicates a new term, an important word, or words that you see onscreen. For instance, words in menus or dialog boxes appear in **bold**. Here is an example: "**RxJS marble diagrams** are a powerful tool for visualizing and understanding the behavior of Observables and operators in reactive programming."

Tips or important notes

Appear like this.

Get in touch

Feedback from our readers is always welcome.

General feedback: If you have questions about any aspect of this book, email us at customercare@ packtpub.com and mention the book title in the subject of your message.

Errata: Although we have taken every care to ensure the accuracy of our content, mistakes do happen. If you have found a mistake in this book, we would be grateful if you would report this to us. Please visit www.packtpub.com/support/errata and fill in the form.

Piracy: If you come across any illegal copies of our works in any form on the internet, we would be grateful if you would provide us with the location address or website name. Please contact us at copyright@packt.com with a link to the material.

If you are interested in becoming an author: If there is a topic that you have expertise in and you are interested in either writing or contributing to a book, please visit authors.packtpub.com.

Share your thoughts

Once you've read *RxJS Cookbook for Reactive Programming*, we'd love to hear your thoughts! Scan the QR code below to go straight to the Amazon review page for this book and share your feedback.

https://packt.link/r/178862405X

Your review is important to us and the tech community and will help us make sure we're delivering excellent quality content.

Free Benefits with Your Book

This book comes with free benefits to support your learning. Activate them now for instant access (see the "*How to Unlock*" section for instructions).

Here's a quick overview of what you can instantly unlock with your purchase:

PDF and ePub Copies

Next-Gen Web-Based Reader

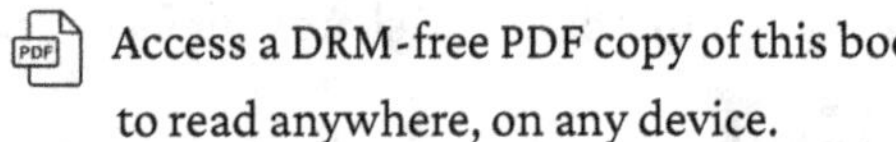 Access a DRM-free PDF copy of this book to read anywhere, on any device.

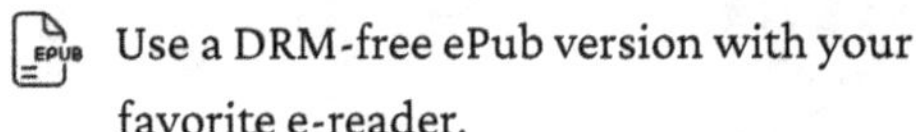 Use a DRM-free ePub version with your favorite e-reader.

Multi-device progress sync: Pick up where you left off, on any device.

Highlighting and notetaking: Capture ideas and turn reading into lasting knowledge.

Bookmarking: Save and revisit key sections whenever you need them.

Dark mode: Reduce eye strain by switching to dark or sepia themes.

How to Unlock

Scan the QR code (or go to packtpub.com/unlock). Search for this book by name, confirm the edition, and then follow the steps on the page.

Note: Keep your invoice handy. Purchases made directly from Packt don't require one.

1

Handling Errors and Side Effects in RxJS

Welcome to the *RxJS Cookbook for Reactive Programming*!

After working with RxJS for a while, and learning all about every operator in RxJS docs, have you ever felt stuck or didn't know how to get your RxJS game to the next level? This book is **Packt(ed)** with advanced recipes and practical use cases to take you to that next level and make you ready for any real-life challenge in the web development world. Buckle up, it's going to be a fun ride!

This chapter explores techniques to manage the inevitable complexities of real-world reactive programming. We'll learn how to gracefully handle errors and maintain stream integrity. We will delve into side effect management to perform tasks such as logging, API calls, and DOM updates without disrupting data flows. Also, we will master strategies to isolate side effects and ensure predictable, testable RxJS code. Finally, we will understand the role of WebSockets as side effects and explore heartbeat techniques to ensure connection integrity in a Reactive way.

In this chapter, we will cover the following recipes:

- Handling DOM updates
- Handling network requests
- Handling network errors
- Debugging RxJS streams
- Understanding HTTP polling
- Handling WebSocket connections

Free Benefits with Your Book

Your purchase includes a free PDF copy of this book along with other exclusive benefits. Check the *Free Benefits with Your Book* section in the Preface to unlock them instantly and maximize your learning experience.

Technical requirements

To follow along in this chapter, you'll need the following:

- Angular v19+
- RxJS v7
- Node.js v22+
- npm v11+ or pnpm v10+

The code for recipes in this chapter is placed in the GitHub repository:

```
https://github.com/PacktPublishing/RxJS-Cookbook-for-Reactive-Programming/tree/
main/Chapter01
```

Handling DOM updates

Due to its declarative and reactive nature, RxJS provides a way to efficiently take care of DOM updates and react to UI updates without directly manipulating DOM elements.

How to do it...

In this example, we will build a small **cooking recipe** app, where we will load a list of recipes from the mocked BE (using MSW) and show them in the list. After that, we will implement two search fields to find desired recipes by name and ingredient. We will do this by handling input updates from both filters in a declarative way, then combining the query results and providing filtered results in the end.

Here's how the app would look in its initial state:

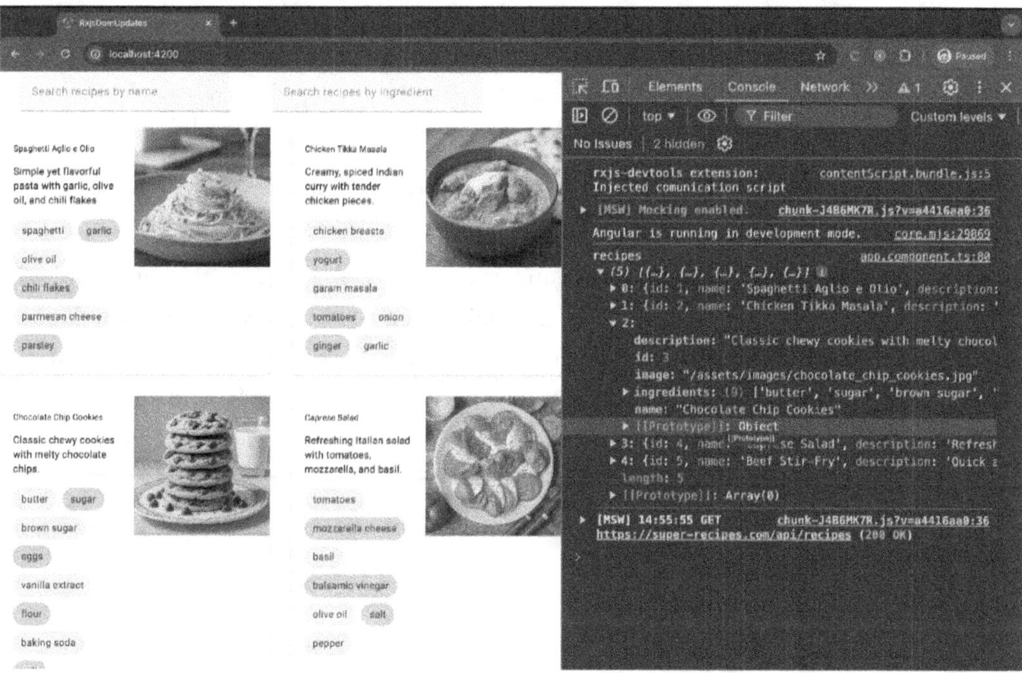

Figure 1.1: Recipe app – initial state

Step 1 – Handling one search input

Let's start easy by implementing search by name filter first. In our Angular component, we will have a `searchNameInput` DOM element reference and a `fromEvent` operator:

```
@ViewChild('searchNameInput')
    searchNameInputElement!: ElementRef;


ngAfterViewInit() {
    fromEvent<InputEvent>(
```

```
        this.searchNameInputElement.nativeElement,'input')
        .pipe(
          map((searchInput: InputEvent) =>
              (searchInput.target as HTMLInputElement)
                  .value),
          startWith(''), debounceTime(500),
          distinctUntilChanged(),
          switchMap((searchName: string) =>
              this.recipesService.searchRecipes$(searchName)))
        .subscribe((recipes) => this.recipes = recipes);
    }
```

Here's a breakdown of what we are doing:

1. With the `map` operator, we will extract the value of the input and state that the starting value should be an empty string with the `startWith` operator.

2. To prevent sending unnecessary requests and increasing load on the server, we will debounce every user keystroke up to 500 milliseconds. Also, we will check whether the search query has changed from the previous one (e.g., if we wanted to search for lasagna, we would type the query "lasag", get the result, and then delete "g" and put "g" back in the query within 500 milliseconds; we won't send another request, because the query hasn't changed).

3. In the end, once we get the search query, we will use `switchMap` to take the query value and send the request to the BE API.

Why switchMap?

The main reason we are using *switchMap* here is the cancellation effect. This is what it means. Assume that a user types a search query, and we have an ongoing request. Now, if the user changes the query to a new one, the previous request will be cancelled automatically, since we are no longer interested in the previous result.

Now, when we type a search query for recipes, we might see the results in the UI:

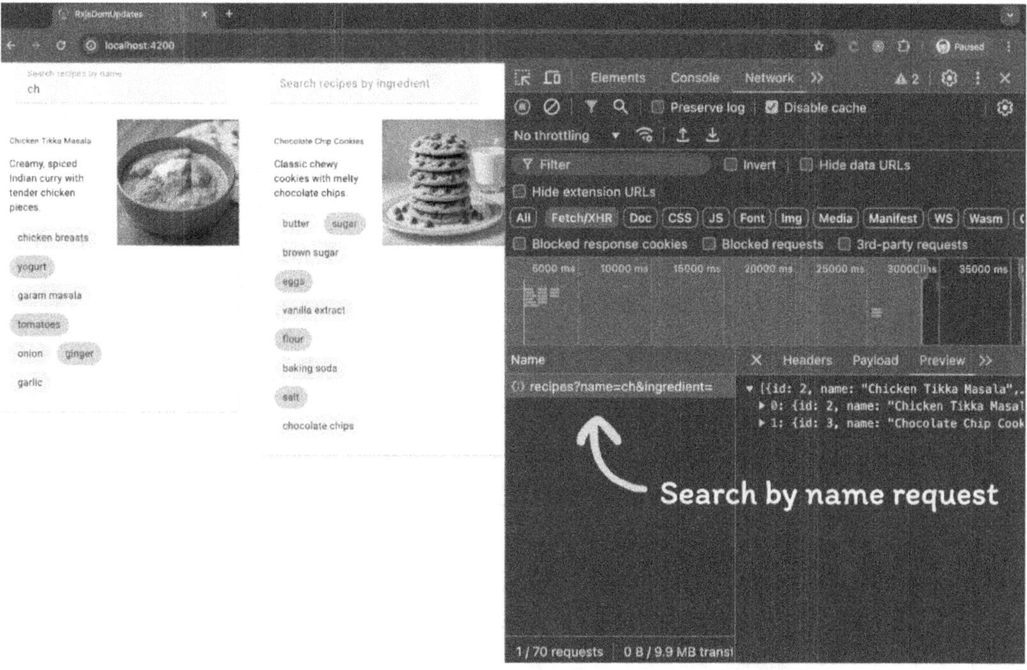

Figure 1.2: Search recipe by name

Step 2 – Handling two search inputs

Now let's add a second search input for ingredients. Again, we will create a stream of search input events from the second input, but this time, we want to combine results with the first input as well. The way we can achieve that is by using the `combineLatest` function that will create a stream of events from multiple sources.

Here the `startWith` operator comes in handy as well, since `combineLatest` won't emit any values until both inputs emit at least once. That would mean that we would see the empty recipes list initially without using `startWith`. This is what our code looks like after adding the second input:

```
const searchNameInputValue$ = fromEvent<InputEvent>(
    this.searchNameInputElement.nativeElement, 'input')
    .pipe(
        map((searchInput: InputEvent) =>
            (searchInput.target as HTMLInputElement) .value),
        startWith('')
```

```
);
const searchIngredientInputValue$ = fromEvent<InputEvent>(
    this.searchIngredientInputElement.nativeElement, 'input')
    .pipe(
        map((searchInput: InputEvent) =>
            (searchInput.target as HTMLInputElement) .value),
        startWith('')
);
combineLatest({
  searchName: searchNameInputValue$,
  searchIngredient: searchIngredientInputValue$
})
.pipe(debounceTime(500),
    distinctUntilChanged(
(prev, curr) => prev.searchName ===
    curr.searchName && prev.searchIngredient ===
        curr.searchIngredient),
    switchMap(({ searchName, searchIngredient }) =>
        this.recipesService.searchRecipes$(
            searchName, searchIngredient)))
.subscribe((recipes) => this.recipes = recipes);
```

Notice one more important change from the previous example with `distinctUntilChange`. One of the most common mistakes when using operator is assuming it does figure out on its own when the stream has changed, but that only works for primitive values coming out of a stream as a result. Previously, we emitted string values from the first search input, but now since we are combining the results of two search inputs, we have a stream of object values. Therefore, we must do a deep check on previous and current object properties, in our case, `searchName` and `searchIngredient`. Alternatively, we could use the `distinctUntilKeyChanged` operator.

If we open our app in the browser, now we can search recipes not only by name but also by ingredient:

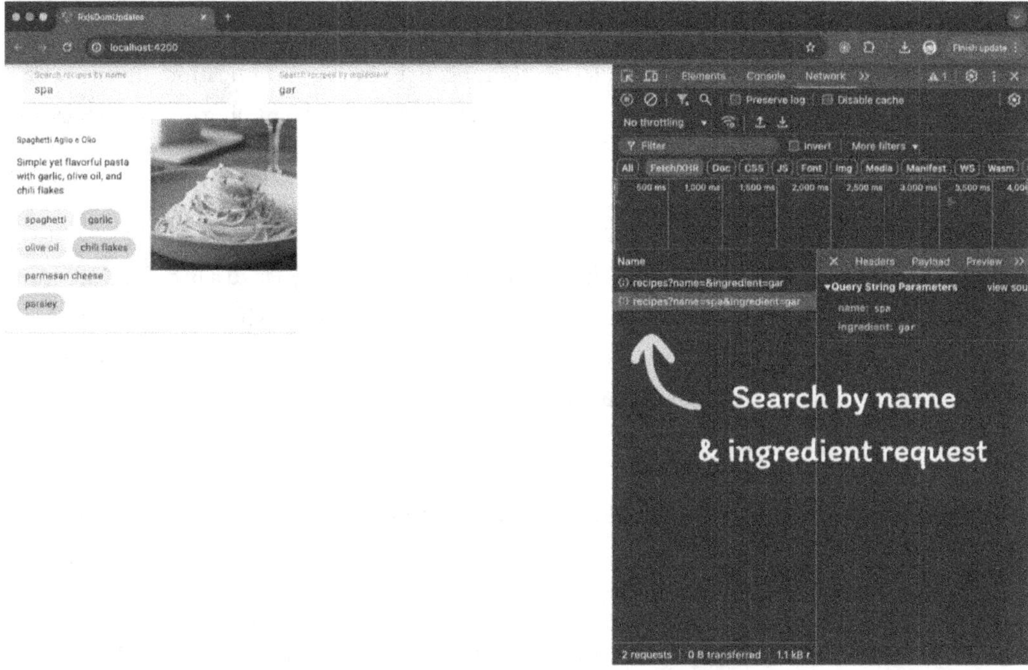

Figure 1.3: Search recipe by name and ingredient

See also

- MSW: `https://mswjs.io/`
- `fromEvent` operator: `https://rxjs.dev/api/index/function/fromEvent`
- `map`: `https://rxjs.dev/api/operators/map`
- `startWith` operator: `https://rxjs.dev/api/operators/startWith`
- `switchMap`: `https://rxjs.dev/api/operators/switchMap`
- `combineLatest` function: `https://rxjs.dev/api/index/function/combineLatest`
- `distinctUntilKeyChanged` operator: `https://rxjs.dev/api/operators/distinctUntilKeyChanged`

Handling network requests

The area where RxJS really excels is in handling side-effects. Given that an **Observable** is a stream of values that arrive over time, this implies asynchronicity. That makes RxJS a perfect fit for managing async state and data flows, such as complex network communication. In this recipe, we're going to explore the most advanced and sophisticated ways of handling different network request scenarios.

How to do it...

In this example, we will build a small cooking recipe app, where we will load a list of recipes from the mocked BE (using MSW) and show them in the list. Then after clicking on a specific recipe, we will show that recipe on a new page with more details, which will require another layer of communication with the BE to fetch those details.

Step 1 – Handling requests in sequence

Let's say we have two different endpoints. One that holds information about the recipe, and the other one only contains details for a recipe with the same ID. This is how the async data flow would look:

1. We would send the request to the `https://super-recipes.com/api/recipes?id=1` endpoint, which would return basic information about the recipe.

2. Then we would take the id of a specific recipe from the response and send a new sequential request to the `https://super-recipes.com/api/recipes/details?id=1` endpoint:

    ```
    getRecipeById$(id: number): Observable<Recipe> {
        return this.httpClient.get<Recipe>(
            `/api/recipes?id=${id}`
        );
    }


    getRecipeDetails$(
        id: number
    ): Observable<{
        recipe: Recipe,
        details: RecipeDetails
    }> {
        return this.getRecipeById$(id).pipe(
    ```

```
        switchMap((recipe: Recipe) => {
            return this.httpClient
            .get<RecipeDetails>(
                `/api/recipes/details?id=${id}`
            )
            .pipe(map((details) => ({
                recipe,
                details
            })
        ));
    })
    );
}
```

3. In the end, we will use the map operator to combine the results from both endpoints, since we're going to need all that information in our details component.

If we click on one of the recipes, that will navigate us to the `RecipeDetails` page, with some specific nutrient info for each recipe:

Figure 1.4: Recipe Details page with nutrition info

Step 2 — Handling requests in parallel

Imagine that we have a high resolution, size-heavy images for our recipes. We want to reduce initial response payload size and offload that initial load for the `RecipeListComponent`. To improve the performance of the app, we have separated loading of images to a different endpoint, so initially, we show the recipe list data from one endpoint. After that, we send multiple requests in parallel to fetch all corresponding images. In our example, first we send a request to the `https://super-recipes.com/api/recipes` endpoint to fetch the list of cooking recipes. In the response, we will have the list of all recipe ids, based on which we can send parallel request to the `https://super-recipes.com/api/recipes/images` endpoint. In the meantime, we will have a loading indicator for each image.

Also, we will leverage the power of the `forkJoin` operator to send image requests in parallel:

```
getRecipesWithImageInParallel$(): Observable<ImageUrl[]> {
    return this.getRecipes$().pipe(
        tap((recipes: Recipe[]) =>
            this.recipes.next(recipes)),
        switchMap((recipes: Recipe[]) => {
            const imageRequests = recipes.map((recipe) =>
                this.httpClient.get<ImageUrl>(
                    `/api/recipes/images?id=${recipe.id}`
                )
            );


        return forkJoin(imageRequests);
        }),
    );
}
```

Now when we open our recipe in the browser, we can see placeholders instead of images, and in the **Network** tab, we can see images being downloaded in parallel:

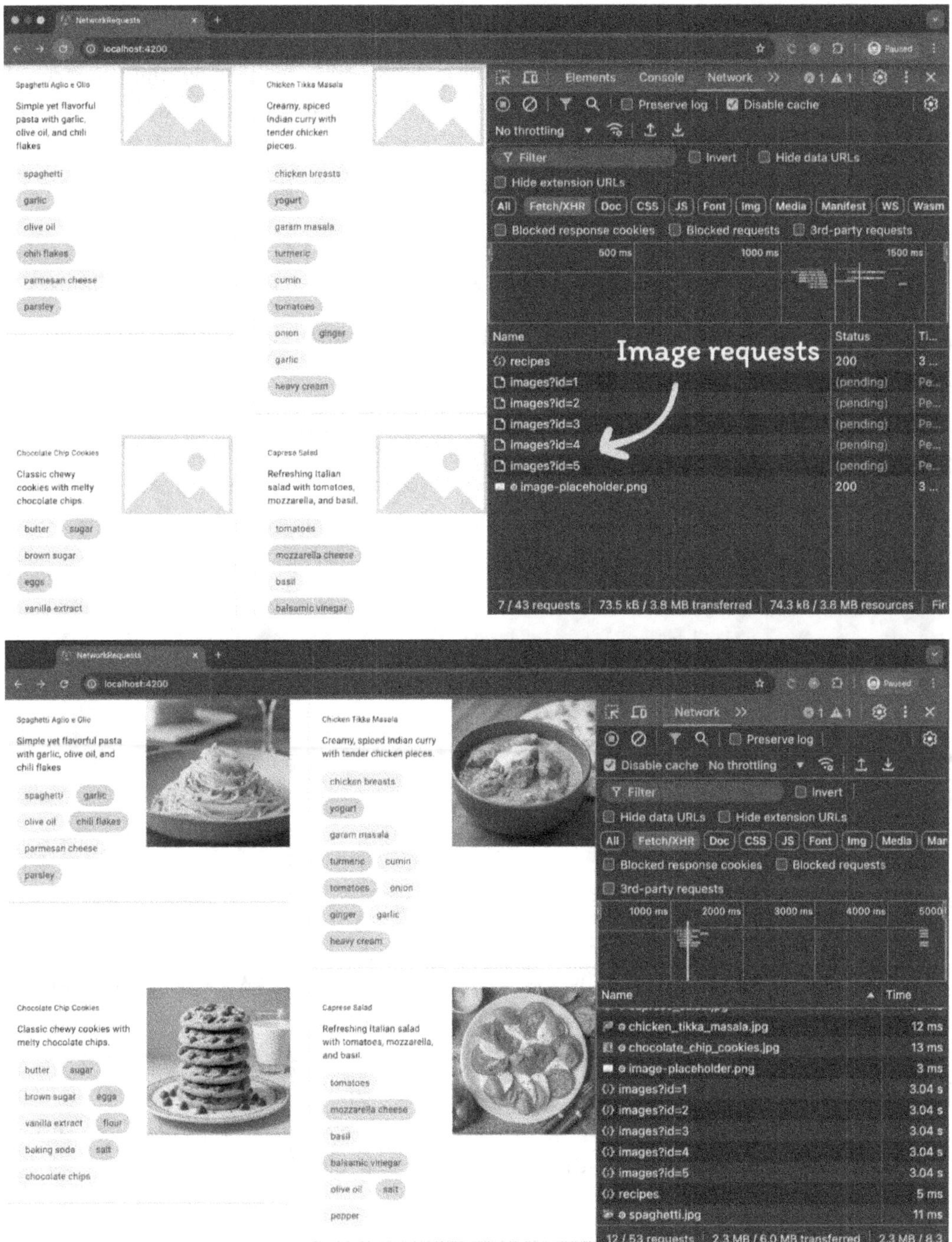

Figure 1.5: Recipe images before (first) and after (second)

Step 3 – Handling concurrent requests

In our example so far, we have been sending multiple requests in parallel, but the drawback of that approach is that we must wait for all image requests to be completed before we show results. Since our images can be a few MBs in size and can overwhelm the server, we can additionally improve the performance of our recipe app by batching image requests concurrently:

1. First, we can load images for the first three recipes.

2. Then, after we get a response for those, we can send request for the remaining images.

The way we can achieve this effect is by using the **RxJS mergeMap concurrent** mode:

```
public recipes = new BehaviorSubject<Recipe[]>([]);


getRecipesWithConcurrentImage$(): Observable<ImageUrl> {
    return this.getRecipes$().pipe(
        tap((recipes: Recipe[]) => this.recipes.next(recipes)),
        switchMap((recipes: Recipe[]) => {
            const imageIds = recipes.map(
                (recipe) => recipe.id);


            return from(imageIds).pipe(
                mergeMap((id) =>  this.httpClient.get(
                    `/api/recipes/images?id=${id}`), 3
            );
        })
    );
}
```

By extracting ids of all images from the first request, we can create a new inner Observable from that array of IDs and send concurrent requests with `mergeMap`. Note the second parameter of `mergeMap`: that parameter will help us to fine-tune how many concurrent requests can go at the same time. By doing so, we can rate-limit the number of requests and prevent our server from having an overwhelming number of ongoing requests. This means that we will load the list of images three by three, which is something we can observe in our Dev Tools.

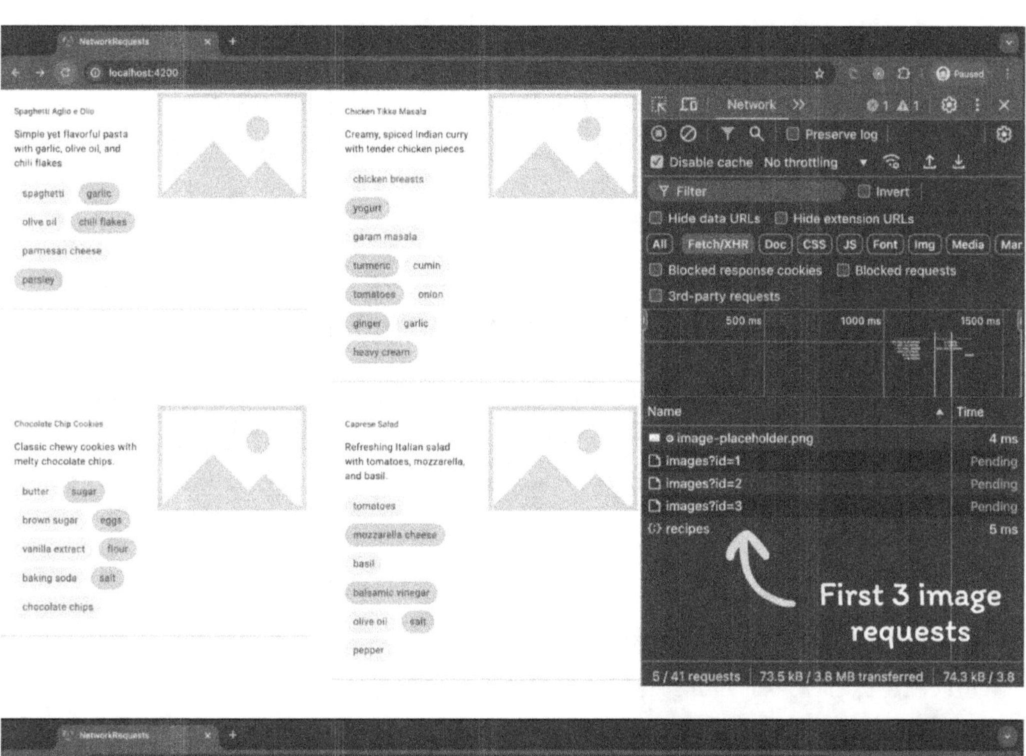

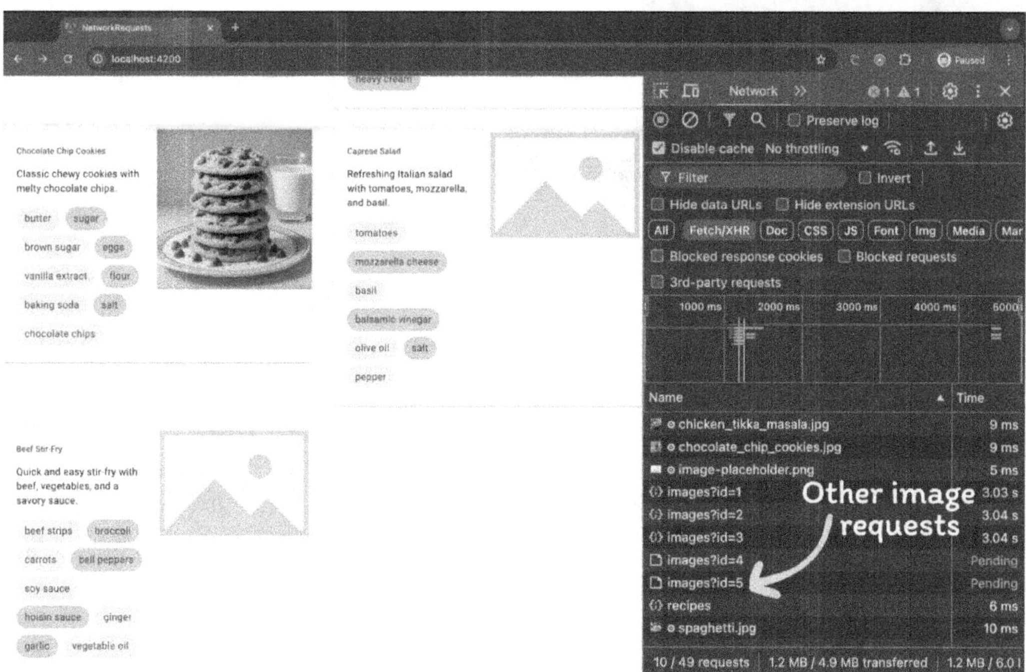

Figure 1.6: Concurrent image requests

See also

- `forkJoin` operator: https://rxjs.dev/api/index/function/forkJoin

- `mergeMap` operator: https://rxjs.dev/api/operators/mergeMap

Handling network errors

So far, we have handled the happy path of dealing with network requests. However, what if things don't go so smoothly? We still need to build robust and resilient apps, which will react to those special events (or to exceptions).

How to do it...

In this example, we are going to discover sophisticated resiliency patterns and learn how to deal with network errors.

Step 1 – Catching errors

The simplest way to react to network error is just to use the catchError operator from RxJS:

```
getRecipes$(): Observable<Recipe[]> {
    return this.httpClient.get<Recipe[]>(
        'https://super-recipes.com/api/recipes'
    ).pipe(
        catchError((error) => {
            this._snackBar.open(
                'Recipes could not be fetched.',
                'Close'
            );
            return EMPTY;
        })
    );
}
```

The strategy here is pretty simple. If there is a request error, catch the error, display a notification in the UI, and gracefully complete the stream. We might also want in some instances to re-throw the error, if we need it later in the stream chain:

```
throwError(() => new Error('Recipes could not be fetched.'))
```

In our browser, we can open Dev Tools, disable network request and see this behavior in action, alongside an error notification when requests fail:

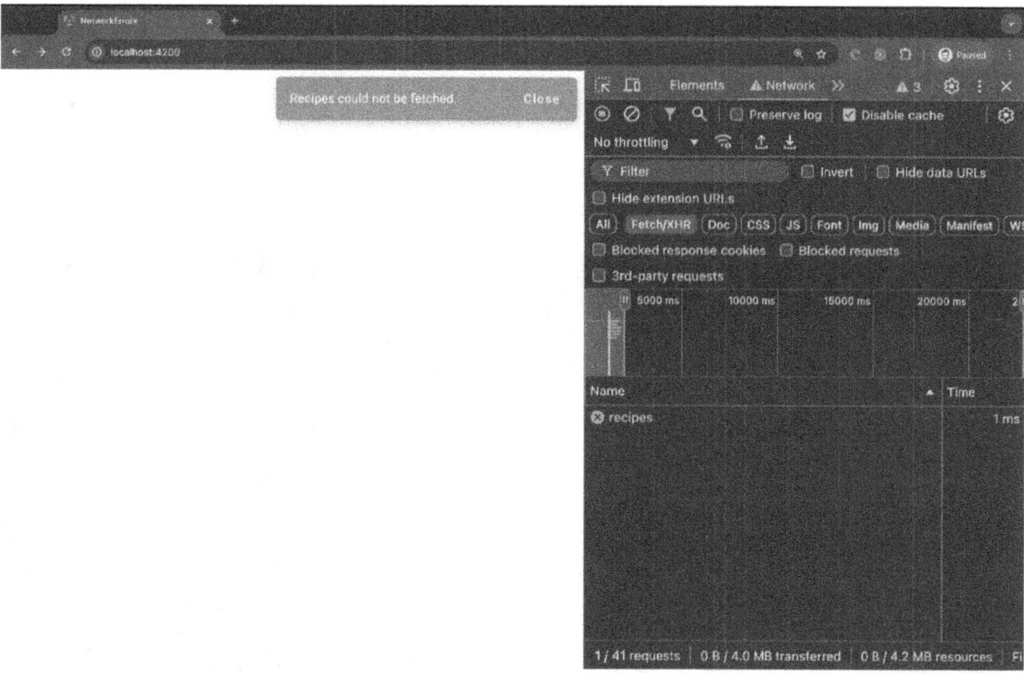

Figure 1.7: Error notification

Step 2 – Using the retry pattern

However, what if there was a just slight hiccup at the server, so this error was a one-time thing? After we close the error notification this way, there is no way to know whether everything is okay a few seconds later but to refresh the page and start over. That's why we need the retry strategy. The way we can achieve that is with the RxJS retry operator.

If we just pass a number as a parameter, this indicates the number of retries that would happen immediately one after the other.

The way we can apply this operator is by chaining it after the catchError operator:

```
getRecipes$(): Observable<Recipe[]> {
    return this.httpClient.get<Recipe[]>('/api/recipes')
    .pipe(
        catchError((error) => {
            this._snackBar.open(
```

```
            'Recipes could not be fetched.', 'Close');
        return throwError(() => new Error(
            'Recipes could not be fetched.'));
    }),
    retry(3)
  );
}
```

Implementing the `retry` pattern would lead to the following:

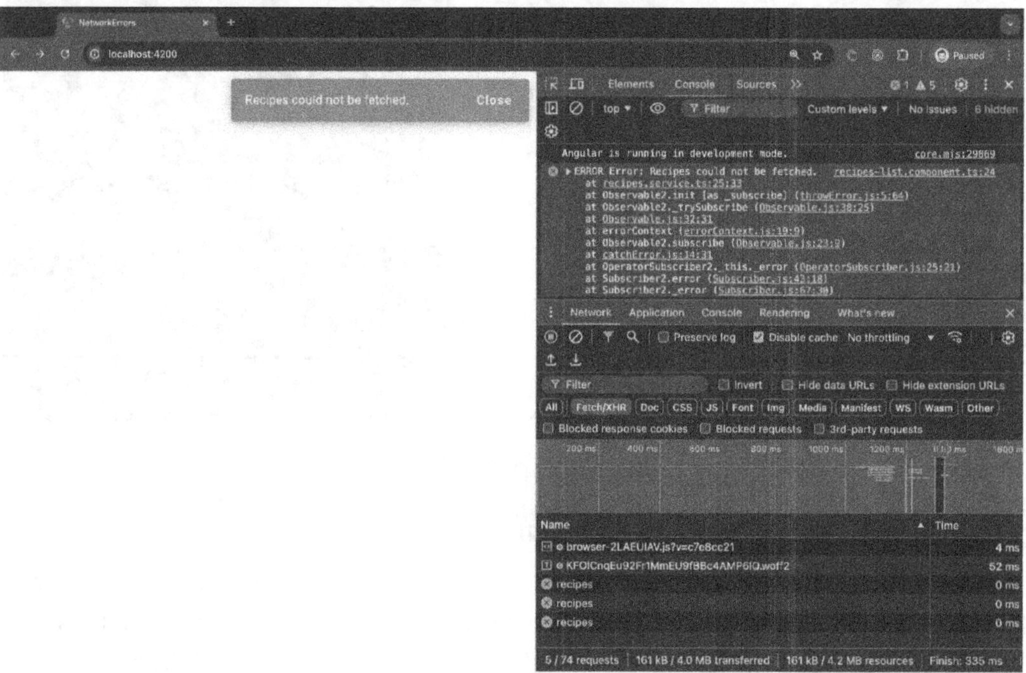

Figure 1.8: Error with number of retries

However, ideally, we would like to leave some time in between two retry attempts for our server to recover. That leads us to the next pattern.

Step 3 — Using the exponential back off pattern

This is a retry pattern whereby we gradually increase the delay between retry attempts, until either we get a successful response, or give up eventually and conclude that the system has an issue at the moment:

```
  getRecipesWithBackoffStrategy$(): Observable<Recipe[]> {
return this.httpClient.get<Recipe[]>('/api/recipes')
.pipe(
    catchError((error) => {
        this._snackBar.open(
            'Recipes could not be fetched.',
            'Close'
        );
        return throwError(() => new Error(error));
    }),
    retry({
        count: 3,
        delay: (error, retryCount) => {
        return timer(Math.pow(2, retryCount) * 1000);
        },
    }),
);
}
```

To implement this pattern, we will introduce a delay as part of the retry configuration. It's a callback function that has error and retryCount parameters. With the help of RxJS timer function, we will emit a new notification for a delay, exponentially increasing the time in between two retry attempts. As a result, we will end up with four failed requests in the Network Dev Tools (one original, and three retried requests).

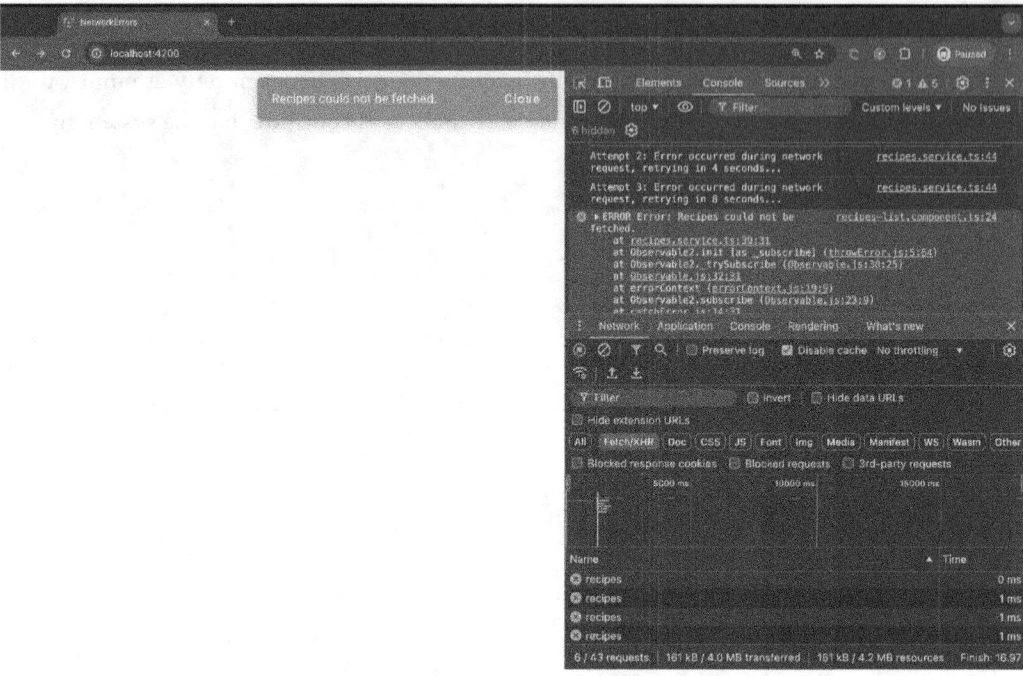

Figure 1.9: Exponential back off strategy

Step 4 – Using the circuit breaker pattern

Imagine an electrical circuit breaker in your home. If there's a power surge or overload, the circuit breaker trips, cutting off the power to protect your appliances and prevent further damage. The **circuit breaker pattern** in software works similarly.

If we experience several cascading errors in the system, we will open the circuit. In this OPEN state, we will immediately reject any new request to the server for a certain period. After that period, we enter the HALF_OPEN state, where we allow several test requests to check whether the system has recovered in the meantime. If the system has recovered and the request is successful, we close the circuit. Otherwise, we open it again for a certain period.

First, let's have methods to represent these states and transitions to these states:

```
private state: 'CLOSED' | 'OPEN' | 'HALF_OPEN' = 'CLOSED';


private openCircuit() {
    if (this.state === 'OPEN') return;
    this.state = 'OPEN';
    timer(15000)
```

```typescript
      .subscribe(() => this.halfOpenCircuit());
  }

  private halfOpenCircuit() {
    this.state = 'HALF_OPEN';
  }

  private closeCircuit() {
    this.state = 'CLOSED';
  }
```

Now we are ready to react to these states in case of network failures. In our `recipe.service.ts`, we will start off by checking whether we should throw an error if we are in the OPEN state:

```typescript
sendRequestIfCircuitNotOpen() {
    if (this.state === 'OPEN') {
        console.error('Circuit is open, aborting request');
        return throwError(() =>
            new Error('Circuit is open'));
    }
    return this.httpClient.get<Recipe[]>('/api/recipes');
}
getRecipesWithCircuitBreakerStrategy$():
    Observable<Recipe[]> {
        return defer(() =>
            this.sendRequestIfCircuitNotOpen());
    }
```

Here's a breakdown of what we've done:

1. First, with the help of the `defer` function, we defer the execution of the request until we figure out the current state of circuit.
2. We check whether the state of circuit is OPEN:

   - If it is, we immediately throw an error and set up a timer for 15 seconds to enter the HALF_OPEN state, so we can try again after that period
   - If not, we will allow at least one request

Now let's check what we have in our pipe operator sequence:

```typescript
getRecipesWithCircuitBreakerStrategy$():
    Observable<Recipe[]> {
        return defer(() =>
            this.sendRequestIfCircuitNotOpen()
        ).pipe(
            catchError((error) => {this._snackBar.open(
                'Recipes could not be fetched.', 'Close');
            return throwError(() => new Error(
                'Recipes could not be fetched.'));
        }),
        retry({
            count: this.state === 'HALF_OPEN' ? 1 : 3,
            delay: (error, retryCount) => {
                if( this.state === 'HALF_OPEN' ||
                    retryCount === 3)
                {
                    this.openCircuit();
                    return throwError(() =>
                        new Error('Circuit is open'));
                }

                return timer(2000);
            },
        }),
    );
}
```

As part of the retry mechanism, here, we can notice that based on a circuit state, we control the number of retries to be one or three. Also, if the current state was HALF_OPEN and we failed again, or initially when we exceed three retries, we enter the OPEN state and throw an error. We enter the retry block every two seconds to check whether there were any changes until the system eventually recovers or we give up and show the error notification.

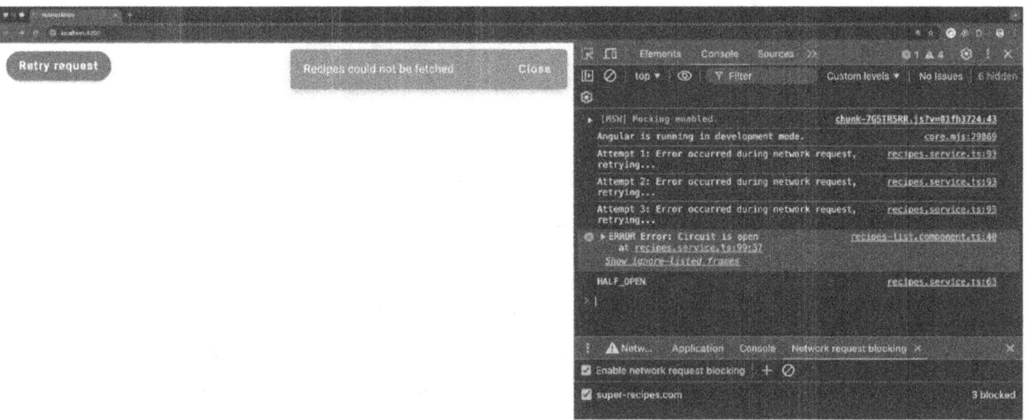

Figure 1.10: Circuit breaker pattern

Once we enter HALF_OPEN state, we can play around in our browser by blocking network request and verify circuit behavior in action.

At the end, if the response was successful, we would simply close the circuit by calling the closeCircuit method and show the recipes list.

There's more...

- **Exponential back off pattern**: The benefit of this approach is that we reduce the load to the server during error cases and give the whole system time to recover in between. It also improves the success rate by allowing transient errors to resolve quickly.

- **Circuit breaker pattern**: The benefit of this approach might be improving system responsiveness. Since we know that there are services unavailable, we will fail fast and let users know about it. Also, it can help us with self-healing and monitoring of the system resiliency. The logic when we enter OPEN and HALF_OPEN states might defer from use case to use case or based on personal preference. We might keep track of the number of success and error requests, and based on a success rate, let the circuit go into an OPEN state or not.

- **Fallback strategy**: One more thing to keep in mind here is the fallback strategy, or what should happen when requests are rejected. Should we return cached data, default values, or something else? It's totally up to you to decide what fits your needs best.

See also

- `catchError` operator: https://rxjs.dev/api/operators/catchError
- `retry` operator: https://rxjs.dev/api/operators/retry
- `timer` function: https://rxjs.dev/api/index/function/timer
- `defer` function: https://rxjs.dev/api/index/function/defer
- *How to implement retry logic like a Pro* article: https://dev.to/officialanurag/javascript-secrets-how-to-implement-retry-logic-like-a-pro-g57
- *How to implement an exponential backoff retry strategy in Javascript* article: https://advancedweb.hu/how-to-implement-an-exponential-backoff-retry-strategy-in-javascript/

Debugging RxJS streams

There are a lot of great tools to debug RxJS streams that can really help us be productive, reproduce issues that may occur, and identify bugs easily. However, what if we don't need to go through the setup of those tools and can rather have a simple network traffic log to observe what is going on in the network?

How to do it...

In this recipe, we will implement a simple network logger to observe the ongoing network traffic in the browser console. For that purpose, we will leverage Angular interceptors. Also, after each error, we will send the error information to our custom analytics endpoint, to increase our system Observability and Error Tracking.

Step 1 – Logging successful responses

In our `network-logger.interceptor.ts`, we will start intercepting ongoing network requests:

```
export const networkLogger: HttpInterceptorFn = (
                            req, next) => {
  const started = Date.now();
  const httpClient = inject(HttpClient);
  const errorSubject = new Subject<HttpErrorResponse>();

  function logSuccessfulResponse(event: any) {
    if (event instanceof HttpResponse) {
      const elapsed = Date.now() - started;
```

```
            console.log(
        `Request took %c${elapsed} ms`, 'color: #ffc26e');
            console.log('%cResponse:', 'color: #d30b8e',
                        event);
        }
    }

    return next(req).pipe(
        tap(() => console.log(
            '------------------'
            `\nRequest for ${req.urlWithParams} started...`
        )
    ),
    tap((event) => logSuccessfulResponse(event)),
    finalize(() => console.log('------------------'))
    );
};
```

Here's a breakdown of what we are doing:

1. First, we log when each request has started.

2. Then, after we get the response, in the `logSuccessfulResponse` function, we display how long the request took alongside the response itself.

Step 2 – Logging network errors

In case of network error, we can use the catchError operator to handle network errors and log the time elapsed and cause of an error:

```
function logFailedResponse(error: HttpErrorResponse):
    Observable<never> {
        const elapsed = Date.now() - started;
        console.log(`Request for ${
            req.urlWithParams} failed after %c${elapsed}
            ms`,'color: #ffc26e'
        );
    console.log('%cError:', 'color: #d30b8e', error);
    errorSubject.next(error);
    throw error;
}
```

```
return next(req).pipe(
    tap(() =>
        console.log(
            ' ------------------ ',
                `\nRequest for ${req.urlWithParams} started...`
        )
    ),
    tap((event) => logSuccessfulResponse(event)),
    catchError((error) => logFailedResponse(error)),
    finalize(() => console.log(' ------------------ '))
);
```

Also, we might notice that whenever an error happens, we are sending that error to `errorSubject`. Now, whenever a new error has been emitted to the **Subject**, we may notify our analytics service and have our own custom error reporting mechanism within our system:

```
errorSubject
    .pipe(
        concatMap((error: HttpErrorResponse) =>
            httpClient.post('/api/analytics', error)
        )
).subscribe();
```

Now, when we open our browser console, we can observe network traffic and improve the debugging experience. Also, note how in the case of an error, we would get one Error Response from an endpoint, and one Successful Response from our analytics endpoint.

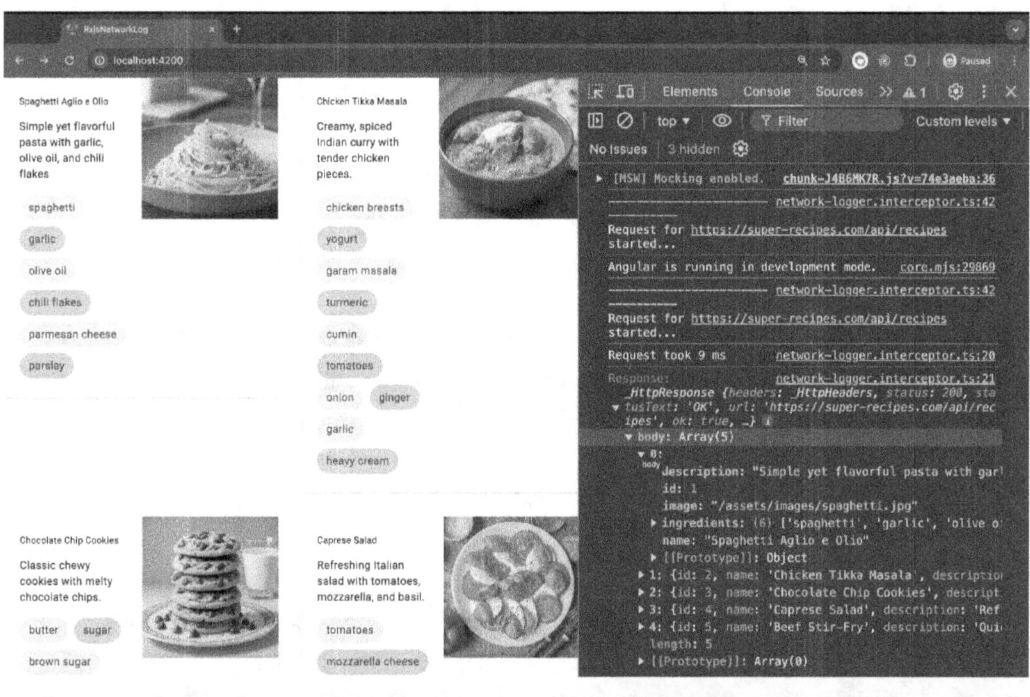

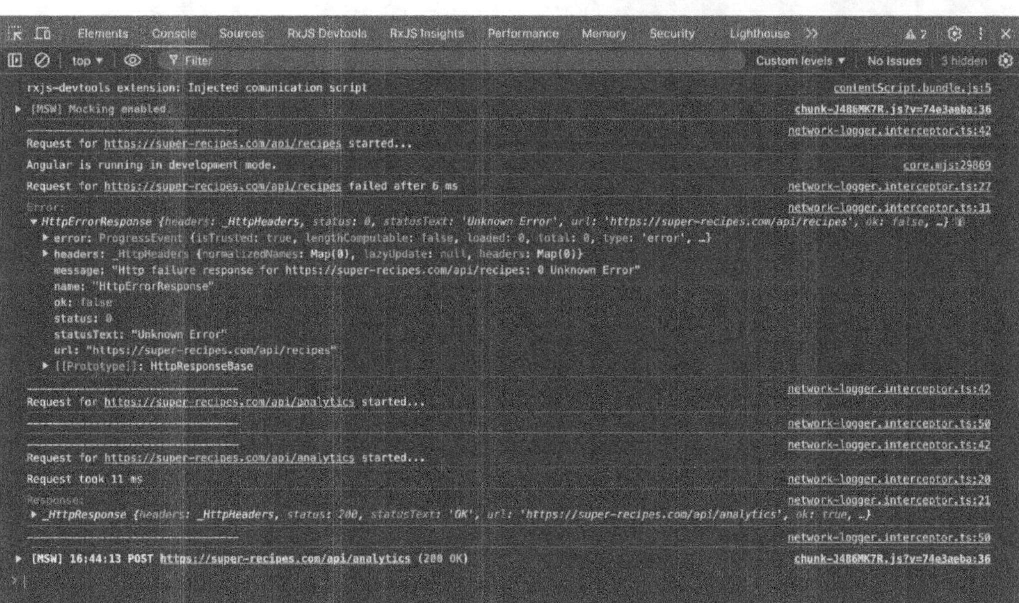

Figure 1.11: Console logger service

Understanding HTTP polling

HTTP polling is one of the most common techniques to keep your data fresh by fetching the data in regular intervals. By doing so, we can get real time updates from a server, monitor the progress of a long-running tasks, or check for frequent data changes. This is a way to simulate a real-time connection with a server over HTTP, which is a stateless protocol.

How to do it...

In this recipe, we are going to explore a reactive approach to the standard HTTP polling, as well as long polling by building a small cooking recipe app. First, we will load a list of recipes from the mocked BE (using MSW) and show them in the list. Then, we will implement a polling mechanism to check continuously whether there are new recipe data to refresh the list with new data.

Step 1 – Standard HTTP polling

In our `http-polling.service.ts`, based on a configurable interval, we set the `timer` for that interval. After each of these intervals, we will send a new request to get the latest data:

```
private stopPolling$ = new Subject<void>();

startPolling<T>(url: string, interval: number = 5000):
    Observable<T> {return timer(0, interval).pipe(
        switchMap(() => this.httpClient.get<T>(url)),
        takeUntil(this.stopPolling$),
        shareReplay({ bufferSize: 1, refCount: true })
    );
}
```

If we open our console in the browser, we can observe network request being sent every five seconds:

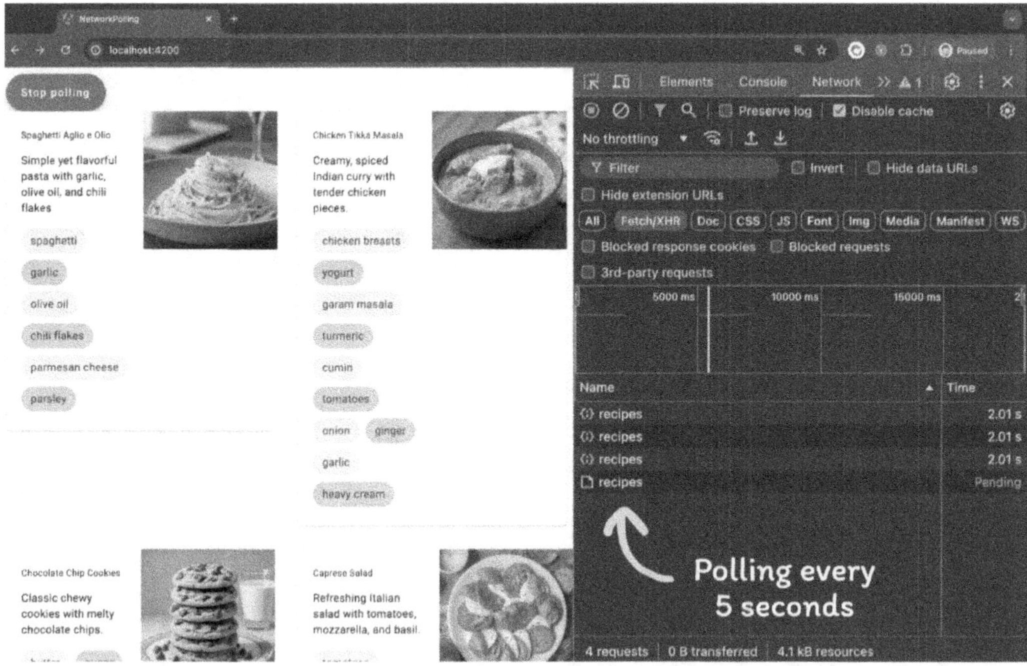

Figure 1.12: HTTP Polling

Step 2 – Long HTTP polling

Long polling is a bit different from standard polling. Instead of sending a request after an interval, which can be wasted bandwidth if the data hasn't changed, the client sends a request and the server holds the connection open until new data becomes available or a timeout occurs:

```
startLongPolling<T>(
    url: string,
    interval: number = 5000
): Observable<T> {
    return timer(0, interval).pipe(
        switchMap(() => this.httpClient.get<T>(url)
        .pipe(timeout(interval))
    ),
    retry({
        count: 3,
```

```
        delay: (error, retryCount) => {
            console.log(
                `Attempt ${retryCount}:
                Error occurred during polling,retrying...`
            );
        this._snackBar.open(
            'Retrying to establish connection...', 'Close'
        );
        return timer(interval);
        },
    }),
    catchError(error => {
        console.error('Long polling error:', error);
        this._snackBar.open(error.message, 'Close');
        return throwError(() => new Error(error));
    }),
    takeUntil(this.stopPolling$),
    shareReplay({ bufferSize: 1, refCount: true }),
    );
}
```

Compared to the standard polling example, note here that we added a timer at the end of our request:

```
switchMap(() => this.httpClient.get<T>(url).pipe(
    timeout(interval),
)),
```

This means that if we establish connection with the server, and the response doesn't arrive before that interval, the request will time out, and then we will go into the retry mechanism.

If we open our browser console, we may observe this behavior in action. If the response hasn't arrived within a defined `interval` (in our case, five seconds), we will retry the same request three times, until we eventually throw an error.

Figure 1.13: HTTP Long Polling retry

How to play around with polling recipes

In the `mocks/handlers.ts` file, there is a `delay` function from MSW that delays the HTTP response for a certain amount of time, so we can play around with this delay. If we set the delay to be under five seconds, in our example, we will see the list of recipes being refreshed every five seconds. If we set the delay to over five seconds, we can simulate slow network responses from BE services and see how our app would behave in the case of the error retry mechanism.

See also

- `interval` function: https://rxjs.dev/api/index/function/interval
- `timeout` operator: https://rxjs.dev/api/operators/timeout
- `retry` operator: https://rxjs.dev/api/operators/retry
- `delay` operator: https://rxjs.dev/api/operators/delay

Handling WebSocket connections

WebSocket is a communication protocol that provides us with real-time communication with client and server. The difference between WebSocket and HTTP is that the former is a two-way communication, where both sides can continuously send data, which is perfect for real-time applications such as chat apps, multiplayer gives, live notifications, IoT apps, and so on.

RxJS provides us with a `webSocket` factory function, a wrapper around the **W3C-compatible** WebSocket object provided by the browser.

How to do it...

In this recipe, we are going to explore a reactive approach for handling real-time updates over WebSocket by building a small cooking recipe app. We will load a list of recipes from the mocked BE (using MSW) over a WebSocket connection and show them in the list. Also, we will automatically update the list over WebSocket if there is a new data entry. Additionally, we will implement a heartbeat mechanism, which is essential when we lose connection with WebSocket.

Step 1 – Connecting to the socket

In our `recipe-list.component.ts`, we call the `connect` method to establish the connection to the WebSocket:

```
export class RecipesListComponent {
    constructor(private recipesService: RecipesService) {}
    ngOnInit() {
        this.recipesService.connect();
    }
    ngOnDestroy() {
        this.recipesService.close();
    }
}
```

In our `recipes.service.ts`, we can see the implementation behind the connect method:

```typescript
import {
    webSocket, WebSocketSubject } from 'rxjs/webSocket';

export interface Message<T> {
    type: string;
    payload?: T;
}


export class RecipesService {
    private socket$!: WebSocketSubject<Message<any>>;
    connect() {
        if (!this.socket$ || this.socket$.closed) {
            this.socket$ = webSocket<Message<any>>({
                url: 'wss://recipes.example.com',
                deserializer: (e) =>
                    JSON.parse(e.data) as Message,
            });
            this.recipes$ = this.socket$.multiplex(
                () => ({ subscribe: 'recipes' }),
                // Subscription message
                () => ({ unsubscribe: 'recipes' }),
                // Unsubscription message
                (message) => message.type === 'recipes'
                // Filter function
            );
        }
    }
    close() {
        this.socket$.complete();
    }
}
```

After successfully connecting to the socket and gaining the ability to parse the messages that come over the TCP connection, we can subscribe to the specific channel of topic, which in WebSocket terms is called **multiplexing**. This is often done for efficiency, to reduce the overhead of establishing and maintaining multiple connections, or when constraints limit the number of possible connections. In our case, we are interested in the list of recipes, so we will subscribe to that channel.

The way we can communicate over a WebSocket connection between client and a server is by implementing the `sendMessage` method:

```
sendMessage(message: Message) {
    this.socket$.next(message);
}
```

Now, back in our component, we can send a message with a `"recipe"` type, which will fetch us the list of recipes:

```
this.recipesService.sendMessage({ type: 'recipes' });
this.recipesSubscription = this.recipesService.recipes$.subscribe(
    (message: Message) => this.recipes = message.payload);
```

In our browser, when we open the console, we may observe the incoming messages from the Websocket connection:

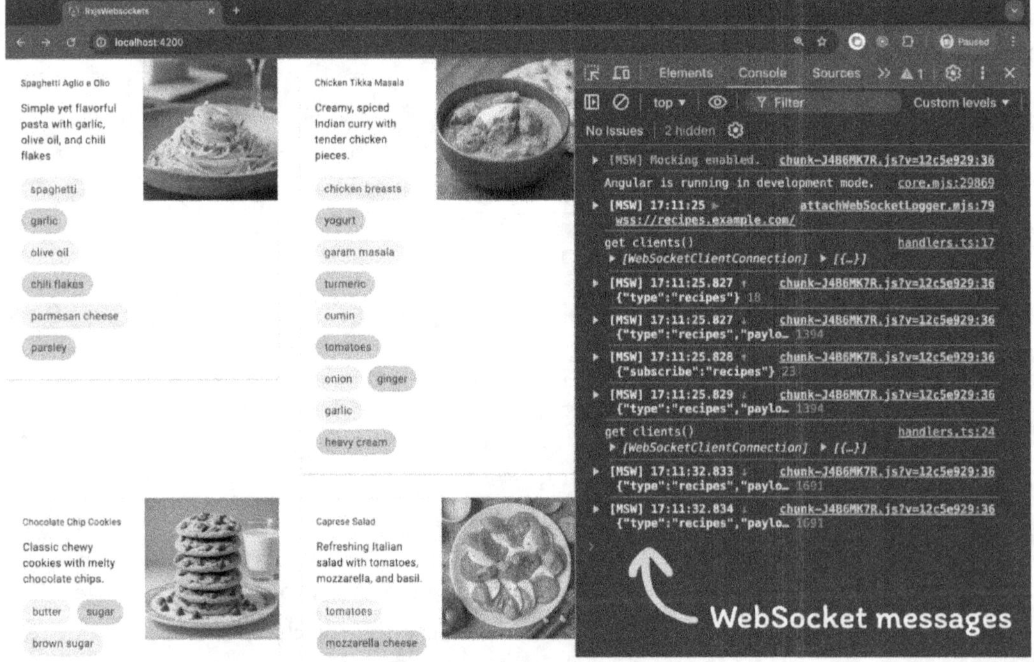

Figure 1.14: WebSocket connection

Step 2 – Implementing a WebSocket heartbeat

When we lose connection to the WebSockets, there are similar retry mechanisms that we can apply as we did for HTTP requests. However, WebSocket has a well-known retry strategy called **heartbeat**. It is a mechanism used to keep the connection alive and ensure that client and the server are still responsive.

In our `recipe.service.ts`, after a retry fails, we can send a heartbeat to our server:

```
this.socket$
  .pipe(
    retry({
      count: 1,
      delay: (error, retryCount) => {
        console.log(`Attempt ${retryCount}:
          Error occurred during websocket
          connection, retrying...`
      );
      return of(error).pipe(delay(1000));
    },
  }),
  catchError((err) => {
    console.error('Error occurred during websocket
            connection:', err);
    this.sendHeartbeat();
    return of(null);
  })
).subscribe();
```

This is the implementation behind the `sendHeartbeat` method:

```
sendHeartbeat() {
timer(0, 5000)
.pipe(
    tap(() => this.sendMessage({ type: 'heartbeat' })),
    switchMap(() =>
        this.socket$.pipe(
            filter((msg) => msg.type === 'heartbeat'),
            timeout(5000 * 2),
            // Allow double the heartbeat interval for
            //response
            catchError(() => {
```

```
                this._snackBar.open(
                    'Lost connection to the WebSocket',
                    'Close');
                this.close();

            return EMPTY;
            // Return null to stop retry attempts after
            //closing
            })
          )
        ),
    ).subscribe();
  }
```

Now we can see that every five seconds, we will send a heartbeat message to the server to check whether we were able to establish the connection again. In case of no luck, we throw an error eventually and show an error notification that states that we have lost connection. The logic around the time interval and retry strategies can be all up to the specific use case or personal preference. Additionally, the same resiliency strategies for building robust web apps in RxJS from the *Handling network errors* recipe in this chapter can be applied to the WebSockets as well.

See also

- WebSocket: `https://rxjs.dev/api/webSocket/webSocket`
- MDN WebSocket API: `https://developer.mozilla.org/en-US/docs/Web/API/WebSocket`

Learn more on Discord

To join the Discord community for this book – where you can share feedback, ask questions to the author, and learn about new releases – follow the QR code below:

`https://packt.link/RxJSCookbook`

2

Building User Interfaces with RxJS

One of the areas where RxJS excels is handling user interactions and orchestrating events in the browser. In this chapter, we're going to explore how to build awesome and interactive UI components that handle any interaction or side effect seamlessly.

In this chapter, we'll cover the following recipes:

- Unlocking a phone with precision using RxJS-powered swipe gestures
- Learning indications with the progress bar
- Streaming image loading seamlessly with Progressive Image
- Optimizing loading tab content
- Reacting to drag-and-drop events
- Crafting your perfect audio player using flexible RxJS controls
- Streamlining real-time updates with RxJS-powered notifications
- Fetching data with the Infinite Scroll Timeline component

Technical requirements

To complete this chapter, you'll need the following:

- Angular v19+
- Angular Material

- RxJS v7
- Node.js v22+
- npm v11+ or pnpm v10+

The code for the recipes in this chapter can be found in this book's GitHub repository: `https://github.com/PacktPublishing/RxJS-Cookbook-for-Reactive-Programming/tree/main/Chapter02`.

Unlocking a phone with precision using RxJS-powered swipe gestures

How cool would it be to have a phone unlock pattern component? In this recipe, we're going to build a component like that so that we can seamlessly react to every user touch swipe, orchestrate all user events, and unlock the phone once a correct combination of numbers is entered.

How to do it...

To create a phone unlock component, we'll create UI controls representing number pads and identify key events to react to user actions. Once the user lifts their finger off the screen, we'll compare the result with the correct pattern to unlock our phone.

Step 1 – Creating number pads

Our `swipe-unlock.component.html` file must contain the following markup for the swipe area and all phone buttons:

```html
<div #swipeArea class="swipe-area">
    <button #one class="number">1</button>
    <button #two class="number">2</button>
    <button #three class="number">3</button>
    <button #four class="number">4</button>
    <button #five class="number">5</button>
    <button #six class="number">6</button>
    <button #seven class="number">7</button>
    <button #eight class="number">8</button>
    <button #nine class="number">9</button>
    <button #zero class="number">0</button>
</div>
```

With a little bit of CSS magic, we can see the component in the UI:

Figure 2.1: Phone swipe component

Meanwhile, in our `swipe-unlock.component.ts` file, we can reference various elements of the number pad's UI so that we can manipulate any events that are performed on them:

```
@ViewChild('swipeArea')
swipeArea!: ElementRef;
@ViewChildren('one, two, three, four, five, six, seven,
            eight, nine, zero')
numbers!: QueryList<ElementRef>;
```

Step 2 – Identifying user touch events

What we're interested in are the events where a user touches the screen, moves (swipes), and lifts their finger off the screen. We can create those streams of events like so:

```
const touchStart$ = fromEvent<TouchEvent>(
    this.swipeArea.nativeElement,
    'touchstart'
);
```

```
const touchMove$ = fromEvent<TouchEvent>(
    this.swipeArea.nativeElement,
    'touchmove'
);
const touchEnd$ = fromEvent<TouchEvent>(
    this.swipeArea.nativeElement,
    'touchend'
);
```

From here, we can react to these events and figure out the coordinates of a touch event, check if
it's intersecting with the number pad area, and highlight it in the UI:

```
const swipe$ = touchStart$.pipe(
    switchMap(() =>
        touchMove$.pipe(
            takeUntil(touchEnd$),
            map((touchMove) => ({
                x: touchMove.touches[0].clientX,
                y: touchMove.touches[0].clientY,
            }))
        )
    ),
);
```

Now, when we subscribe to those swipe coordinates, we can perform the required actions in
sequence, such as selecting the number pad and creating a dot trail:

```
swipe$.pipe(
    tap((dot) => this.selectNumber(dot)),
    mergeMap((dot) => this.createTrailDot(dot)),
).subscribe();
```

Step 3 – Marking selected number pads

After getting the coordinates from each swipe, we can easily check whether it's intersecting the
area surrounding the number pad:

```
private selectNumber(dot: PixelCoordinates): void {
    this.numbersElement.forEach((number) => {
        if (
```

```
        dot.y > number.getBoundingClientRect().top &&
        dot.y < number.getBoundingClientRect().bottom &&
        dot.x > number.getBoundingClientRect().left &&
        dot.x < number.getBoundingClientRect().right
    ) {
        number.classList.add('selected');
        this.patternAttempt.push(parseInt(
            number.innerText)
        );
    }
});
}
```

By adding a `selected` class to each intersecting element, we can visually represent the selected number pads:

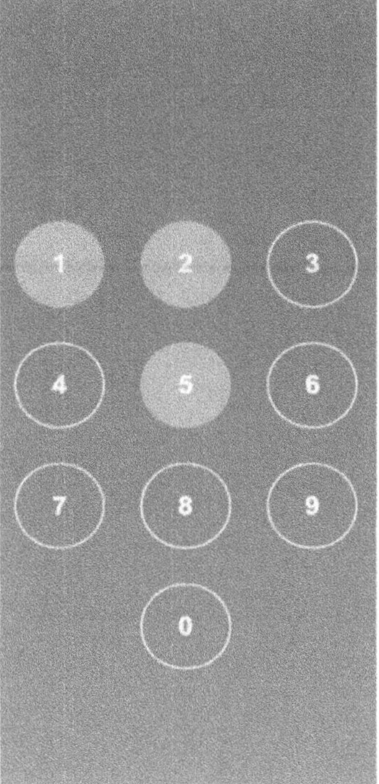

Figure 2.2: Marking the selected number pads

Step 4 – Creating a trail

With the help of the `mergeMap` operator, we can assemble all swipe events and their coordinates, create a dot in the DOM representing the trail of user action, and, after a certain delay, remove the trail from the DOM. Additionally, a nice performance consideration might be grouping many swipe events into one buffer. We can do this by using `bufferCount`, an operator that helps us to ensure optimal memory usage and computational efficiency:

```
private createTrailDot(
    dotCoordinates: PixelCoordinates
): Observable<string[]> {
    const dot = document.createElement('div');
    dot.classList.add('trail-dot');
    dot.style.left = `${dotCoordinates.x}px`;
    dot.style.top = `${dotCoordinates.y}px`;
    this.swipeArea.nativeElement.appendChild(dot);

    return of('').pipe(
        delay(1000),
        bufferCount(100, 50),
        finalize(() => dot.remove())
    );
}
```

Now, in our browser's Dev Tools, we can inspect the creation of the trail by looking at the DOM:

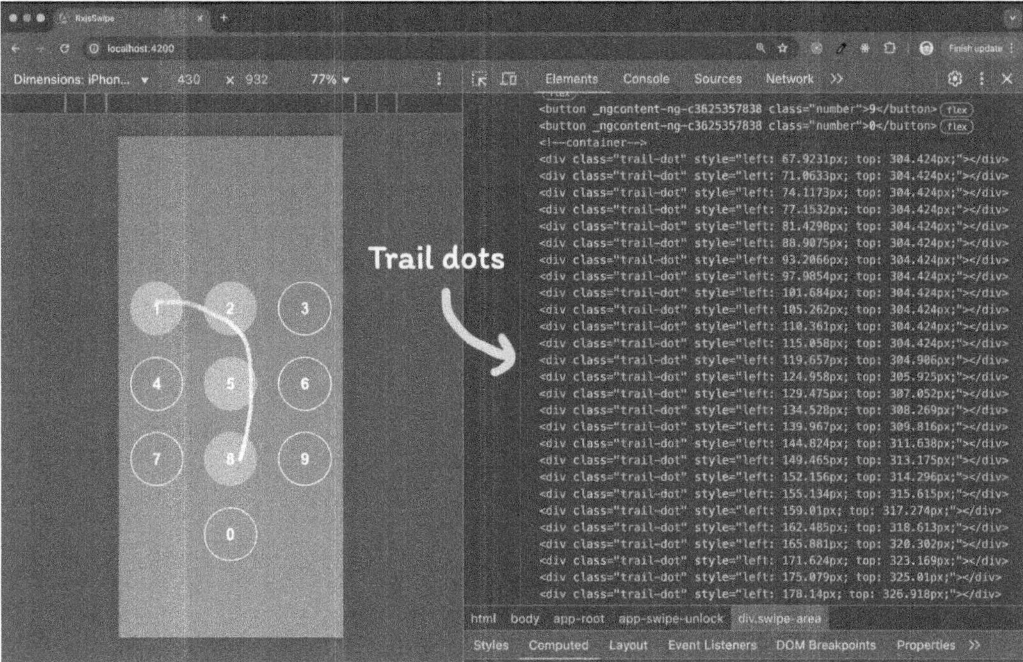

Figure 2.3: Swipe trail

Step 5 – Checking the result

Finally, at the end of the stream in the `showMessage` method, we must check whether the `patternAttempt` array, which was filled with each selected number pad, matches our pattern for unlocking the phone, which is 1 2 5 8 7.

Pattern matching

Since this is **pattern matching** and not exact password matching, the phone can be unlocked by inputting those buttons in any order, so long as those numbers in the pattern are included.

See also

- The `fromEvent` function: https://rxjs.dev/api/index/function/fromEvent
- The `switchMap` operator: https://rxjs.dev/api/operators/switchMap
- The `takeUntil` operator: https://rxjs.dev/api/operators/takeUntil

- The `finalize` operator: https://rxjs.dev/api/operators/finalize
- The `mergeMap` operator: https://rxjs.dev/api/operators/mergeMap
- The `bufferCount` operator: https://rxjs.dev/api/operators/bufferCount

Learning indications with the progress bar

Providing feedback to the user while performing actions when using web applications is one of the key aspects of a good user experience. A component like this helps users understand how long they need to wait and reduces uncertainty if the system is working. Progress bars can be also useful for gamification purposes, to make the overall UX more engaging and motivating.

How to do it...

In this recipe, we'll simulate upload progress to the backend API by implementing a progress indicator that produces a random progress percentage until we get a response. If we still haven't received a response after we get to the very end of the progress bar, we'll set its progress to 95% and wait for the request to be completed.

Step 1 – Creating a progress loading stream

Inside our `recipes.service.ts` service, we'll start a stream of random numbers at a given interval. This will be stopped after we get a response from the backend:

```
private complete$ = new Subject<void>();
private randomProgress$ = interval(800).pipe(
    map(() => Number((Math.random() * 25 + 5))),
    scan((acc, curr) =>
        +Math.min(acc + curr, 95).toFixed(2), 0),
    takeUntil(this.complete$)
);
```

With the help of the `scan` operator, we can decide whether we should produce the next increment of a progress percentage or whether we shouldn't go over 95%.

Step 2 – Merging progress and request streams

Now, we can combine the `randomProgress$` stream with the HTTP request and notify the progress indicator component whenever we get either random progress or complete the request:

```
postRecipe(recipe: Recipe): Observable<number> {
    return merge(
        this.randomProgress$,
```

```
    this.httpClient.post<Recipe>(
        '/api/recipes',
        recipe
    ).pipe(
        map(() => 100),
        catchError(() => of(-1)),
        finalize(() => this.unsubscribe$.next())
    )
  )
}
```

Once we call the `postRecipe` service method inside a component, we can track the request progress:

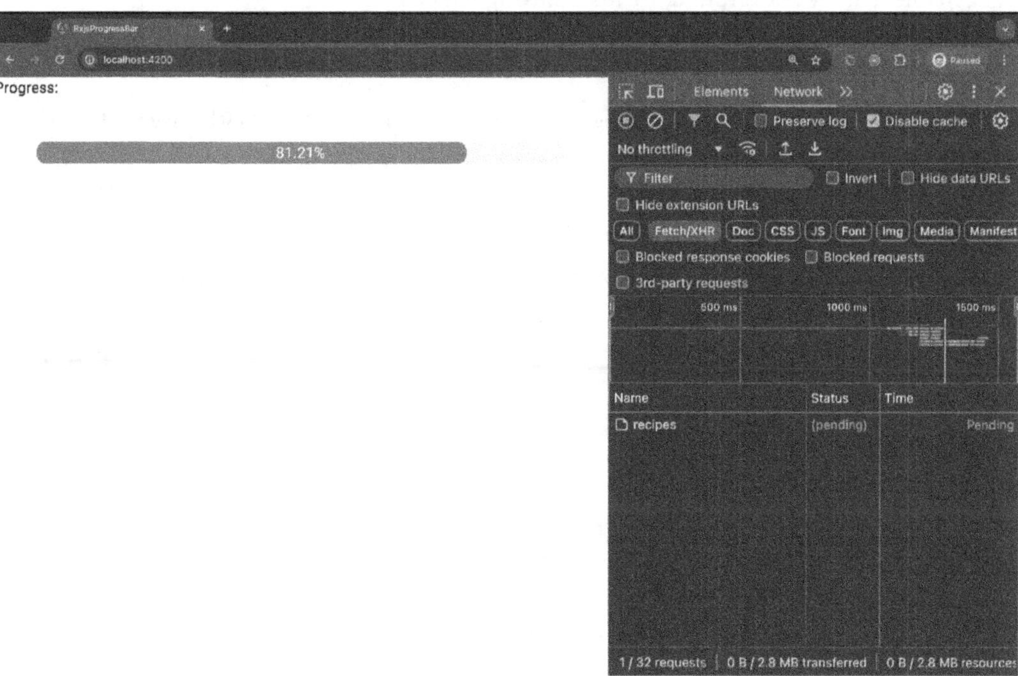

Figure 2.4: Progress indicator

See also

- The `interval` function: https://rxjs.dev/api/index/function/interval
- The `takeUntil` operator: https://rxjs.dev/api/operators/takeUntil
- The `scan` operator: https://rxjs.dev/api/operators/scan

- The `finalize` operator: `https://rxjs.dev/api/operators/finalize`
- The `merge` operator: `https://rxjs.dev/api/operators/merge`

Streaming image loading seamlessly with Progressive Image

In the modern web, we must handle resources that are MBs in size. One such resource is images. Large images can harm performance since they have slower load times, something that could lead to a negative user experience and frustration. To address these issues, one of the common patterns to use is the **LowQualityImagePlaceholder** pattern, also known as **Progressive Image**, where we load an image in stages. First, we show the lightweight version of an image (placeholder image). Then, in the background, we load the original image.

How to do it...

In this recipe, we'll learn how to handle the Progressive Image pattern with ease with the help of RxJS magic.

Step 1 – Defining image sources

Inside our `pro-img.component.ts` file, we must define paths to our local image and a placeholder/blurry version of the same image from our `assets` folder:

```
src = 'image.jpg';
placeholderSrc = 'blurry-image.jpeg';
const img = new Image();
img.src = this.src;
const placeholderImg = new Image();
placeholderImg.src = this.placeholderSrc;
```

Step 2 – Creating a progress stream

While the image is loading, every 100 milliseconds, we'll increase the progress percentage, until the `load` event is triggered. This indicates that the image has been fully loaded. If an error occurs, we'll say that the progress is at –1:

```
const loadProgress$ = timer(0, 100);
const loadComplete$ = fromEvent(img, 'load')
    .pipe(map(() => 100));
const loadError$ = fromEvent(img, 'error')
    .pipe(map(() => -1));
```

Now, we can merge these load events and stream them into the Progressive Image load:

```
loadingProgress$ = new BehaviorSubject<number>(0);


this.imageSrc$ = merge(loadProgress$, loadComplete$,loadError$).pipe(
    tap((progress) => this.loadingProgress$.next(progress)),
    map((progress) => (progress === 100 ?img.src :placeholderImg.src)),
    startWith(placeholderImg.src),
    takeWhile((src) => src === placeholderImg.src, true),
    catchError(() => of(placeholderImg.src)),
    shareReplay({ bufferSize: 1, refCount: true })
);
```

We'll use startWith on the placeholder image and show it immediately in the UI while continuously tracking the progress of the original image load. Once we get 100%, we'll replace the placeholder image source with the original image.

Step 3 – Subscribing to the image stream in the template

Meanwhile, in the component template, pro-img.component.html, we can subscribe to the progress that's been made while the image is loading in the background:

```
<div class="pro-img-container">
    @if ((loadingProgress$ | async) !== 100) {
        <div class="progress">
        {{ loadingProgress$ | async }}%
        </div>
    }
    <img
    [src]="imageSrc$ | async"
    alt="Progressive image"
    class="pro-img"

    >
</div>
```

Finally, if we open our browser, we may see this behavior in action:

Figure 2.5: Progressive Image

Common gotcha

In this recipe, for simplicity, we've chosen to artificially increase the download progress of an image. The obvious drawback is that we don't get the actual progress of the image download. There's a way to achieve this effect: by converting the request of an image's `responseType` into a **blob**. More details can be found here: `https://stackoverflow.com/questions/14218607/javascript-loading-progress-of-an-image`.

See also

- *The Ultimate LQIP Technique*, by Harry Roberts: `https://csswizardry.com/2023/09/the-ultimate-lqip-lcp-technique/`

- The HTML load event: `https://developer.mozilla.org/en-US/docs/Web/API/Window/load_event`

- The `takeWhile` operator: `https://rxjs.dev/api/operators/takeWhile`

- The `startWith` operator: `https://rxjs.dev/api/operators/startWith`

Optimizing loading tab content

When tabs contain complex data or media-rich content, it's beneficial to load the content of tabs lazily. By doing so, we aim to minimize initial page load times, conserve bandwidth, and ensure a smooth and responsive interface. So, let's create a component like that.

How to do it...

In this recipe, we'll have a simple tab group of two tabs. Only when a tab is selected will we lazy-load the component representing the contents of that tab. Each tab is represented in the URL, so whenever we change tabs, we're navigating to a separate page.

Step 1 – Defining a tab group and an active tab

In our `tabs.component.html` file, we'll use the **Angular Material** tab to represent a tab group in the UI:

```html
<mat-tab-group
    [selectedIndex]="(activeTab$ | async)?.index"
    (selectedTabChange)="selectTab($event)"
>

    <ng-container *ngFor="let tab of tabs">
```

```html
        <mat-tab [label]="tab.label"></mat-tab>
    </ng-container>
</mat-tab-group>
```

Now, inside `tabs.component.ts`, we need to define the `activeTab` and `loading` states, as well as the content of a tab stream that we can subscribe to:

```typescript
activeTab$ = new BehaviorSubject<TabConfig | null>(null);
activeTabContent$!: Observable<
    typeof TabContentComponent |
    typeof TabContent2Component |
    null
>;
loadingTab$ = new BehaviorSubject<boolean>(false);
```

Now, we can hook into **Angular Router events**, filter events when navigation ends, and, based on an active URL, mark the corresponding tab as active:

```typescript
this.router.events.pipe(
    filter((event) => event instanceof NavigationEnd),
    takeUntil(this.destroy$)
).subscribe({
    next: () => {
        const activeTab = this.tabs.find(
            (tab) => tab.route === this.router.url.slice(1)
        );
        this.activeTab$.next(activeTab || null);
    },
});
```

Step 2 — Loading tab content

Since we know which tab is active, we can start loading the content of that tab:

```typescript
private loadTabContent(tab: TabConfig) {
    const content$ = tab.route === 'tab1'
    ? of(TabContentComponent)
    : of(TabContent2Component);
```

```
    return content$.pipe(delay(1000));
}


this.activeTabContent$ = this.activeTab$.pipe(
    tap(() => this.loadingTab$.next(true)),
    switchMap((tab) =>
        this.loadTabContent(tab!).pipe(
            startWith(null),
            catchError((error) => {
                this.errors$.next(error);
                return of(null);
            }),
        finalize(() => this.loadingTab$.next(false))
        )
    ),
    shareReplay({ bufferSize: 1, refCount: true })
);
```

Inside the `loadTabContent` method, we'll create an Observable out of the Angular component that's matched based on the current route. Once we've done this, we're ready to stream into the tab content whenever the active tab changes. We can do this by starting the loading state, switching to the stream that's loading content, and resetting the loading state once the content has arrived.

Now, all we need to do is represent the content in the UI. Back in our `tabs.component.html` file, we can simply add the following code:

```
@if (loadingTab$ | async) {
    <p>Loading...</p>
}
<ng-container
    *ngComponentOutlet="activeTabContent$ | async"
></ng-container>
```

Now, by going to our browser, we'll see that the content of a tab will only be loaded when we click on that specific tab:

Figure 2.6: Loading tabs

See also

- The `of` function: `https://rxjs.dev/api/index/function/of`
- The `startWith` operator: `https://rxjs.dev/api/operators/startWith`
- Angular's Router' `NavigationEnd` event: `https://angular.dev/api/router/NavigationEnd`
- The Angular Material tab component: `https://material.angular.io/components/tabs/overview`

Reacting to drag-and-drop events

Creating a drag-and-drop component for file uploads is quite a common task for a web developer. If you've ever worked on such a component, you may already know that it isn't a trivial task and that there's a lot of hidden complexity behind a component like this. Luckily for us, we have RxJS to help us streamline the experience of reacting to drag-and-drop events in a reactive and declarative way.

Getting ready

In this recipe, to provide support for tracking image upload progress, we need to run a small Node.js server application located in the `server` folder. We can run this server application by using the following command:

```
node index.js
```

After that, we're ready to go to the `client` folder and dive into the reactive drag-and-drop component.

How to do it...

In this recipe, we'll define a drag-and-drop area for `.png` images. Then, we'll add support for multiple uploads to be made at the same time, show the upload progress of each image, and display error messages if the format of the image isn't correct. We'll also implement a retry mechanism in case a file upload fails over the network.

Step 1 – Defining a dropzone

In our `dnd-file-upload.component.html` file, we must place markup for the dropzone area:

```html
<div #dropzoneElement class="drop-zone-element">
    <p>Drag and drop png image into the area below</p>
</div>
```

After getting the `dropzoneElement` reference with `@ViewChild()`, we can start reacting to the drag-and-drop events in the dropzone area:

```
@ViewChild('dropzoneElement') dropzoneElement!: ElementRef;


ngAfterViewInit(): void {
    const dropzone = this.dropzoneElement.nativeElement;
    const dragenter$ = fromEvent<DragEvent>(
        dropzone,
        'dragenter'
    );
    const dragover$ = fromEvent<DragEvent>(
        dropzone,
        'dragover'
    ).pipe(
        tap((event: DragEvent) => {
            event.preventDefault();
            event.dataTransfer!.dropEffect = 'copy';
            (event.target as Element).classList.add('dragover');
        })
    );
    const dragleave$ = fromEvent<DragEvent>(
        dropzone,
        'dragleave'
    ).pipe(
        tap((event: DragEvent) => {
            (event.target as Element).classList.remove('dragover');
        })
    );
    const drop$ = fromEvent<DragEvent>(
        dropzone,
        'drop'
    ).pipe(
        tap((event: DragEvent) => {
            (event.target as Element).classList.remove('dragover');
```

```
        })
    );


    const droppable$ = merge(
        dragenter$.pipe(map(() => true)),
        dragover$.pipe(map(() => true)),
        dragleave$.pipe(map(() => false))
    );
}
```

While creating these events, we can track when the file(s) have entered the dropzone and when they're leaving. Based on this, we can style the component by adding the corresponding classes. We've also defined all droppable even so that we know when to stop reacting to the stream of new images that's being dragged over.

Step 2 – Validating files

Now, we can hook into a stream of drop events and validate the format of each image; if the format is OK, we can start uploading each image to the backend API:

```
drop$.pipe(
    tap((event) => event.preventDefault()),
    switchMap((event: DragEvent) => {
        const files$ = from(Array.from(
            event.dataTransfer!.files));

        return this.fileUploadService.validateFiles$(
            files$);
    }),
    ...the rest of the stream
```

Back in our `FileUploadService` service, we have a validation method that checks whether we've uploaded a `.png` image:

```
validateFiles$(files: Observable<File>): Observable<{
    valid: boolean,
    file: FileWithProgress
}> {
```

```
        return files.pipe(
            map((file File) => {
                const newFile: FileWithProgress = new File(
                    [file],
                    file.name,
                    { type: file.type }
                );
                if (file.type === 'image/png') {
                    newFile.progress = 0;
                } else {
                    newFile.error = 'Invalid file type';
                }
            return newFile;
            }),
            map((file: FileWithProgress) => {
                return of({
                    valid: !file.error,
                    file
                });
            }),
            mergeAll()
        );
}
```

Here, we check the file type. If it's expected, we set the progress to 0 and start the upload. Otherwise, we set the error message for that specific file upload.

Step 3 – Uploading files and tracking progress

Once we've validated each file, we can start upload them to the backend:

```
drop$.pipe(
    // validation steps from Step 1
    map((file: FileWithProgress) =>
        this.fileUploadService.handleFileValidation(file)
    ),
    mergeAll(),
    takeUntil(droppable$
        .pipe(filter((isDroppable) => !isDroppable))
```

```
        ),
    repeat()
)
handleFileValidation$(file: FileWithProgress):
    Observable<FileWithProgress | never> {
        if (!file.valid) {
            this._snackBar.open(
                `Invalid file ${file.name} upload.`,
                'Close',
                { duration: 4000 }
            );
        return EMPTY;
    }
    return this.fileUploadService
        .uploadFileWithProgress$(file);
}
```

If the file is invalid, we'll immediately return that file and show the error in the UI:

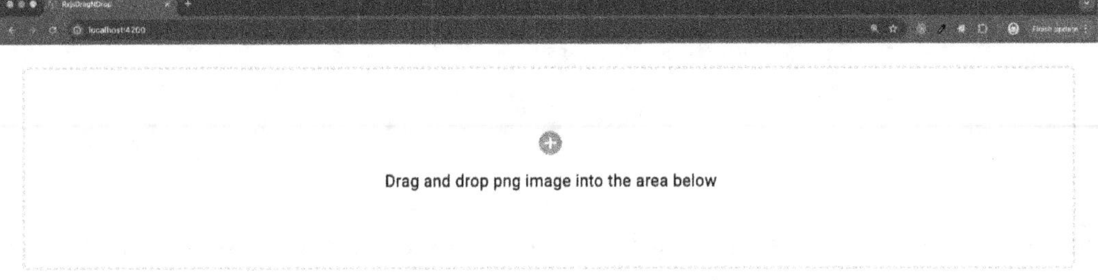

Figure 2.7: Invalid file format upload

If it's a valid file upload, then we initiate an upload request to our API. In Angular, if we want to track the actual progress of a request, there are a few things we must do:

1. We need to send the request payload as `FormData`.

2. We need to set `responseType` to `'blob'`.

3. We need to set the `reportProgress` flag to `true`.

After applying all these steps, our `uploadFiles$` method should look like this:

```
uploadFile$(file: File): Observable<number> {
    const formData = new FormData();
    formData.append('upload', file);
    const req = new HttpRequest(
        'POST', '/api/recipes/upload', formData, {
            reportProgress: true,
            responseType: 'blob'
        }
    );
    return this.httpClient.request(req).pipe(
        map((event: HttpEvent<Blob>) =>
            this.getFileUploadProgress(event)),
        filter(progress => progress < 100),
    );
}
```

Now, when we send this request, we'll get a series of HTTP events that we can react to. If we check the `getFileUploadProgress` method, we'll see this in action:

```
getFileUploadProgress(event: HttpEvent<Blob>): number {
    const { type } = event;
    if (type === HttpEventType.Sent) {
        return 0;
    }
    if (type === HttpEventType.UploadProgress) {
        const percentDone = Math.round(
            100 * event.loaded / event.total!);
        return percentDone;
    }
    if (type === HttpEventType.Response) {
```

```
        return 100;
    }
    return 0;
}
```

With this approach, we know the exact progress of the file upload due to the `UploadProgress` event.

Finally, we can call the `uploadFileWithProgress$` method from our service and return each file with progress information attached to each corresponding file:

```
uploadFileWithProgress$(file: FileWithProgress):
Observable<FileWithProgress> {
    return this.uploadFile$(file).pipe(
        map((progress: number) =>
            this.createFileWithProgress(file, progress)),
        endWith(this.createFileWithProgress(file, 100))
    );
}
```

After emitting a progress value, we'll return the file with information attached about its progress so that we can display it in the UI.

Step 4 – Showing file uploads in the UI

Finally, once we subscribe to this whole stream of file upload events inside of our component, we can show the list of all the files that are being uploaded with corresponding progress bars. This also allows us to show an error message if an error has occurred:

```
drop$.pipe(
    // validation steps from Step 1
    // file upload steps from Step 2
).subscribe({
    next: (file) => {
        if (file.valid) {
            this.validFiles.set(file.name, file);
            return;
        }
        if (!file.valid) {
            this._snackBar.open(
                'Invalid file upload.',
                'Close',
```

```
                {}
            );
        }
    }
});
```

Once we open our browser and drag multiple valid `.png` images, we can handle those uploads concurrently and observe their progress:

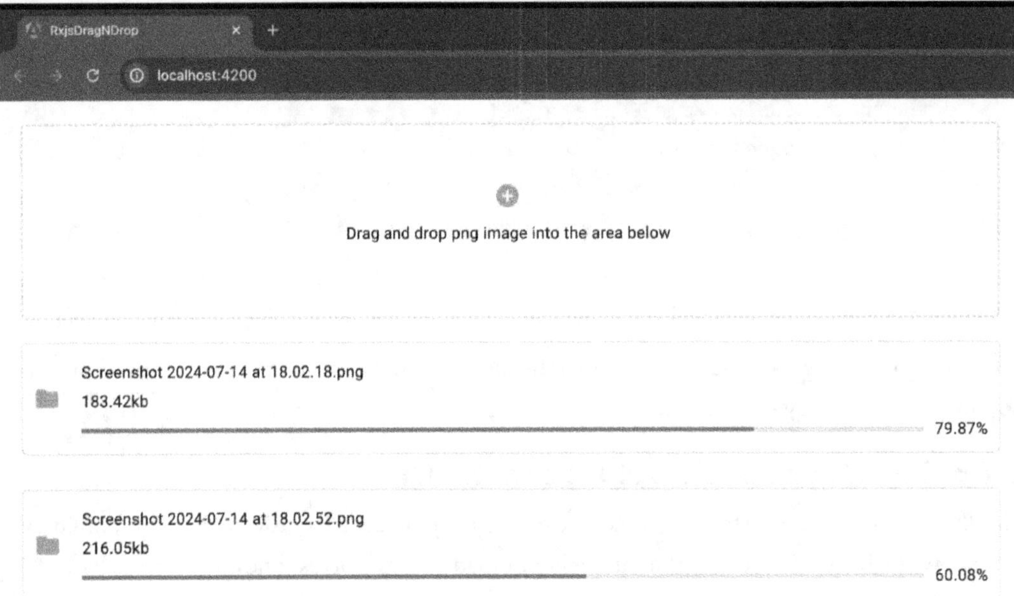

Figure 2.8: A reactive drag-and-drop file upload

Step 5 — Handling file upload errors

Imagine that, in the middle of our image upload, the network fails. One of the key aspects of a component like this is that it must be resilient to these kinds of errors and provide a recovery or retry mechanism. We can do this by catching that network error in the file upload stream and showing a retry button in the UI next to the failed upload. We can extend our service method by adding an error catch mechanism:

```
uploadFileWithProgress$(file: FileWithProgress):
Observable<FileWithProgress> {
    return this.uploadFile$(file).pipe(
        map((progress: number) =>
```

```
            this.createFileWithProgress(file, progress)),
        endWith(this.createFileWithProgress(file, 100)),
        catchError(() => {
            const newFile: FileWithProgress =
                this.createFileWithProgress(
                    file,
                    -1,
                    'Upload failed'
                );
            return of(newFile);
        })
    );
}
```

Back in our component template, `dnd-file-upload.component.html`, we can add a retry button if the file's upload progress is at –1, meaning that it failed previously:

```
@if (file.value.progress !== -1) {
    {{ file.value.progress }}%
} @else {
    <button
        mat-icon-button
        (click)="retryUpload(file.value)"
        >
        <mat-icon aria-hidden="false" fontIcon="redo">
        </mat-icon>
    </button>
}
retryUpload(file: FileWithProgress): void {
    this.recipeService.uploadFileWithProgress$(
        file).subscribe({ next: (file: FileWithProgress) =>
            this.validFiles.set(file.name, file),
            error: (err) => console.error(err),
        });
}
```

If we open our browser, if an upload error has occurred, we may notice the retry button in the UI. If the network recovers, we can trigger another upload request for the failed uploads:

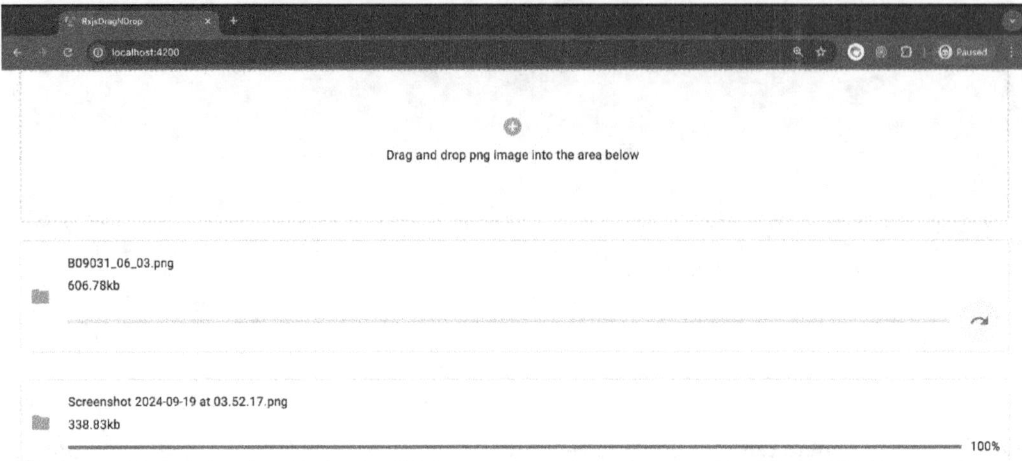

Figure 2.9: Retry on file upload

See also

- The HTML input file: `https://developer.mozilla.org/en-US/docs/Web/HTML/Element/input/file`

- The `interval` function: `https://rxjs.dev/api/index/function/interval`

- The `repeat` operator: `https://rxjs.dev/api/operators/repeat`

- The `scan` operator: `https://rxjs.dev/api/operators/scan`

- The `finalize` operator: `https://rxjs.dev/api/operators/finalize`

- The `merge` operator: `https://rxjs.dev/api/operators/merge`

- The `mergeAll` operator: `https://rxjs.dev/api/operators/mergeAll`

- The `endWith` operator: `https://rxjs.dev/api/operators/endWith`

Crafting your perfect audio player using flexible RxJS controls

Everybody likes music. Whether you use Spotify, Deezer, YouTube, or something else to listen to your favorite jams, having control over your playlist with a sophisticated audio player is one of the essential conditions for providing an awesome user experience. In this recipe, we'll create a lightweight RxJS audio player with reactive controls for playing and pausing songs, controlling volume, as well as skipping to the next song in the playlist.

How to do it...

The essential thing to understand in this recipe is the **native HTMLAudioElement** and, based on that, which events are the most important to react to.

Step 1 – Creating audio player events

In our `audio-player.component.html` file, we must implement markup for the audio player:

```
<audio #audio></audio>
```

Concerning that audio HTML element, in the component `audio-player.component.ts` file, we'll define all the key events for that element:

```typescript
@ViewChild('audio') audioElement!:
    ElementRef<HTMLAudioElement>;
ngAfterViewInit(): void {
    const audio = this.audioElement.nativeElement;
    const duration$ = fromEvent(audio,
        'loadedmetadata').pipe(map(() => (
            { duration: audio.duration }))
    );
    const playPauseClick$ = fromEvent(audio, 'play').pipe(
        map(() => ({ isPlaying: true }))
    );
    const pauseClick$ = fromEvent(audio, 'pause').pipe(
        map(() => ({ isPlaying: false }))
    );
    const volumeChange$ = fromEvent(audio,
        'volumechange').pipe(
            map(() => ({ volume: audio.volume })),
    );
    const time$ = fromEvent(audio, 'timeupdate').pipe(
        map(() => ({ time: audio.currentTime }))
    );
    const error$ = fromEvent(audio, 'error');
}
```

Using the audio element, we can react to play, pause, volumechange, and timeupdate events, as well as metadata that holds information about the duration value of a song. Also, in case network interruptions occur when we fetch the audio file or corrupted audio files, we can subscribe to the error event from the audio element.

Now, we can combine all those events and hold the state of a song in a centralized place:

```
merge(
    duration$,
    playPauseClick$,
    pauseClick$,
    volumeChange$
).subscribe((state) =>
    this.audioService.updateState(state));
```

Step 2 – Managing song state

In our audio.service.ts file, we'll store the state of the current song:

```
public audioState$ = new BehaviorSubject<AudioState>({
    isPlaying: false,
    volume: 0.5,
    currentTrackIndex: 0,
    duration: 0,
    tracks: []
});

updateState(state: Partial<AudioState>): void {
    this.audioState$.next({
      ...this.audioState$.value,
      ...state
    });
}
```

Now, we can subscribe to all state changes in the component and have reactive audio player controls over user actions.

Step 3 – Playing/pausing a song

Back in our audio-player.component.ts file, whenever play or pause events are being emitted, the state will update, at which point we can subscribe to the state change:

```
this.audioService.audioState$.subscribe(({ isPlaying }) =>
    this.isPlaying = isPlaying;
);
```

Now, in the audio-player.component.html file, we can present either a **play** or **pause** icon based on the following condition:

```
<button mat-fab class="play-pause-btn" (click)="playPause()">
    @if (isPlaying) {
        <mat-icon>pause</mat-icon>
    } @else {
        <mat-icon>play_arrow</mat-icon>
    }
</button>
```

We can also control the audio when playing a song:

```
playPause(): void {
    if (!this.isPlaying) {
        this.audioElement.nativeElement.play();
    } else {
        this.audioElement.nativeElement.pause();
    }
}
```

Step 4 – Controlling the song's volume

By subscribing to the audio player state, we also have information about the volume based on the previously emitted volumechange event:

```
this.audioService.audioState$.subscribe(({ volume }) => {
    this.volume = volume;
});
```

We can represent this state in the UI like so:

```html
<div class="volume">
    @if (volume === 0) {
        <mat-icon>volume_off</mat-icon>
    } @else {
        <mat-icon>volume_up</mat-icon>
    }
    <input
        type="range"
        [value]="volume"
        min="0"
        max="1"
        step="0.01"
        (input)="changeVolume($event)"
    />
</div>
```

Now, we can emit the same event by changing the volume of the audio player by invoking the `changeVolume()` method:

```typescript
changeVolume({ target: { value } }): void {
    this.audioElement.nativeElement.volume = value;
}
```

This will automatically update the `volume` state reactively on the audio player element.

Step 5 – Switching songs

Back in our `audio.service.ts` file, we've implemented methods for changing the current song index in the list of tracks:

```typescript
previousSong(): void {
    let prevIndex =
        this.audioState$.value.currentTrackIndex - 1;
    const tracks = this.audioState$.value.tracks;
    if (prevIndex < 0) {
        prevIndex = tracks.length - 1; // Loop back to the
                                       // end

    }
```

```
        this.updateState({
            isPlaying: false,
            currentTrackIndex: prevIndex
        });
    }


nextSong(): void {
    let nextIndex =
        this.audioState$.value.currentTrackIndex + 1;
    const tracks = this.audioState$.value.tracks;
    if (nextIndex >= tracks.length) {
        nextIndex = 0; // Loop back to the beginning
    }
    this.updateState({
        isPlaying: false,
        currentTrackIndex: nextIndex
    });
}
```

Also, when we come to the end of the list, we'll loop to the beginning of the playlist.

Inside the audio-player.component.ts component, we can subscribe to this state change and change the song using the audio element:

```
this.audioService.audioState$.subscribe(({
    currentTrackIndex,
    tracks
}) => {
    if (
        tracks[currentTrackIndex].title !==
            this.currentTrack.title
    ) {
        this.audioElement.nativeElement.src =
            tracks[currentTrackIndex].song;
        this.currentTrack = tracks[currentTrackIndex];
    }
});
```

This means that we have all the information we need about the current song, which means we can display that data in our `audio-player.component.html` template.

Step 6 — Skipping to the middle of a song

In our audio element, there's a `timeupdate` event that lets us track and update the current time of a song:

```
const time$ = fromEvent(audio, 'timeupdate').pipe(
    map(() => ({ time: audio.currentTime }))
);
time$.subscribe(({ time }) => this.currentTime = time);
```

In the UI, we can combine this current time information with the previous song metadata, show it in a slider, and watch the song progress:

```
<p>{{ currentTime | time }}</p>
<audio #audio></audio>
<mat-slider [max]="duration" class="song">
    <input matSliderThumb
    [value]="currentTime"
    (dragEnd)="skip($event)"
    >
</mat-slider>
<p>{{ duration | time }}</p>
```

Finally, if we open our browser, we can inspect all these features and play our favorite jam:

Figure 2.10: Reactive audio player

See also

- The `BehaviorSubject` class: `https://rxjs.dev/api/index/class/BehaviorSubject`

- The `fromEvent` function: `https://rxjs.dev/api/index/function/fromEvent`

- The `map` operator: `https://rxjs.dev/api/operators/map`

- The HTML `audio` tag: `https://developer.mozilla.org/en-US/docs/Web/HTML/Element/audio`

Streamlining real-time updates with RxJS-powered notifications

Notifications are one of the main ways we can prompt users about relevant events or changes within the system. By utilizing **Observables** and **operators**, RxJS provides a powerful framework for managing these asynchronous notifications efficiently and effectively.

How to do it...

In this recipe, we'll have an array of notifications to represent incoming notifications based on a user action, store them by ID, and remove them after a certain period. We'll also provide support to manually remove notifications from a stack.

Step 1 – Stacking incoming notifications

To streamline the stack of notifications efficiently, inside `NotificationService`, we'll use `BehaviorSubject` to represent all the notifications that may arrive over time asynchronously. We'll also have a **Subject** that triggers an event when we want to add a new notification to the stack and another for dismissal:

```
private notifications$ = new BehaviorSubject<Notification[]>([]);
private addNotification$ = new Subject<Notification>();
private removeNotification$ = new Subject<string>();


addNotification(notification: Notification) {
    this.addNotification$.next(notification);
}


removeNotification(id: string) {
    this.removeNotification$.next(id);
}
```

So, whenever there's an ongoing request for posting new data, we'll combine these two actions with the latest state of the notification stack with the help of the `withLatestFrom` operator and update its state:

```
get notifications(): Observable<Notification[]> {
    return merge(
        this.addNotification$,
        this.removeNotification$
```

```
        ).pipe(
        withLatestFrom(this.notifications$),
        map(([changedNotification, notifications]) => {
            if (changedNotification instanceof Object) {
                this.notifications$.next([
                    ...notifications,
                    changedNotification
                ]);
            } else {
                this.notifications$.next(notifications.filter
                    (notification =>
                        notification.id !== changedNotification)
                );
            }
            return this.notifications$.value;
        })
    )
}
```

Based on the latest emitted value's type, we can decide whether a new notification needs to be added or filtered from the stack.

Step 2 – Reacting to a user action and displaying notifications

In our app.component.html file, we have a simple button that will trigger a POST request to add a new random cooking recipe:

```html
<button (click)="sendRequest()">Add recipe</button>
```

Clicking that button will invoke a function:

```
sendRequest() {
    this.recipeService.postRecipes();
}
```

In `RecipeService`, we must implement the service method for sending the request to the BE API.
If we get a successful response, we'll perform a side effect to add a notification to the stack. If we
get an error, we'll display a notification that's of the error type:

```
getRecipes(): void {
    this.httpClient.get<Recipe[]>('/api/recipes').pipe(
        tap(() => {
            this.notificationService.addNotification({
                id: crypto.randomUUID(),
                message: 'Recipe added successfully.',
                type: 'success'
            });
        }),
        catchError((error) => {
            this.notificationService.addNotification({
                id: crypto.randomUUID(),
                message: 'Recipe could not be added.',
                type: 'error'
            });
            return throwError(() =>
                new Error('Recipe could not be added.'));
        }),
    ).subscribe();
}
```

Finally, in `NotificationComponent`, we can subscribe to the changes on `notifications$` and
display notifications:

```html
<div class="container">
    <div
      *ngFor="let notification of notifications | async"
      class="notification {{ notification.type }}"
    >
      {{ notification.message }}
        <mat-icon
            (click)="removeNotification(notification.id)"
            class="close">
            Close
        </mat-icon>
```

```
      </div>
  </div>
```

Now, when we open our browser, we'll see incoming notifications stacked on each other:

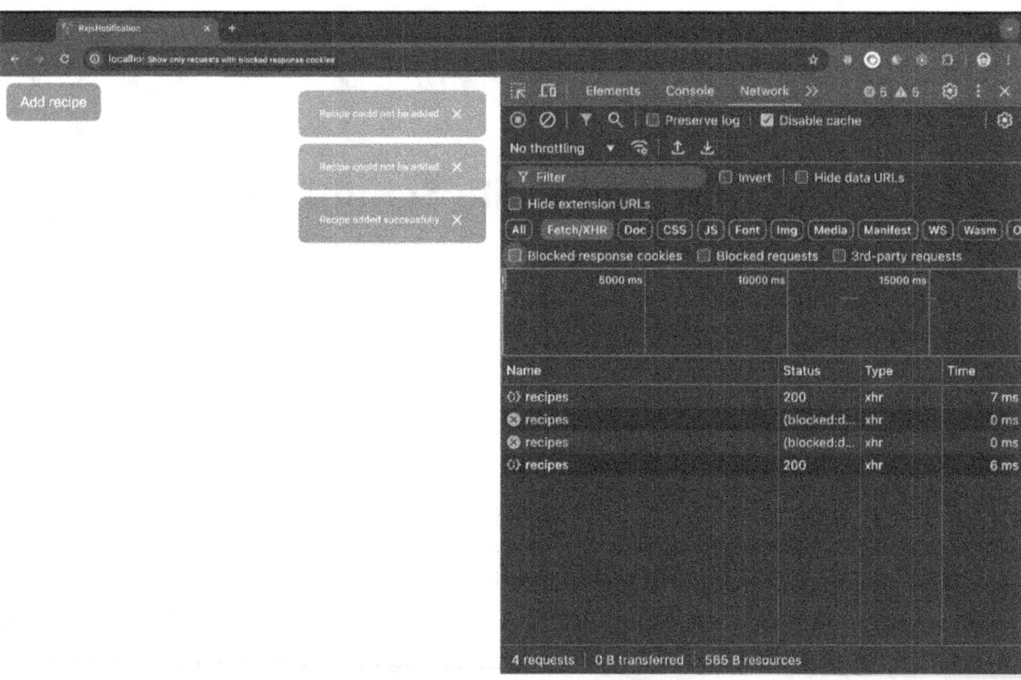

Figure 2.11: A reactive stack of notifications

Step 3 – Automatic notification dismissal

Previously, we could manually remove notifications from the stack by clicking the close button. Now, after a certain period, we want a notification to be automatically removed from the stack. Back in `NotificationService`, when adding a notification to the stack initially, we'll simply define a timer, after which we'll call the `removeNotification` method:

```
addNotification(
    notification: Notification,
    timeout = 5000
) {
    this.addNotification$.next(notification);
    timer(timeout).subscribe(() =>
        this.removeNotification(notification.id));
}
```

See also

- The `BehaviorSubject` class: `https://rxjs.dev/api/index/class/BehaviorSubject`
- The `Subject` class: `https://rxjs.dev/api/index/class/Subject`
- The `withLatesFrom` operator: `https://rxjs.dev/api/operators/withLatestFrom`
- Web API Crypto's `randomUUID` method: `https://developer.mozilla.org/en-US/docs/`
- `Web/API/Crypto/randomUUID`

Fetching data with the Infinite Scroll Timeline component

Imagine going through your favorite cooking web application and getting the latest updates on delicious new recipes. To show this latest news, one of the common UX patterns is to show this recipe news in a timeline component (such as Facebook's news feed). While you scroll, if there are new recipes, you'll be updated that there are fresh new recipes so that you can scroll back to the top and start over.

How to do it...

In this recipe, we're going to build a timeline component that shows the list of your favorite latest cooking recipes. Since there are a lot of delicious recipes out there, this would be a huge list to fetch initially. To increase the performance of the application and to improve the general UX, we can implement an infinite scroll list so that once the user scrolls to the end of a list of 5 initial recipes, we can get a set of 5 new recipes. After some time, we can send a new request to check whether there are new recipes and refresh our timeline of recipe news.

Step 1 – Detecting the end of a list

In our `RecipesList` component, we'll create a stream of scroll events. On each emission, we'll check whether we're near the end of the list in the UI based on a certain threshold:

```
private isNearBottom(): boolean {
    const threshold = 100; // Pixels from bottom
    const position = window.innerHeight + window.scrollY;
    const height = document.documentElement.scrollHeight;
    return position > height - threshold;
}


const isNearBottom$ = fromEvent(window, 'scroll').pipe(
    startWith(null),
```

```
    auditTime(10), // Prevent excessive event triggering
    observeOn(animationFrameScheduler),
    map(() => this.isNearBottom()),
    distinctUntilChanged(), // Emit only when near-bottom
                            //state changes
)
```

As you can imagine, with the scroll event emissions, there's the potential for performance bottlenecks. We can limit the number of scroll events that are processed by the stream using the auditTime operator. This is especially useful since we want to ensure that we are always processing the latest scroll event, and auditTime will always emit the most recent value within the specified time frame. Also, with observeOn(animationFrameScheduler), we can schedule tasks to be executed just before the browser's next repaint. This can be beneficial for animations or any updates that cause a repaint as it can help to prevent **jank** and make the application feel smoother.

auditTime versus throttleTime

You might be wondering why we used auditTime in our scroll stream and not throttleTime. The key difference between these two operators is that auditTime emits the last value in a time window, whereas throttleTime emits the first value in a time window. Common use cases for throttleTime might include rate-limiting API calls, handling button clicks to prevent accidental double clicks, and controlling the frequency of animations.

Once we know we're getting near the end of a list, we can trigger a loading state and the next request with a new set of data.

Step 2 – Controlling the next page and loading the state of the list

At the top of our RecipesList component, we'll define the necessary states to control the whole flow and know when we require the next **page**, when to show the **loader**, and when we've reached the end of the list:

```
private page = 0;
public loading$ = new BehaviorSubject<boolean>(false);
public noMoreData$ = new Subject<void>();
private destroy$ = new Subject<void>();
```

Now, we can continue our `isNearBottom$` stream, react to the next page, and specify when to show the loader:

```
isNearBottom$.pipe(
    filter((isNearBottom) =>
        isNearBottom && !this.loading$.value),
    tap(() => this.loading$.next(true)),
    switchMap(() =>
        this.recipesService.getRecipes(++this.page)
        .pipe(
            tap((recipes) => {
                if (recipes.length === 0)
                    this.noMoreData$.next();
            }),
            finalize(() => this.loading$.next(false))
        )
    ),
    takeUntil(merge(this.destroy$, this.noMoreData$))
    )
    .subscribe((recipes) => (
        this.recipes = [...this.recipes, ...recipes])
    );
}
```

Here's a breakdown of what we've done:

1. First, we check whether we're near the bottom of the page or whether there's already an ongoing request.

2. We start a new request by showing a loading spinner.

3. We send a new request with the next page as a parameter.

4. When we get a successful response, we can check whether there's no more data or we can continue scrolling down the timeline.

5. Once the stream has finished, we remove the loading spinner:

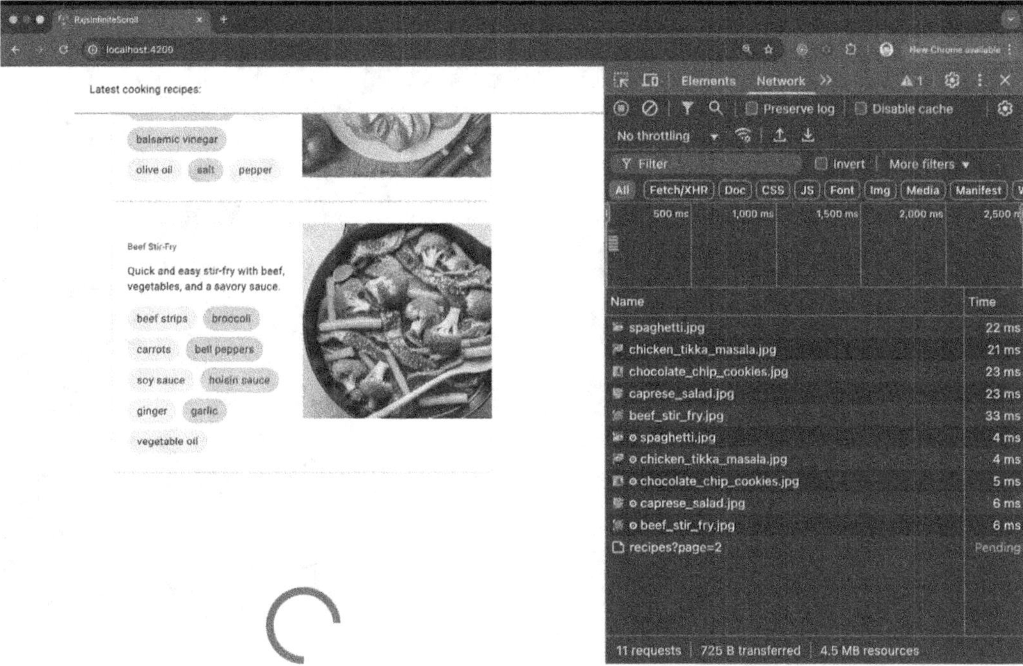

Figure 2.12: Reactive infinite scroll

Step 3 — Checking for new recipes

In our `recipes.service.ts` file, we've implemented a method that will check whether there are new recipes periodically and whether we should scroll to the top of the timeline and refresh it with new data:

```
checkNumberOfNewRecipes(): Observable<number> {
    return interval(10000).pipe(
        switchMap(() =>
            this.httpClient.get<number>(
                '/api/new-recipes'))
    );
}
```

Once we receive several new recipes, we can subscribe to that information inside
`NewRecipesComponent` and display it in the UI:

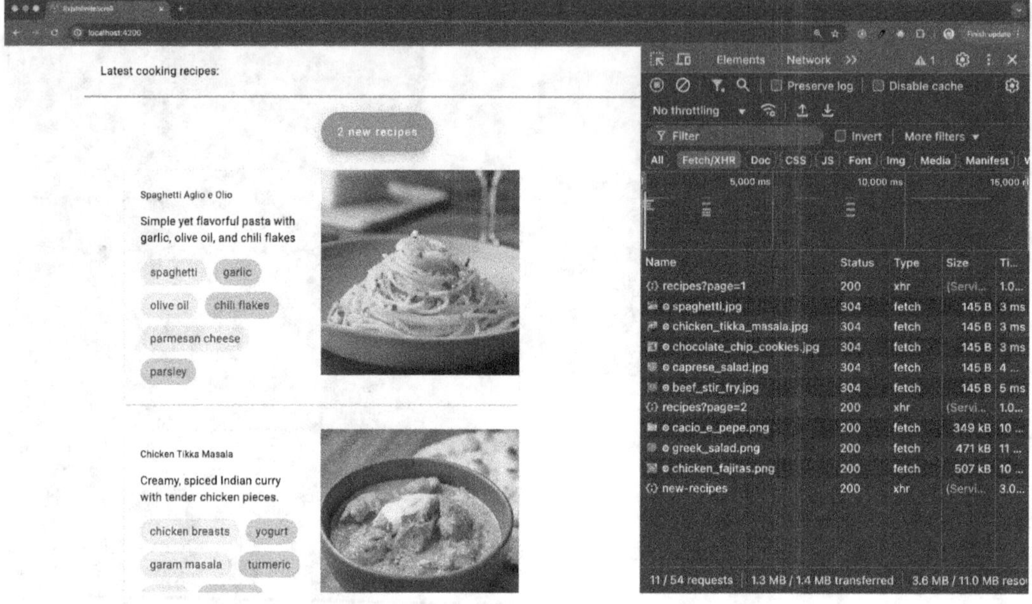

Figure 2.13: Reactive timeline updates

Now, once we click the `2 new recipes` button, we can scroll to the top of the timeline and get
the newest data.

See also

- The `fromEvent` function: https://rxjs.dev/api/index/function/fromEvent

- The `auditTime` operator: https://rxjs.dev/api/operators/auditTime

- The `animationFrameScheduler` operator: https://rxjs.dev/api/index/const/
  animationFrameScheduler

- The `observeOn` operator: https://rxjs.dev/api/operators/observeOn

- The `distinctUntilChanged` operator: https://rxjs.dev/api/operators/
  distinctUntilChanged

- The `switchMap` operator: https://rxjs.dev/api/operators/switchMap

- The `takeUntil` operator: https://rxjs.dev/api/operators/takeUntil

Get This Book's PDF Version and Exclusive Extras

Scan the QR code (or go to packtpub.com/unlock). Search for this book by name, confirm the edition, and then follow the steps on the page.

Note: Keep your invoice handy. Purchases made directly from Packt don't require one.

3

Understanding Reactive Animation Systems with RxJS

Animations in web apps are much more than just decorative elements. When used thoughtfully, they can significantly enhance the **user experience** (**UX**) and create a *wow* effect for the end users. When it comes to animations, RxJS can really become handy when creating complex animations because of its superpower to orchestrate multiple events.

In this chapter, we are about to explore some of the coolest ways to add visual delight for our users with RxJS animations by implementing the following recipes:

- Simulating realistic ball-bouncing physics using RxJS
- Creating mesmerizing fluid particle effects using RxJS
- Adding subtle elegance to components with RxJS transitions

Technical requirements

To follow along in this chapter, you'll need the following:

- Angular v19+
- RxJS v7
- Node.js v22+
- npm v11+ or pnpm v10+

The code for the recipes in this chapter is placed in the GitHub repository here: `https://github.com/PacktPublishing/RxJS-Cookbook-for-Reactive-Programming/tree/main/Chapter03`

Simulating realistic ball-bouncing physics using RxJS

Grab your physics textbook, and let's bounce into the world of realistic ball physics with RxJS! We're about to find out how to translate real-world physics principles into a reactive RxJS stream of events that simulates smooth ball movement in the UI.

How to do it...

In this recipe, we're going to implement a reactive bouncing ball animation, ensuring that it runs 60 frames per second. We are striving to be as realistic as possible with the physics of a bouncing ball, applying gravity, falling velocity, and energy loss on each bounce.

Step 1 – Animating a ball falling

Isn't it just annoying when you see janky animation on the web? In order to avoid that, and provide the best possible user experience, the first thing we're going to do is to ensure that our animation runs at 60 fps. We can achieve this by using RxJS's `animationFrameScheduler`, which will perform a browser task when `requestAnimationFrame` fires.

In `bouncing-ball.component.ts`, we are going to start off by defining an Observable stream for animation frames:

```
const ballLoop$ = interval(0, animationFrameScheduler);
```

Now we can pipe into the `animationFrame$` stream and update the ball position on every new animation frame:

```
const initialHeight = 0;


ngAfterViewInit() {
    const initialHeight = 0;
    this.ballLoop$ = animationFrame$.pipe(
        scan(({ y, dy}, velocity) => {
            dy += gravity;
            y += dy;
        return { y, dy };
        }, { y: initialHeight, dy: 0 }),
        tap(({ y }) => {
            ball.style.top = `${y}px`;
        }),
```

```
    );
    this.ballLoop$.subscribe();
}
```

At this point, we will see an animation where we update the ball's y position on each frame, where dy is the direction of movement of the ball.

Anybody who paid attention to physics class in high school will know about gravity laws. They essentially say that if we have gravity acceleration of 9.81m/s^2, it means that each second the ball is falling, it is going to get additional velocity of 9.81m/s. In our recipe, if we map one animation frame as a second in real life, it means that we can achieve a similar effect if we just accumulate gravity value to dy. By saying dy += gravity, we can simulate how the ball would gain velocity over time.

Step 2 – Bouncing off the ground

What we want now is for the ball to recognize the *ground* and bounce off it each time:

```
@ViewChild('ball', { static: true }) ballRef!: ElementRef;
bounceCount = 0;

ngAfterViewInit() {
    const ball = this.ballRef.nativeElement;
    const container = document.documentElement;
    let energyLoss = 0.8;
    this.ballLoop$ = animationFrame$.pipe(
        scan(({ y, dy}, velocity) => {
            dy += gravity;
            y += dy;
            // Bounce off the ground
            if (y + ball.offsetHeight >
                container.clientHeight) {
                    y = container.clientHeight -
                        ball.offsetHeight;
                    dy = -dy * energyLoss;
                    // Reverse direction and reduce energy
                    this.bounceCount++;
            }
            return { y, dy };
```

```
        }, { y: initialHeight, dy: 0 }),
    tap(({ y }) => {
        ball.style.top = `${y}px`;
    }),
);
```

Here, we can see that we have updated the logic so that we know when the ball is hitting the ground (has reached the end of a viewport), bouncing off it by reverting the direction and factoring in the energy loss on each bounce.

Step 3 – Stopping and repeating the animation

To prevent memory leaks, complete the stream when the ball stops falling, and have control over the animation, we are going to apply the RxJS takeWhile operator:

```
private bounceRepeat$ = new Subject<void>();
message = signal<string>('');


ngAfterViewInit() {
    this.ballLoop$ = interval(
        0,
        animationFrameScheduler
    ).pipe(
        // the rest of the stream
        takeWhile(
            ({ y, dy }) =>
                y < this.container.clientHeight -
                    ball.offsetHeight - 10 ||
                    Math.abs(dy) > 5
        ),
        finalize(() => {
            this.message.set(`Bouncing stopped after ${
                this.bounceCount} bounces`);
        }),
        repeat({ delay: () => this.bounceRepeat$ })
    );
}
```

```
startBouncing() {
    this.bounceRepeat$.next();
}
```

Here, we are simply saying that the stream should stop whenever we are 10 px away from the ground and the current movement of the ball is not larger than 5 px, up or down.

Also, whenever we click on the ***START BOUNCING*** button, we will trigger the animation again by leveraging the RxJS repeat operator. One more great thing about the repeat operator is that it won't trigger new animations if we repeatedly click on a button, since it will only re-subscribe to the stream once the initial stream is completed.

Figure 3.1: RxJS bouncing ball

See also

- RxJS animationFrameScheduler: https://rxjs.dev/api/index/const/animation FrameScheduler

- RxJS repeat operator: https://rxjs.dev/api/operators/repeat

Creating mesmerizing fluid particle effects using RxJS

Prepare to be captivated! One of the most beautiful and mesmerizing UI effects is provided by the **particles.js** library. Although it looks like a visual symphony, crafting such an effect can be really challenging. Luckily for us, RxJS can help us out by orchestrating the movement, interaction, and behavior of individual particles, resulting in a fluid, organic, and truly captivating visual experience.

How to do it...

In this recipe, we are going to re-create the default version of the particles.js animation, only this time with the power and elegance of RxJS.

Step 1 – Drawing particles

When working with complex animations like this, the crucial step is to break the animations into a lot of small, manageable tasks. We're going to start off easy by generating and drawing static particles on a canvas. In particles.component.html, we will have the following:

```
<canvas #canvas class="canvas" width="2300" height="1200">
</canvas>
```

To increase the resolution of canvas elements, the dimensions of the canvas are higher than the dimensions of the screen. Increasing the width and height of a canvas element increases its resolution because it increases the number of pixels available for rendering. This results in more detailed, higher-quality graphics, but it also requires more resources to process and render the additional pixels.

In the particles.component.ts component, we can set up a canvas element reference and generate a particles array:

```
@ViewChild('canvas', { static: true })
canvas!: ElementRef<HTMLCanvasElement>;
private ctx!: CanvasRenderingContext2D;
private particles$!: Observable<Particle[]>;
```

```
private generateParticle(): Particle {
    return {
        x: Math.random() * this.canvas.nativeElement.width,
        y: Math.random() * this.
            canvas.nativeElement.height,
        radius: Math.random() * 0.5 + 2.5,
        vx: Math.random() < 0.5
            ? (Math.random() + 0.8)
            : -(Math.random() + 0.8),
        vy: Math.random() < 0.5
            ? (Math.random() + 0.8)
            : -(Math.random() + 0.8),
        color: `rgba(255,255,255,0.5)`
    }
};
```

When generating particles, we will have the following properties:

- Particle coordinates x and y

- The size and color of the particle

- The direction of particle movement, defined with vx and vy

Now we can call the `generateParticles()` method and draw particles on the canvas:

```
ngOnInit() {
this.ctx = this.canvas.nativeElement.getContext('2d')!;
const initialParticles: Particle[] = Array.from(
    { length: 123 },
    this.generateParticle,
    this
);
const animationFrame$ = animationFrames();
this.particles$ = animationFrame$.pipe(
    scan((particles: Particle[], event: IAnimationFrame) =>
    {
        return particles.map(particle => {
            let newX = particle.x + particle.vx;
            let newY = particle.y + particle.vy;
```

```
            return {
                ...particle,
                x: newX,
                y: newY,
                vx: particle.vx,
                vy: particle.vy
            };
        });
    }, initialParticles),
    tap(particles => this.drawParticles(particles))
);
```

Here, you may notice that we are using the RxJS animationFrames function to ensure smooth animation and render particles within the browser rendering cycle. Whenever we enter a new rendering cycle, we can update the position of each particle on the canvas, and call the drawParticles() method:

```
drawParticles(particles: Particle[]) {
    this.ctx.clearRect(
        0,
        0,
        this.canvas.nativeElement.width,
        this.canvas.nativeElement.height
    );
    particles.forEach(particle =>
        this.drawParticle(particle));
}


drawParticle(particle: Particle) {
    this.ctx.beginPath();
    this.ctx.arc(
        particle.x,
        particle.y,
        particle.radius,
        0,
        Math.PI * 2
    );
```

```
        this.ctx.fillStyle = particle.color;
        this.ctx.fill();
    }
```

Step 2 – Detecting wall collision

With the current state of our particle's recipe, we may notice that, after a certain period, all particles fly away from the screen. This happens because we are not detecting the border of the canvas container we are observing. We can use the `checkWallCollision()` method to check whether the particles are hitting the wall and change the direction of movement for each particle:

```
detectWallCollision(
    particle: Particle,
    newX: number,
    newY: number
): Particle {
    if (newX + particle.radius >
        this.canvas.nativeElement.width ||
        newX - particle.radius < 0
    ) {
    particle.vx = -particle.vx;
    particle.x = newX + particle.radius >
        this.canvas.nativeElement.width
        ? this.canvas.nativeElement.width - particle.radius
        : particle.radius;
    }

    if (newY + particle.radius >
        this.canvas.nativeElement.height
        || newY - particle.radius < 0
    ) {
    particle.vy = -particle.vy;
    particle.y = newY + particle.radius >
        this.canvas.nativeElement.height
        ? this.canvas.nativeElement.height -
            particle.radius
        : particle.radius;
    }
```

```
        return particle;
}
```

Once we have implemented the `checkWallCollision()` method, we can detect wall collision for each particle in the stream:

```
this.particles$ = animationFrame$.pipe(
    scan((particles: Particle[],
          event: IAnimationFrame) => {
        return particles.map(particle => {
            let newX = particle.x + particle.vx;
            let newY = particle.y + particle.vy;

            return {
                ...particle,
                x: newX,
                y: newY,
                vx: particle.vx,
                vy: particle.vy
            };
        });
    }, initialParticles),
    map(particles => particles.map(particle =>
        this.detectWallCollision(
            particle,
            particle.x + particle.vx,
            particle.y + particle.vy))
    ),
);
```

Step 3 — Drawing connections

After drawing and animating the movement of all particles, we can calculate the distance between them and draw a connection. The connection line will increase its opacity each time it gets closer and closer to another particle:

```
this.particles$ = animationFrame$.pipe(
    // the rest of the stream
    tap(particles => this.drawParticles(particles)),
    tap(particles => this.drawConnections(particles)),
);


drawConnections(particles: Particle[]) {
    for (let i = 0; i < particles.length; i++) {
        for (let j = i + 1; j < particles.length; j++) {
            const particle1 = particles[i];
            const particle2 = particles[j];
            const distance = Math.sqrt(
                (particle1.x - particle2.x) ** 2 +
                    (particle1.y - particle2.y) ** 2
            );
            if (distance <= 250) {
                const opacity = 1 - distance / 250;
                this.drawLine(particle1, particle2, opacity);
            }
        }
    }
}
```

Who said we won't need the **Pythagorean theorem** ever in our lives? In the `drawConnections()` method, we are calculating the distance between two particles based on their coordinates. If they are in a radius of 250 px, we will call the `drawLine()` method, which will draw a connection between particles on the canvas.

Figure 3.2: RxJS particles

Step 4 — Moving particles with a hover effect

In this step, we will match the interaction with particles in the same way as the `particles.js` library does:

```
const mouseMove$ = fromEvent<MouseEvent>(
    this.canvas.nativeElement,
    'mousemove'
).pipe(
    throttleTime(5),
    map((event: MouseEvent) => {
        const rect =
        this.canvas.nativeElement.getBoundingClientRect();
        return {
            x: (event.clientX - rect.left) *
                (this.canvas.nativeElement.width / rect.width),
            y: (event.clientY - rect.top) *
                (this.canvas.nativeElement.height / rect.height),
```

```
            };
        }),
        takeUntil(
            merge(
                fromEvent(this.canvas.nativeElement,
                    'mouseout'),
                fromEvent(this.canvas.nativeElement,
                    'mouseleave')
            )
        )
    );
```

Since the dimensions of the canvas are scaled compared to screen dimensions, we need to transform mouse coordinates proportionally. After doing that, we can include the mouseMove$ stream in the main particles$ stream:

```
this.particles$ = merge(mouseMove$, animationFrame$).pipe(scan(
    (particles: Particle[],
     event: { x: number, y: number } | IAnimationFrame
) => {
    if ('x' in event && 'y' in event) {
        this.mouseX = event.x;
        this.mouseY = event.y;
    return particles;
    }
    return particles.map(particle => {
        const mouseMoveCoordinates =
            this.handleMouseInteraction(particle);
        let newX = mouseMoveCoordinates?.newX ||
                particle.x + particle.vx;
        let newY = mouseMoveCoordinates?.newY ||
                particle.y + particle.vy;
    return {
        particle,
        x: newX,
        y: newY,
        vx: particle.vx,
        vy: particle.vy
```

```
};
    });
}, initialParticles));
```

Finally, we can call the `handleMouseInteraction()` method and move the particles away from
the hover radius:

```
handleMouseInteraction(
    particle: Particle
): { newX: number; newY: number } | undefined {
    // Mouse hover radius avoidance
    const distanceToMouse = Math.sqrt(
        (this.mouseX - particle.x) ** 2 +
        (this.mouseY - particle.y) ** 2
    );

    if (distanceToMouse > 200) return;
    // Calculate angle between particle and mouse
    const angle = Math.atan2(
        particle.y - this.mouseY,
        particle.x - this.mouseX
    );
    const normalX = Math.cos(angle);
    const normalY = Math.sin(angle);
    const influenceFactor = Math.max(
        0, 1 - distanceToMouse / 200);
    particle.vx += normalX * influenceFactor * 2;
    // Adjust the factor as needed
    particle.vy += normalY * influenceFactor * 2;
    // Adjust the factor as needed
    particle.x = this.mouseX + 200 * normalX + particle.vx;
    particle.y = this.mouseY + 200 * normalY + particle.vy;

    return {
        newX: particle.x,
        newY: particle.y,
    };
}
```

Another day in life not using trigonometry's sin, co.... oh wait. Math professors were right all along! Here is how we know where to move particles if the distance between the particle and the mouse hover radius is less than 200 px:

- `Math.atan2` calculates the angle (in radians) between the particle and the mouse. This angle is measured counterclockwise from the positive x axis to the line connecting the particle and the mouse.

- `Math.cos(angle)` and `Math.sin(angle)` give the x and y components of the unit vector pointing from the mouse to the particle. This vector is normalized, meaning it has a length of 1.

- The dot product of the particle's velocity vector and the normalized direction vector is calculated. This measures how much of the particle's velocity is in the direction of the mouse.

- The new position of the particle is calculated by moving it 200 units away from the mouse in the direction opposite to the angle, plus the adjusted velocity.

The trigonometry behind the particle movement involves calculating the angle and direction from the particle to the mouse, determining the influence of the mouse on the particle's velocity, and then updating the particle's position to move it away from the mouse. By doing so, we are able to avoid the mouse cursor and adjust particle velocities based on their relative positions.

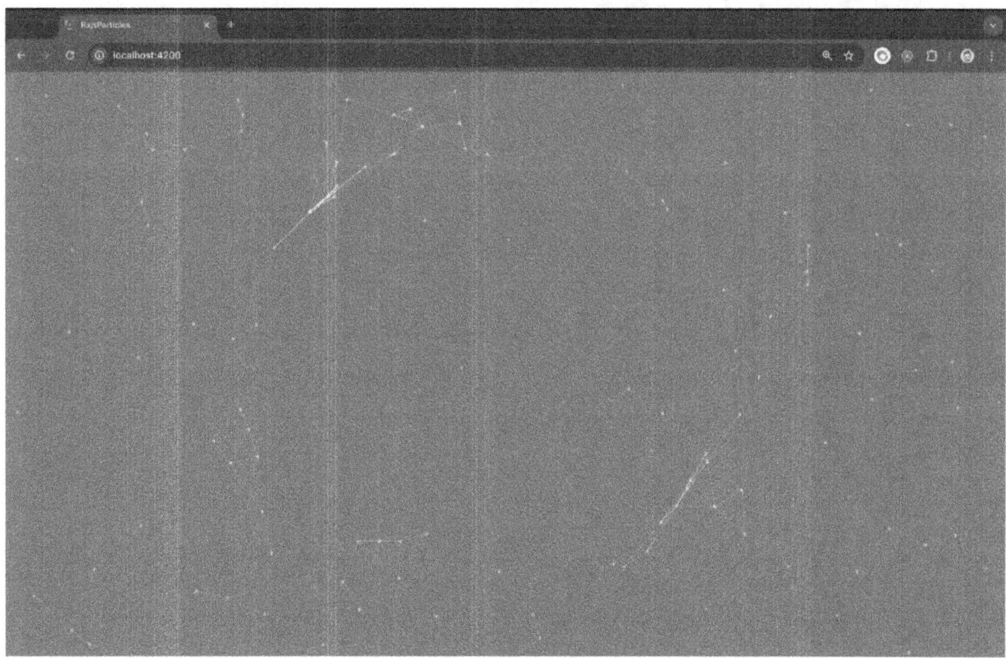

Figure 3.3: RxJS particles hover effect

See also

- `Particles.js`: https://vincentgarreau.com/particles.js/

Adding subtle elegance to components with RxJS transitions

The way we can improve the user experience of our UI components is by adding clear and visually appealing feedback. And what could be a better way to do so, than adding a sophisticated reactive animation to a component? Let's imagine that, for our brand-new design system, we need to create an upload button with a visually appealing progress indicator that gracefully updates.

How to do it...

In this recipe, we are going to be creative and craft a recipe for an upload button where we are gradually going to increase the progress and control animation states in between until the upload is fully over.

Step 1 – Increasing the upload progress

As the first step, we are going to define a random progress stream that emits values from 0 to 100:

```
const uploadProgress$ = range(0, 101).pipe(
    zipWith(interval(50)),
    map(([value, _]) => value),
    take(101)
);
```

Here, we could get creative in how we generate the upload progress or retrieve the actual progress from a server. The current approach is just a simulation, and the focus of this recipe is on animating the upload progress.

Step 2 – Animating the upload progress

After we effectively manage different button upload progress, we can leverage RxJS BehaviorSubject state transitions, and animate button upload progress accordingly:

```
const clickStream$ = this.upload$.pipe(
    tap(() => this.btnState$.next(EBtnStates.LOADING)),
    switchMap(() => animationFrames()),
    withLatestFrom(uploadProgress$, this.btnState$),
    distinctUntilChanged(
```

```
        ([_, progress], [__, prevProgress]) =>
            progress === prevProgress),
    tap(([_, progress]) => {
        if (progress === 100) {
            this.btnState$.next(EBtnStates.DONE);
        }
    }),
    takeWhile(([_, __, btnState]) =>
        btnState !== EBtnStates.DONE, true)
);
```

Whenever we click a button, we are going to switch to the `animationFrames()` stream, which gives us a timeframe to update and render performant animations. We are going to take the animation frames stream as long as we are not in the DONE state. After that, we are going to combine that stream with the latest stream from `uploadProgress$` and increase the progress background width of the button.

In the template of `button-upload.component.html`, we can bind the `buttonWidth` signal value to the upload background effect:

```html
<button #button id="submitButton" (click)="startUpload()">
<span
  class="upload"
  [style.width.px]="buttonProgressWidth()"
></span>
  @if ((btnState$ | async) === 'loading') {
      <span class="spinner"></span>
  } @else if ((btnState$ | async) === 'done') {
      <span class="checkmark"></span>
  } @else {
      <span class="upload-text">Upload</span>
  }
</button>
```

Finally, when we open our browser, we can see this animation in action:

Figure 3.4: Animated upload progress

See also

- RxJS animationFrame: https://rxjs.dev/api/index/function/animationFrames

Get This Book's PDF Version and Exclusive Extras

Scan the QR code (or go to packtpub.com/unlock). Search for this book by name, confirm the edition, and then follow the steps on the page.

Note: Keep your invoice handy. Purchases made directly from Packt don't require one.

4

Testing RxJS Applications

Code testing is one of the best and most vital practices in modern software development. Establishing code testing as a practice ensures the reliability and correctness of our code, improves code quality, makes our code more resilient to errors, and acts as a safety net when we want to introduce a change in our code. We can use unit testing to verify that all components are working as expected in isolation. Then, we can write integration tests to verify that components in our system work together in certain scenarios or to check if they are well integrated with external systems, such as backend APIs. Tests can also serve us as documentation of the expected behavior of the code. All these benefits apply to testing RxJS code as well, especially for complex streams. By testing Observables, subscriptions, and operators, we can verify that data flows as expected and asynchronous operations are handled correctly.

Testing can be challenging, especially with RxJS, because of its asynchronous nature, where operations execute over time and not in a predictable, linear fashion. That's why we have a lot of cool testing tools and libraries to make our lives easier when dealing with async code and event coordination. Key elements in RxJS unit testing include the following:

- **TestScheduler**: A virtual time environment to control and simulate time-based operations, making testing asynchronous code deterministic
- **Marble diagrams**: A visual representation to describe the expected behavior of Observables and operators over time, aiding in test case design
- **Assertion libraries**: Utilize libraries such as Jasmine or Jest to define expectations and verify that the actual output matches the desired outcome

In this chapter, we'll cover the following recipes:

- Mastering time-based RxJS operators with marble testing
- Mocking HTTP dependencies with Observables in Angular
- Mocking API calls with **Mock Service Worker (MSW)**
- Testing complex state management with NgRx

Technical requirements

To follow along in this chapter, you'll need the following:

- Angular v19+
- Karma
- Jasmine
- Jest
- RxJS v7
- MSW
- Node.js v22+
- npm v11++ or pnpm v10+

The code for recipes in this chapter is placed in the GitHub repository here: `https://github.com/PacktPublishing/RxJS-Cookbook-for-Reactive-Programming/tree/main/Chapter04`

Mastering time-based RxJS operators with marble testing

RxJS marble diagrams are a powerful tool for visualizing and understanding the behavior of Observables and operators in reactive programming. They provide a clear, timeline-based representation of how values, events, and errors flow through Observable streams. By using intuitive symbols and a visual timeline, marble diagrams simplify the communication and comprehension of RxJS concepts, aiding in the design, debugging, and documentation of reactive code. That can help us understand how complex reactive systems work and make testing of reactive code way easier, especially when dealing with asynchronous operations and state transitions.

Getting ready

To demonstrate the power of RxJS marbles, we are going to write a marble unit test for the *Streamlining real-time updates with RxJS-powered notifications* recipe from *Chapter 2* (https://github.com/PacktPublishing/RxJS-Cookbook-for-Reactive-Programming/tree/main/Chapter02/rxjs-notification).

To understand the marble diagram syntax and help us follow along with this recipe, here is a quick cheat sheet:

- `-`: Represents a single frame of virtual time passing
- `[a-z0-9]`: Represents a value emitted by the Observable.
- `(abc)`: Groups multiple values emitted in the same frame
- `|`: Represents the completion of the Observable
- `#`: Represents an error thrown by the Observable
- `^`: Represents the point at which a subscription starts
- `!`: Represents the point at which a subscription ends (unsubscribes)
- `[0-9]+(ms|s|m)`: Represents a specific duration of time (milliseconds, seconds, minutes)

How to do it...

In this recipe, we will test the stream of notifications that are incoming asynchronously over time and stacking in the UI. To accomplish this, we will present incoming notifications with marble diagrams and then assert the given sequence of events to make sure we get timely state transitions, which will be represented in the UI.

Step 1 – Setting up TestScheduler

At the beginning of the test, we'll set up `TestScheduler`. We'll need `TestScheduler` to execute our Observable streams in a controlled, virtual time environment:

```
describe('NotificationService', () => {
    let service: NotificationService;
    let testScheduler: TestScheduler;

    beforeEach(() => {
        TestBed.configureTestingModule({
            providers: [NotificationService]
        });
```

```
        testScheduler = new TestScheduler(
            (actual, expected) => {
                expect(actual).toEqual(expected);
        });
    service = TestBed.inject(NotificationService);
});
```

Step 2 – Testing simple RxJS streams

In this step, for the simplicity of the test, we will comment out the automatic dismissal of notifications inside of the addNotification$() method, just for now:

```
addNotification$(
    notification: Notification,
    autodismiss = true,
    timeout = 5000
) {
    this.addNotification$.next(notification);

    // if (autodismiss) {
    // timer(timeout).subscribe(() =>
      this.removeNotification(notification.id));
  // }
}
```

Here, we will demonstrate how notifications are added to the stack over time and how we can represent that timeline with RxJS marble diagrams:

```
it('should add notifications', fakeAsync(() => {
    testScheduler.run(({ cold, expectObservable,
        expectSubscriptions }) => {
            const notification1:
                Notification = { id: '1',
                    message: 'Recipe added successfully.',
                    type: 'success' };
            const notification2:
                Notification = { id: '2',
                    message: 'Recipe added successfully.',
                    type: 'success' };
        const add1$ = cold('a', { a: notification1 });
```

```
        const add2$ = cold('--a', { a: notification2 });
        const expected$ = 'a-b';
        const expectedValues = {
            a: [notification1],
            b: [notification1, notification2]
        };
        add1$.subscribe(notification =>
            service.addNotification(notification));
        add2$.subscribe(notification =>
            service.addNotification(notification));
            service.notifications.subscribe();
        // Delay the subscription to notifications$ to
        //ensure addNotification has been called
        testScheduler.schedule(() =>
            expectObservable(service.notifications$)
            .toBe(expected$, expectedValues));
    });
}));
```

Let's break down the example a bit:

1. First, we create a cold Observable for the first notification at the first frame of time. The reason for that is that compared to hot Observables, cold Observables offer us better control and predictability for testing asynchronous behavior since they start emitting values only when we subscribe to the stream.

2. For the second notification, nothing will happen at the first two frames, then we will wait at the third frame and finally emit a value.

Imagine this as a timeline of events that we can visually represent in our code, where each '-' instance in the timeline represents 1 ms. We emit the first notification immediately. Meanwhile, the second notification waits for two frames and then emits a value. When we look at a timeline of events, we can clearly see that the order was as follows:

1. First frame – The first notification emits a value; the second notification waits. At this point, we are expecting to have one notification in the stack.

2. Second frame – Nothing happens, we still have one notification in the stack.

3. Third frame – The second notification emits a value. Once we emit the second notification, we expect to have two notifications in the stack.

Step 3 – Testing complex RxJS streams

Now that we understand the basics of marble testing, we are ready to test more complex
streams, such as auto-dismissing notifications after varying delays. We are about to see how this
functionality affects a timeline where we are adding multiple notifications but also dismissing
them in between. After uncommenting the code from the `addNotification$()` method we did
in *step 2*, our test might look like this:

```
it('should add and remove notification after 5 seconds',
fakeAsync(() => {
    testScheduler.run((({ cold, expectObservable }) => {
        const notification1: Notification = { id: '1',
            message: 'Recipe added successfully.',
            type: 'success' };
        const notification2: Notification = { id: '2',
            message: 'Recipe could not be added.',
            type: 'error' };
        const notification3: Notification = { id: '3',
            message: 'Recipe could not be added.',
            type: 'error' };
        const add1$ = cold('a', { a: notification1 });
        const add2$ = cold('1500ms a', { a: notification2
});
    const add3$ = cold('4000ms a', { a: notification3 });
    const expected$ =
        'a 1499ms b 2499ms c 999ms d 3999ms e';
    const expectedValues = {
        a: [notification1],
        b: [notification1, notification2],
        c: [notification1, notification2, notification3],
        d: [notification2, notification3],
        e: [notification2]
    };
    add1$.subscribe(notification =>
        service.addNotification(notification));
    add2$.subscribe(notification =>
        service.addNotification(notification, false));
    add3$.subscribe(notification =>
```

```
        service.addNotification(notification));
        service.notifications.subscribe();

        testScheduler.schedule(() => {
            expectObservable(service.notifications$).toBe(
                expected$,
                expectedValues
            );
        });
    });
}));
```

Let's break down this example as well to reinforce understanding:

1. We create a cold Observable for the first notification, which we emit right away.

2. After 1500 ms, we emit the second notification, which won't be auto dismissible. That means that the notification will stay in the stack until we remove it manually.

3. After 4000 ms, we emit the third notification.

Now, the fun part starts. At first, by looking at the expected timeline, some values might seem strange, but there is a good reason behind these values. Every emission of a value takes 1 ms of virtual time. That means that if we want to create a 1500 ms gap between two emitted values, we can describe this timeline as with marble diagrams: `'a 1499ms b'`. Now, if we look closely at the expected timeline, `'a 1499ms b 2499ms c 999ms d 3999ms e'`, things start to make sense:

1. First, we emit a value for the first notification, which will be dismissed after 5000 ms. At that point, we have the first notification in the stack.

2. We wait 1499 ms, then we emit the second notification that takes 1 ms, which won't be auto-dismissed from the stack. At that point, we have the first two notifications in the stack.

3. The third notification should be emitted 4000 ms after the first notification. So far, 1500 ms have passed in virtual time. That means we must wait 2499 ms to emit a value for the third notification. At that point, we have all three notifications in the stack.

4. So far, 4000 ms have passed in the timeline after we emitted the first value. That means we wait for 999 ms until the first notification is auto-dismissed from the stack. Once that happens, we have the second and third notifications left in the stack.

5. At this point in virtual time, since we emitted the third notification, 1000 ms have passed. We wait for 3999 ms more and remove the third notification from the stack. Finally, we are left with only the second notification in the stack.

Wasn't that hard as it seemed at first, right? These marble diagrams are fun! By following this pattern, with marble diagrams, we can describe any asynchronous stream of events, which can help us be more descriptive about our test.

See also

- Marble syntax: `https://rxjs.dev/guide/testing/marble-testing#marble-syntax`
- RxJS marble testing blog: `https://betterprogramming.pub/rxjs-testing-write-unit-tests-for-observables-603af959e251`
- *Getting Started with Marble Tests* course: `https://rxjs-course.dev/course/testing/getting-started-with-marble-tests`
- Ben Lesh's article *Hot vs Cold Observables*: `https://benlesh.medium.com/hot-vs-cold-observables-f8094ed53339`
- *Testing asynchronous RxJs operators* article: `https://medium.com/angular-in-depth/testing-asynchronous-rxjs-operators-5495784f249e`
- *How to test Observables* article: `https://medium.com/angular-in-depth/how-to-test-observables-a00038c7faad`
- Marble testing helpers for RxJS and Jasmine: `https://www.npmjs.com/package/jasmine-marbles`

Mocking HTTP dependencies with Observables in Angular

In Angular, every HTTP call is represented as an Observable. That means whenever we are writing an integration test with an external service, we have to mock HTTP dependencies as we don't want the real request being triggered from a test itself.

Getting ready

In this recipe, we're going to test network request services that we implemented in *Chapter 1* (`https://github.com/PacktPublishing/RxJS-Cookbook-for-Reactive-Programming/tree/main/Chapter01/network-requests`).

How to do it...

In order to mock HTTP calls to external services, we will take the help of the `@angular/common/http/testing` module and learn how to test requests being sent in sequence as well as in parallel.

Step 1 — Setting up TestBed

To be able to mock HTTP communication with external services, we first need to set up the `TestBed` module at the beginning of each test. In our `recipe.service.spec.ts` file, we will have the following configuration in place:

```
beforeEach(() => {
    TestBed.configureTestingModule({
        providers: [
            provideHttpClient(),
            provideHttpClientTesting(),
            RecipesService
        ],
    });
    service = TestBed.inject(RecipesService);
    httpMock = TestBed.inject(HttpTestingController);
});

afterEach(() => {
    httpMock.verify();
});
```

Now, when we run our tests, instead of hitting the real backend, a request will be sent to our test mock backend. We can also notice that we are injecting `HttpTestingController`, which helps us to interact with the mocked backend, send requests to it, and assert responses that come back from the mocked backend.

After each test execution, we call the `httpMock.verify()` function to confirm that all mocked HTTP requests within the test have been properly handled and asserted, thus preventing accidental omissions and maintaining test integrity.

Step 2 — Testing a simple HTTP request

In our `recipe.service.ts` file, we have a getRecipes$ service method that is sending an HTTP request:

```
getRecipes$(): Observable<Recipe[]> {
    return this.httpClient.get<Recipe[]>('/api/recipes');
}
```

The response from an HTTP call such as this would look something like this:

```
const mockResponse = [
    {
    "id": 1,
    "name": "Spaghetti Aglio e Olio",
    "description": "Simple yet flavorful pasta with garlic,
                    olive oil, and chili flakes",
    "ingredients": ["spaghetti", "garlic", "olive oil",
                    "chili flakes", "parmesan cheese",
                    "parsley"]
    },
    {
    "id": 2,
    "name": "Chicken Tikka Masala",
    "description": "Creamy, spiced Indian curry with tender
                    chicken pieces.",
    "ingredients": ["chicken breasts", "yogurt",
                    "garam masala", "turmeric", "cumin",
                    "tomatoes", "onion", "ginger",
                    "garlic", "heavy cream"]
    },
];
```

Now, we can assert this response by calling the getRecipes$ method within the test.

In our integration test, we will define a test-case scenario for fetching a list of recipes:

```
it('should fetch a list of recipes', fakeAsync(async () => {
    const recipes$ = service.getRecipes$();
    const recipes = firstValueFrom(recipes$);
```

```
    const request = httpMock.expectOne('/api/recipes');
    request.flush(mockResponse);

    expect(await recipes).toEqual(mockResponse);
}));
```

Let's break down what we did here:

1. First, we assign an HTTP call to the `recipes$` variable.
2. Then, we use the `firstValueFrom` function from RxJS, which subscribes automatically to an Observable, sends the HTTP request, and converts the value into a Promise.
3. Next, we assert the request with `HttpTestingController` and check if the correct request has been sent.
4. Then, we deliver the mock response with the `flush` method.
5. Finally, we assert the response.

Step 3 – Testing multiple requests in sequence

In our `recipe.service.ts` file, we have a `getRecipeDetails$()` method that sends two requests in sequence, one after the other:

```
getRecipeById$(id: number): Observable<Recipe> {
    return this.httpClient
    .get<Recipe>(`/api/recipes?id=${id}`);
}
getRecipeDetails$(
    id: number
): Observable<{ recipe: Recipe; details: RecipeDetails }> {
    return this.getRecipeById$(id).pipe(
        switchMap((recipe: Recipe) => {
            return this.httpClient
            .get<RecipeDetails>(`/api/recipes/details?id=
                                ${id}`)
            .pipe(
                map((details) => ({ recipe, details }))
            );
        })
    );
}
```

This means that in our test, we must assert both ongoing requests and responses since we are combining them as the result of the whole stream.

Our mocked response will look something like this:

```
const dummyRecipe = {
    "id": 1,
    "name": "Spaghetti Aglio e Olio",
    "description": "Simple yet flavorful pasta with garlic,
                    olive oil, and chili flakes",
    "ingredients": ["spaghetti", "garlic", "olive oil",
                    "chili flakes", "parmesan cheese",
                    "parsley"]
};
const dummyDetails = {
    "id": 1,
    "prepTime": 7200000,
    "cuisine": "Italian",
    "diet": "Vegetarian",
    "url": "/assets/images/spaghetti.jpg",
    "nutrition": {
        "calories": 450,
        "fat": 15,
        "carbs": 70,
        "protein": 10
    }
};
```

Now, let's test fetching recipe details:

```
it('should fetch recipe details', async () => {
    const recipeDetails$ = service
    .getRecipeDetails$(dummyRecipe.id);
    const recipeDetails = firstValueFrom(recipeDetails$);
    const req1 = httpMock.expectOne(`/api/recipes?id=${dummyRecipe.id}`);
    req1.flush(dummyRecipe);
    const req2 = httpMock.expectOne(
        `/api/recipes/details?id=${dummyRecipe.id}`);
    req2.flush(dummyDetails);
```

```
        expect((await recipeDetails).recipe)
        .toEqual(dummyRecipe);
        expect((awaitrecipeDetails).details)
        .toEqual(dummyDetails);
    });
```

Here, we can notice that we are asserting ongoing requests as well as the responses from both.

Step 4 — Testing multiple requests in parallel

In our service, we have a `getRecipesWithImageInParallel$` method that sends multiple image requests in parallel:

```
getRecipesWithImageInParallel$(): Observable<Object[]> {
    return this.getRecipes$().pipe(
        tap((recipes: Recipe[]) => this.recipes.next(
                                            recipes)),
        switchMap((recipes: Recipe[]) => {
            const imageRequests = recipes.map((recipe) =>
            this.httpClient.get(`/api/recipes/images? id=${recipe.id}`
          ));
            return forkJoin(imageRequests);
        }),
    );
}
```

The `getRecipes$` service will return the same response as we had in *step 3*. Once we get a list of recipes, we will send multiple requests in parallel for each recipe's image:

```
const dummyImages = [
    {
    "id": 1,
    "url": "/assets/images/spaghetti.jpg"
    },
    {
    "id": 2,
    "url": "/assets/images/chicken_tikka_masala.jpg"
    },
];
```

Now, when we test this HTTP call, we should be able to assert the image responses for each recipe:

```
it('should fetch recipes with images in parallel', async () => {
    const recipeImages$ = service
    .getRecipesWithImageInParallel$();
    const recipeImages = firstValueFrom(recipeImages$);
    const req = httpMock.expectOne('/api/recipes');
    expect(req.request.method).toBe('GET');
    req.flush(dummyRecipes);
    dummyRecipes.forEach((recipe, index) => {
        const imgReq = httpMock.expectOne(
            `/api/recipes/images?id=${recipe.id}`);
        expect(imgReq.request.method).toBe('GET');
        imgReq.flush(dummyImages[index]);
    });
    expect(await recipeImages).toEqual(dummyImages);
});
```

Note that in this test, we are using `forEach` to iterate through each recipe that we're about to send a request to and extract images for each individual recipe.

Step 5 — Testing errors

In our service, let's extend the `getRecipes$` method to handle the error case:

```
getRecipes$(): Observable<Recipe[]> {
    return this.httpClient.get<Recipe[]>('/api/recipes'
    ).pipe(
        catchError(
            () => of(new Error('Error fetching recipes'))
        )
    );
}
```

The way we can test this error scenario is by flushing the error to `httpMock` and asserting the error instance and message in the end:

```
it('should handle error when fetching recipes', async () => {
    const recipes$ = service.getRecipes$();
    const recipes = firstValueFrom(recipes$);
    const req = httpMock.expectOne('/api/recipes');
    expect(req.request.method).toBe('GET');
    req.flush('Failed!', {
        status: 500,
        statusText: 'Error fetching recipes'
    });
    const recipesResponse = await recipes;
    expect(recipesResponse).toBeInstanceOf(Error);
    expect(recipesResponse.message).toEqual(
                    'Error fetching recipes');
});
```

See also

- Angular docs guide on testing: `https://angular.dev/guide/http/testing#expecting-and-answering-requests`

- Angular docs guide on testing services: `https://angular.dev/guide/testing/services#httpclienttestingmodule`

Mocking API calls with MSW

In the preceding recipe, we have seen how Angular's `HttpTestingController` class helped us mock integration with external services and prevent real HTTP requests from being triggered.

In this recipe, we're going to explore how we can simplify this process even further with the **Mock Service Worker (MSW)** library. In general, MSW is like a proxy between the browser and external services, so it is ideal to intercept all ongoing requests and return what we desire instead of pinging the real backend service. This is especially useful for writing integration tests.

Getting ready

In this recipe, we're going to test network request services that we implemented in *Chapter 1* (`https://github.com/PacktPublishing/RxJS-Cookbook-for-Reactive-Programming/tree/main/Chapter01/network-requests`).

How to do it...

Since MSW works only with Jest, we first need to set up the test configuration in the Angular project to use Jest, and not default testing frameworks Jasmine and Karma. The way we can do it is by using the `jest-preset-angular` library. We'll go through the same test-case scenarios we looked at in the preceding recipe, but this time, we will see the power of MSW and how we can simplify the testing process of RxJS side effects such as network requests and errors.

Jest setup

To keep the focus of the recipe on writing tests, we will skip the Jest setup part. But if you need more info on how to do it, you can check this fantastic blog from Tim Deschryver on how to integrate Jest into an Angular application and library: `https://timdeschryver.dev/blog/integrate-jest-into-an-angular-application-and-library#`.

Step 1 – Setting up TestBed

To be able to mock HTTP communication with external services, we first need to start MSW before each test by importing the server from the `mocks/node.ts` file. After that, we will set up the `TestBed` module at the beginning of each test.

In our `recipe.service.spec.ts` file, we have the following configuration in place:

```
beforeEach(() => {
    TestBed.configureTestingModule({
        providers: [
            provideHttpClient(),
            RecipesService
        ],
    });

    service = TestBed.inject(RecipesService);
});

beforeAll (() => {
    server.listen();
});
```

Now, the difference from the preceding recipe is that we omitted the need to put `provideHttpClientTesting` into the `providers` array as well as injecting `HttpTestingController`. Also, note that before running all tests, we need to call the `listen()` method on a mocked server provided by MSW. This will start MSW and intercept all API calls to the real backend service.

Step 2 – Testing a simple HTTP request

In our `recipe.service.ts` file, we have the `getRecipes$` service method that sends an HTTP request, so the integration test for that external communication would look like this:

```
test('should fetch a list of recipes', async () => {
    const recipes$ = service.getRecipes$()
    const response = await firstValueFrom(recipes$)
    expect(response).toStrictEqual([{
        "id": 1,
        "name": "Spaghetti Aglio e Olio",
        "description": "Simple yet flavorful pasta with
                        garlic, olive oil, and chili
                        flakes",
        "ingredients": ["spaghetti", "garlic", "olive oil",
                        "chili flakes", "parmesan cheese",
                        "parsley"]
    }])
});
```

Let's see what we did in the preceding test:

1. We call the `getRecipes$` method to trigger a request.
2. Then, the request is automatically intercepted by MSW and a mocked response is returned.
3. Next, with the `firstValueFrom` operator, we extract the response value.
4. Finally, we do Jest assertion to check if the response is indeed the one that we are expecting to have.

Step 3 – Testing multiple requests in sequence

In our `recipe.service.ts` file, we have the `getRecipeDetails$()` method that sends two requests in sequence, one after the other.

This means that in our test, we must assert both ongoing requests and responses since we are combining them as the result of the whole stream:

```
test('should fetch recipe details', (done) => {
    const dummyRecipe = {
        id: 1,
        name: 'Spaghetti Aglio e Olio',
        description: 'Simple yet flavorful pasta with
                        garlic, olive oil, and chili flakes',
        ingredients: ['spaghetti', 'garlic']
    };
    const dummyDetails = {
        id: 1,
        prepTime: 7200000,
        cuisine:: 'Italian',
        diet: 'Vegetarian',
        url: '/assets/images/spaghetti.jpg',
        nutrition: {
            calories: 450,
            fat: 15,
            carbs: 70,
            protein: 10
        }
    };

    const recipes$ = service.getRecipeDetails$(
                            dummyRecipe.id)
    const {
        recipe,
        details
    } = await firstValueFrom(recipes$)
    expect(recipe).toEqual(dummyRecipe);
    expect(details).toEqual(dummyDetails);
```

Let's see what we did in the preceding test:

1. We call the `getRecipesDetails$` method to trigger two requests in sequence, one after the other.

2. The requests are automatically intercepted by MSW, and a mocked response is returned.

3. With the `firstValueFrom` operator, we extract the response value.

4. We do Jest assertion to check if both responses are the ones we expect to have.

Step 4 – Testing multiple requests in parallel

In our service, we have the `getRecipesWithImageInParallel$` method that sends multiple image requests in parallel.

Here's how we can test these requests:

```
test('should fetch recipes with images in parallel', (done) => {
    const dummyRecipes = // same value as in previous step
    const dummyImages = [
    {
        "id": 1,
        "url": "/assets/images/spaghetti.jpg"
    },
    {
        "id": 2,
        "url": "/assets/images/chicken_tikka_masala.jpg"
    },
    ]

    const recipes$ = service.getRecipesWithImageInParallel$()
    const images = await firstValueFrom(recipes$)
    expect(images).toStrictEqual(dummyImages);
});
}
```

Comparing this approach to that in the preceding recipe, note how simplified our integration test looks, thanks to the power of MSW.

Step 5 – Testing errors

In our service, we have the getRecipes$ method that sends simple HTTP requests but also has a catchError handler in case of an error:

```
test('request error', waitForAsync(async () => {
    server.use([
        http.get('/api/recipes', async ({ request }) => {
            return HttpResponse.error()
        })
    ])
    const recipes$ = service.getRecipes$()
    const errorResponse = await firstValueFrom(recipes$)
    expect(errorResponse.message).toStrictEqual(
                       'Something went wrong.');
}));
```

Here is where it gets a little bit tricky with MSW. There is no way to have both success and error cases within the same MSW handler, so if we want to simulate an error within the test, we must override the original handler with the error one to return a mocked error response.

After that, the process is standard to the previous approach: we call the service method, extract the response with the firstValueFrom operator, and assert the error message.

See also

- jest-preset-angular library: https://www.npmjs.com/package/jest-preset-angular
- MSW docs: https://mswjs.io/

Testing complex state management with NgRx

NgRx is a powerful state management library built on the principles of Redux, tailored for Angular applications. With its emphasis on structured state management, NgRx is a popular choice for large-scale Angular applications where state complexity can easily become overwhelming.

Getting ready

In *Chapter 6*, we will use NgRx as state management in Angular. Here, we will use the same recipe and write unit tests for the provided functionality (https://github.com/PacktPublishing/RxJS-Cookbook-for-Reactive-Programming/tree/main/Chapter06/ngrx-state-management).

How to do it...

In this recipe, we will go over the cooking recipe app example and write unit and integration tests for different parts of NgRx, such as the following:

- Store
- Selectors
- Actions
- Effects

Step 1 – Setting up a mock store

To test if the selector is slicing the correct piece of a state that we can subscribe to within our component, we first need to set up a mock store inside of our unit test. We can do that easily with the `provideMockStore` method from the `ngrx/store/testing` package:

```
describe('RecipesSelectors', () => {
    const initialState: AppState = {
        recipesState: {
            recipes: [
            {
              "id": 1,
              "name": "Spaghetti Aglio e Olio",
              "description": "Simple yet flavorful pasta
                             with garlic, olive oil, and
                             chili flakes",
              "ingredients": ["spaghetti", "garlic", "olive
                             oil", "chili flakes",
                             "parmesan cheese",
                             "parsley"],
              "image": "/assets/images/spaghetti.jpg"
            },
            ],
            selectedRecipe: null,
            error: null,
            loading: false
        }
    };
    let store: MockStore;
```

```
    beforeEach(() => {
        TestBed.configureTestingModule({
            providers: [provideMockStore()]
        });
        store = TestBed.inject(MockStore);
    });
});
```

Step 2 – Testing store selectors

After we have the mock store in place, we can call the `projector` function on that selector and
pass the slice of state we want to unit test:

```
it('should select the recipes state', () => {
    const result = selectRecipesState.projector(
        initialState.recipesState
    );
    expect(result.recipes.length).toEqual(1);
    expect(result.recipes[0].id).toEqual(1);
});
```

An alternative way to do the same thing is to provide a selector state through `provideMockStore`
as follows:

```
provideMockStore({
    selectors: [
        {
            selector: selectRecipesState,
            value: [
                {
                    "id": 1,
                    "name": "Spaghetti Aglio e Olio",
                    "description": "Simple yet flavorful pasta with
                                    garlic, olive oil, and chili
                                    flakes",
                    "ingredients": ["spaghetti", "garlic", "olive
                                     oil", "chili flakes",
                                    "parmesan cheese", "parsley"],
                    "image": "/assets/images/spaghetti.jpg"
```

```
            },
        ]
      },
    ]
  }),
```

After that, we can subscribe to the store selector within the test. In that case, our test would look like this:

```
it('should select the recipes state', (done) => {
    store.select(selectRecipesState).subscribe(
        (mockBooks) => {
        expect(mockBooks).toEqual([
        {
            id: 'mockedId',
            volumeInfo: {
                title: 'Mocked Title',
                authors: ['Mocked Author'],
            },
        },
    ]);
    done();
  });
});
```

Step 3 – Setting up integration test and mock actions

In our `recipes.store.spec.ts` file, we'll start off by configuring the test suite:

```
describe('RecipesEffects', () => {
    let actions$: Observable<Action>;
    let effects: RecipesEffects;
    let recipesService: RecipesService;
    let testScheduler: TestScheduler;

    beforeEach(() => {
        TestBed.configureTestingModule({
            imports: [],
            providers: [
                RecipesService,
```

```
            RecipesEffects,
            provideHttpClient(),
            provideHttpClientTesting(),
            provideMockActions(() => actions$)
        ]
    });

    effects = TestBed.inject(RecipesEffects);
    recipesService = TestBed.inject(RecipesService);
});
```

Let's break down what we have done here:

1. We are calling the `TestBed.configureTestingModule()` method before each test execution.

2. We then pass the necessary dependencies for `TestBed`.

3. We finally inject the services and effects we want to test.

Step 4 – Testing effects and dispatching actions

Now, we are ready to write our integration test. In the `recipes.effects.ts` file, we can notice that the `loadRecipe$` effect is going to observe whether `loadRecipesAction()` is being dispatched. The `getRecipes$` service method will be called with an HTTP request, which will return a response of a recipes list and dispatch `loadRecipesActionSuccess()` with the payload of that list:

```
it('should dispatch loadRecipesActionSuccess when the service responds
with recipes', async () => {
    // list of recipes, check mocks/mock.json file
    const mockRecipes = []
    spyOn(
        recipesService,
        'getRecipes$'
    ).and.returnValue(of([mockRecipes]));
    actions$ = of(loadRecipesAction());
    const effectResult =
        await firstValueFrom(effects.loadRecipes$);
    expect(effectResult).toEqual(
        loadRecipesActionSuccess({ recipes })
    );
});
```

When writing tests, it is always good practice to check the **reverse error** case, where we cause the test to fail on purpose, just to be sure if the test is working properly:

```
spyOn(recipesService, 'getRecipes$').and.returnValue(of([
    ...recipes,
    {
        "id": 6,
        "name": "Spaghetti Carbonara",
        "description": "Rich and creamy pasta with
                        pancetta, eggs, and cheese.",
        "ingredients": ["spaghetti", "pancetta", "eggs",
                        "parmesan cheese", "black pepper"],
        "image": "/assets/images/spaghetti_carbonara"
    }
]));
```

So, if we add, let's say, one more recipe as a return value of a service, our test should fail with the following error:

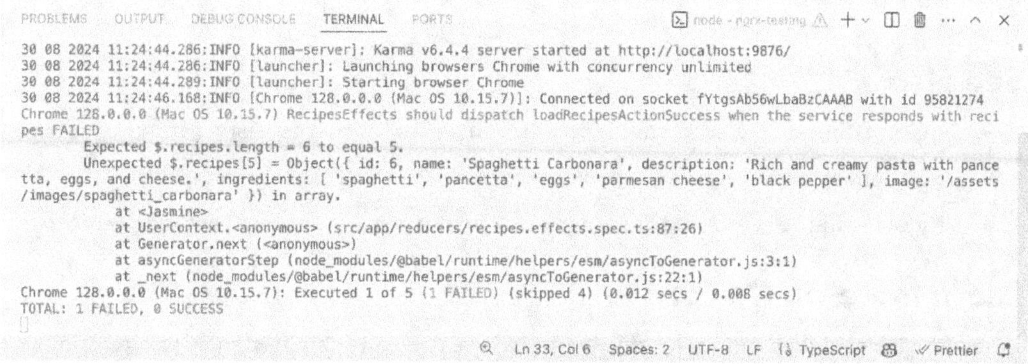

Figure 4.1: Failing test error

Now, we can safely say that our test is working as expected and not producing false positive test cases.

Step 5 – Testing effect errors

In this step, we are going to test the scenario when the service returns an error. First, we would mock an error response, then dispatch the `loadRecipesAction()` action, and finally check if our effect will catch that error and the dispatched `loadRecipesActionError()` action:

```
it('should dispatch loadRecipesActionError when the service responds with
an error', async () => {
    const error = new Error('Error loading recipes');
```

```
    spyOn(recipesService, 'getRecipes$').and.returnValue(
        throwError(() => 'error')
    );
    actions$ = of(loadRecipesAction());

    const effectResult =
        await firstValueFrom(effects.loadRecipes$);
    expect(effectResult).toEqual(loadRecipesActionError({
        error: error.message
    }));
});
```

Testing practices

As per the NgRx documentation, there are multiple strategies to write unit and integration tests, such as marble diagrams, `TestScheduler`, and `ReplaySubject`. The strategy that has been chosen in this recipe is Observables, but we can accommodate our tests to any strategy of preference.

See also

- NgRx testing strategies: `https://ngrx.io/guide/effects/testing#testing-practices`
- NgRx effect testing: `https://ngrx.io/guide/effects/testing#examples`
- NgRx testing selectors: `https://ngrx.io/guide/store/testing#testing-selectors`

Learn more on Discord

To join the Discord community for this book – where you can share feedback, ask questions to the author, and learn about new releases – follow the QR code below:

`https://packt.link/RxJSCookbook`

5

Performance Optimizations with RxJS

One of the key aspects of having amazing user experiences across the web is web performance. Performance optimization in RxJS involves carefully managing data flow and strategically using operators to streamline asynchronous operations within your applications. Key techniques include filtering unnecessary emissions, asynchronous handling, efficient data combination, and preventing memory leaks. By employing these strategies, you can minimize redundant calculations, reduce rendering overhead, and create a more responsive and smooth user experience.

In this chapter, we'll cover the following recipes:

- Optimizing RxJS streams with strategic operator selection
- Creating a custom Core Web Vitals performance monitoring system
- Using Web Workers alongside RxJS

Technical requirements

To complete this chapter, you'll need the following:

- Angular v19+
- RxJS v7
- Node.js v22+
- npm v11+ or pnpm v10+

The code for the recipes in this chapter can be found in this book's GitHub repository: `https://github.com/PacktPublishing/RxJS-Cookbook-for-Reactive-Programming/tree/main/Chapter05`.

Optimizing RxJS streams with strategic operator selection

Although RxJS is considered a very performant library, if we aren't careful, we can introduce performance bottlenecks within our system. To prevent this scenario from happening, we need to understand what might lead to inefficient RxJS streams:

- Over-subscription and memory leaks
- Inefficient operators and complex pipelines
- Complex data flows
- Misunderstanding cold and hot Observables

How to do it...

In this recipe, we're going to address and prevent most of the potential performance bottlenecks in one simple RxJS stream, such as search input that sends HTTP requests based on a search query. We'll also create a simple custom RxJS operator to benchmark the speed of stream execution.

Step 1 – Creating a stream of events

First, we'll define a simple input in the UI and create a stream of user input events. In `app.component.html`, input the following:

```
<input #input type="text" />
```

Then, in the `app.component.ts` file, we can use the `fromEvent` operator to create a stream of events:

```
@ViewChild('input') input!: ElementRef;


ngAfterViewInit(): void {
    const input$ = fromEvent<KeyboardEvent>(
        this.input.nativeElement, 'input'       );
}
```

Step 2 – Transforming the data stream for efficiency

If we subscribe to the current stream, we'll get an Observable stream of `InputEvent` values. But we're only interested in the input value, nothing else. Also, we don't want to send the request if the input is empty, in which case we know that the result should be an empty list. We can achieve this by using RxJS's `map` and `filter` operators:

```
input$.pipe(
    map((event: Event) =>
        (event.target as HTMLInputElement).value),
    filter((value) => value.trim().length > 0),
)
```

Step 3 – Filtering to reduce data flow

At the moment, whenever the user types something, a new value will be emitted. This isn't efficient since the new request will be sent to the API on each emission. Also, we want to prevent our application from reacting too quickly to every single change so that we get a smoother and more responsive user experience. We can narrow down the data and optimize the stream further by rate-limiting events with `debounceTime` and `distinctUntilChanged`:

```
input$.pipe(
    debounceTime(300),
    map((event:Event) =>
        (event.target as HTMLInputElement).value),
    distinctUntilChanged(),
    filter((value) => value.trim().length > 0),
)
```

Step 4 – Canceling unnecessary requests

While the user types the search query and we get the latest, filtered queries, we want to send an HTTP request to the API to get the result based on that query. To ensure that only the latest search term triggers an API request and all previous ones are canceled when the user types quickly, we can use the higher-order `switchMap` Observable. By doing this, we can optimize how we deliver results from the API to the user:

```
input$.pipe(
    debounceTime(300),
    map((event: Event) =>
        (event.target as HTMLInputElement).value),
    distinctUntilChanged(),
```

```
        filter((value) => value.trim().length > 0),
        switchMap((value) =>
            this.recipesService.getRecipes$(value)),
    )
```

Here are some of the ways `switchMap` can help us:

- **Prevents memory leaks**: It prevents potential memory leaks that could occur if multiple inner Observables remain subscribed and active concurrently, consuming resources even when they're no longer needed.

- **Prevents resource accumulation**: Without `switchMap`, you might end up with multiple pending asynchronous operations accumulating if the source Observable emits values quickly. The `switchMap` Observable ensures only the latest operation is active, preventing resource wastage.

- **Simplifies nested subscriptions**: In complex data flows, you might need to subscribe to multiple Observables in a nested fashion. The `switchMap` Observable flattens this nesting, making the code more readable and maintainable.

- **Avoids subscription management overhead**: Manual subscription management in nested scenarios can be error-prone and lead to memory leaks if it's not handled meticulously. The `switchMap` Observable automates this process, reducing the risk of leaks.

Step 5 — Caching the results

Let's imagine a scenario where multiple components want the same result that we got when the user searches for a term. Each of these new subscriptions will trigger an Observable stream again, which might be inefficient because of unnecessary execution. To ensure that multiple subscribers receive the same values and also cache and replay a portion of the emitted values to new subscribers, we can use the `shareReplay` operator:

```
input$.pipe(
    map((event: Event) =>
        (event.target as HTMLInputElement).value),
    debounceTime(300),
    distinctUntilChanged(),
    filter((value) => value.trim().length > 0),
    switchMap((value) =>
        this.recipesService.getRecipes$(value)),
    shareReplay(1)
)
```

In this case, `shareReplay` creates a hot Observable out of a cold one.

Hot versus cold Observables

Understanding the difference between **hot** and **cold** Observables is crucial for managing resources and data flows effectively, as well as avoiding unexpected behaviors in your RxJS applications. We can think of cold Observables as a factory that creates a product line each time someone wants a product. Cold Observables are more resource-efficient in simple scenarios, since they produce data only when needed and execute once per subscription. We refer to cold Observables as unicast as each subscriber receives an independent sequence of data. We can think of hot Observables as a radio station that's always broadcasting, whether someone is listening or not. Hot Observables are more performant on a larger scale and when implementing caching mechanisms. That's why we refer to hot Observables as multicast – the stream will be executed once, and all subscribers will get the same value.

Step 6 – Preventing memory leaks

Ironically, usage of the `shareReplay` operator can cause memory leaks across our application. The way we used it here will cause the stream to always be active, even when the component is destroyed. We can control this by passing `refCount` as an argument to the `shareReplay` operator:

```
input$.pipe(
    map((event: Event) =>
        (event.target as HTMLInputElement).value),
    debounceTime(300),
    distinctUntilChanged(),
    filter((value) => value.trim().length > 0),
    switchMap((value) =>
        this.recipesService.getRecipes$(value)),
    shareReplay({ bufferSize: 1, refCount: true }),
    takeUntil(this.destroy$)
)
```

Let's take a closer look at this code, step by step:

1. We keep `bufferSize` set to 1 so that we only replay the latest cached value.

2. We pass `refCount` to keep track of the number of active subscribers. When the subscriber count drops to 0, the underlying Observable is automatically unsubscribed, and its resources are cleaned up.

3. Finally, we unsubscribe from the stream with `takeUntil` once the component has been destroyed.

How does shareReplay work under the hood?

Under the hood, the `shareReplay` operator leverages `ReplaySubject` to be able to manage multicast values that are emitted from the source Observable to multiple subscribers. By default, `shareReplay` will cache the number of passed buffer values forever. Even when the number of subscribers drops to zero, it won't unsubscribe from `ReplaySubject`. If we aren't careful, this might cause memory leaks in our application, but we might want to do this when we want to avoid expensive computations for Observables that are frequently used. If we want to have programmatic control over this behavior, `shareReplay` provides a configuration object that can be passed as an argument. Also, if we would like un-subscriptions to be automatically handled by RxJS, we might consider using the `share` operator.

Another commonly used technique is to use the `takeUntil` operator, which helps us manage the life cycle of Observable subscriptions gracefully. While it's often used for component destruction, it can have broader applications for controlling the flow of data based on external events or conditions.

takeUntil – a common pitfall

One of the most common misconceptions about the `takeUntil` operator is its placement within the stream. Order matters! The position of `takeUntil` determines which operators are affected by the notifier and in what order. The most common and straightforward placement is at the end of the operator chain. This allows the entire stream of operators to process values until the notifier Observable emits. If we place `takeUntil` in the middle of a stream, we can selectively control which parts of the stream are affected by the notifier. It can also be placed within a higher-order Observable such as `switchMap`, `mergeMap`, or `concatMap` to control the lifespan of inner Observables. Being able to place the `takeUntil` operator flexibly gives us fine-grained control over our Observable streams and helps manage their life cycle effectively.

Step 7 – Measuring RxJS stream performance

In the same way that we can measure performance with the built-in **Performance API**, we can create something similar in RxJS to mark the start and the end of a stream. For this purpose, we'll create custom operators that we'll carefully place within the stream we want to monitor:

```
export function startMeasurePerformance<T>() {
    return (source$: Observable<T>) => new Observable<T>(
        observer => {
        const subscription = source$.pipe(
            skipUntil(source$)
        ).subscribe({
        next(value) {
            performance.mark('start')
            observer.next(value);
        },
        error(err) { observer.error(err); },
        complete() { observer.complete(); }
    });

    return subscription;
});
}
```

Once we place the `startMeasurePerformance` operator at the beginning of the stream and mark the start of Performance Monitor, we can place `measurePerformance` at the end of the stream:

```
export function measurePerformance<T>() {
    return (source$: Observable<T>) => new Observable<T>(
        observer => {
        const subscription = source$.subscribe({
            next(value) {
                observer.next(value);
                performance.mark('end');
                performance.measure(
                    'Measure between start and end',
                    'start',
                    'end'
                );
```

```
                  const measure = performance
                  .getEntriesByName(
                      'Measure between start and end')
                  [0];
                  console.log(`
                      Duration between start and end:
                          ${measure.duration} milliseconds.
                  `);
                  performance.clearMarks();
                  performance.clearMeasures();
              },
          error(err) { observer.error(err); },
          complete() { observer.complete(); }
      });


      return subscription;
  });
}
```

See also

- Dmytro Mezhenskyi's video about the hidden pitfalls of shareReplay: `https://www.youtube.com/watch?v=mVKAzhlqTx8&t`

- Joshua Morony's fantastic video about improved performance with the share and shareReplay operators: `https://www.youtube.com/watch?v=H542ZSyubrE`

- Dominic Elm's advanced caching mechanism blog: `https://blog.thoughtram.io/angular/2018/03/05/advanced-caching-with-rxjs.html`

- The shareReplay operator: `https://rxjs.dev/api/index/function/shareReplay`

- The share operator: `https://rxjs.dev/api/index/function/share`

- Mastering RxJS Memory Leaks: The Leak Detective Handbook: `https://hackernoon.com/mastering-rxjs-memory-leaks-the-leak-detective-handbook`

- Async Pipe in Angular: `https://medium.com/@softwaretechsolution/async-pipe-in-angular-bf0c691faaf2`

Creating a custom Core Web Vitals performance monitoring system

As part of the Web API specification, one of the functionalities that's included in web browsers as part of their runtime is `PerformanceObserver`. This observer can measure performance events that are recorded in the browser's performance timeline and helps us to track the most important performance metrics of our web application.

How to do it...

In this recipe, we'll build a small custom performance analytics observer to track the **Core Web Vitals** metrics and improve the performance of our web application, something we'll do once we've identified performance bottlenecks. Once we've gathered the necessary metric information, we can send that data to our API analytics service.

Step 1 – Setting up Performance Observer

Since the `PerformanceObserver` Web API doesn't follow the standard **addEventListener/ removeEventListener pattern** for registering events, we can't use RxJS's `fromEvent` operator. Instead, we'll have to use the `fromEventPattern` operator, which helps us emit events based on a custom event pattern and create an RxJS wrapper around `PerformanceObserver`.

First, inside the `service/web-vitals-observer.ts` service, we'll set up `PerformanceObserver`:

```
public observePerformanceEntry(
    entryType: string
): Observable<PerformanceObserverEntryList> {
    this.performanceObserver$ =
        fromEventPattern<PerformanceObserverEntryList>(
            (handler) => {
                const observer = new PerformanceObserver(
                    (list) =>handler(list.getEntries()));
                observer.observe({
                    entryTypes: [entryType],
                    buffered: true
                });
                return observer;
            },
            (handler, observer) => observer.disconnect()
```

```
    );
  return this.performanceObserver$;
}
```

Let's break down what we've done so far:

1. First, we instantiated `PerformanceObserver` and passed the handler callback function that will be called once we call the `observe()` method and performance entry is recorded for one of the `entryType` properties.

2. Then, we specified the set of performance entries to be observed by the browser. Here are the values that we may pass as `entryType` properties:

    *   `largest-contentful-paint`
    *   `layout-shift`
    *   `first-input`
    *   `paint`

3. Finally, we returned `performanceObserver$` so that we can subscribe to it from any component wish.

Step 2 – Observing performance entries

In our `app.component.ts` file, we must define different performance streams based on different entry types:

```
private firstInputPaint$ =
    this.webVitalsObserverService
        .observePerformanceEntry('paint');
private firstContentfulPaint$ =
    this.webVitalsObserverService
        .observePerformanceEntry('first-input');
private cumulativeLayoutShift$ =
    this.webVitalsObserverService
        .observePerformanceEntry('layout-shift');
private largestContentfulPaint$ =
    this.webVitalsObserverService
        .observePerformanceEntry(
            'largest-contentful-paint');
```

Now, we can merge all these streams, gather performance metrics for our custom analytics, and gain important insights about our web application's page load times, cumulative layout shifts, user timing interactions, and more:

```
loading = true;

ngOnInit(): void {
    setTimeout(() => {
        // Simulate Cummulative Layout Shift
        this.loading = false;
    }, 2000);
    merge(
        this.firstInputPaint$,
        this.largestContentfulPaint$,
        this.firstContentfulPaint$,
        this.cumulativeLayoutShift$
    ).subscribe((entry) => console.log(entry));
}
```

See also

- The `PerformanceObserver` Web API: `https://developer.mozilla.org/en-US/docs/Web/API/PerformanceObserver`

- Web Vitals articles: `https://web.dev/articles/vitals`

- RxJS's `fromEventPattern` operator: `https://rxjs.dev/api/index/function/fromEventPattern`

Using Web Workers alongside RxJS

We all know that JavaScript is a single-threaded language, at least in the browser runtime environment. This means that browsers can process one operation at a time. So, if we have a long-running task, it can block the main thread, meaning that the browser would freeze and block the whole user experience. Usually, on the client side, we don't have to deal with computationally intensive or long-running tasks, but when we do, we can offload heavy workloads to the separate thread that runs in the background, similar to Web Workers, which can help us prevent UI freezes and ensure smooth interactions, even when we're performing resource-intensive operations.

How to do it...

In this recipe, we'll simulate computationally intensive operations by creating a web worker and running one million iterations of some simple transformations.

Step 1 – Setting up a web worker in Angular

If we want our web worker to be located in `src/app/app.component.ts`, we can simply run the following command in our terminal:

```
ng generate web-worker app
```

In our example, the web worker will run one million iterations. To simulate some form of data processing, we'll do the following:

1. On every fifth iteration, we'll return `null` as a result.

2. On every tenth iteration, we'll return the previous result, not the current one.

3. Otherwise, we'll double the iteration number as a result.

4. We'll call the `postMessage()` method to get the result from the web worker and send it back to the main thread.

Step 2 – Subscribing to web worker messages

To get to the worker file, we must instantiate a new `Worker` class and provide the path to our worker. Then, we can start the worker by sending a message where we provide the number of iterations:

```typescript
ngOnInit(): void {
    const worker = new Worker(new URL(
        './app.worker',
        import.meta.url
    ));
    worker.postMessage({ iterations: 1_000_000 });
    const message$ = fromEvent<MessageEvent>(
        worker,
        'message'
    );
    message$.subscribe((data) => {
        console.log('Received message from worker:', data);
    });
}
```

After that, we're ready to create a stream of message events and react to them. But if we open Dev Tools and start using the application, after some time, the application will get slower and slower, even though we're processing a long task in the background.

This means that we can take message subscriptions and apply additional performance optimizations.

Step 3 – Optimizing the worker messages stream

At the moment, we can see room for improvement in several areas:

- We get the whole MessageEvent interface as a result of the stream, but we're only interested in data.
- Null values are included in the result.
- There are duplicated successive values.
- The number of events is causing the console to break due to memory overload.

We can address and fix these issues by applying certain RxJS operators:

```
const message$ = fromEvent<MessageEvent>(
    worker,
    'message'
).pipe(
    filter(( { data } ) => data !== null),
    map(({ data }) => data),
    distinctUntilChanged(),
    bufferCount(1000),
    throttleTime(10),
    share()
);
```

Let's break down what we've done here:

1. First, we used the filter operator to exclude null values.
2. Then, we transformed the stream by mapping data values, not the whole event from the web worker.
3. We filtered out duplicate values with the distinctUntilChanged operator.
4. Then, we collected 1,000 events and placed them into a buffer with bufferCount. We significantly improved memory usage by doing so.

5. By using `throttleTime`, we skipped collecting messages every 10 milliseconds since not all messages are that important, and we're looking to round up the result.

6. Finally, we used `share` to return the cached result immediately to multiple subscribers.

Now, our message stream is much more efficient and performant in delivering worker messages.

See also

- Angular docs guide about Web Workers: `https://angular.dev/ecosystem/web-workers#adding-a-web-worker`
- MDN Web Workers docs: `https://developer.mozilla.org/en-US/docs/Web/API/Web_Workers_API/Using_web_workers`
- RxJS's `bufferCount` operator: `https://rxjs.dev/api/operators/bufferCount`
- RxJS's `throttleTime` operator: `https://rxjs.dev/api/operators/throttleTime`
- RxJS's `share` operator: `https://rxjs.dev/api/operators/share`

Get This Book's PDF Version and Exclusive Extras

Scan the QR code (or go to `packtpub.com/unlock`). Search for this book by name, confirm the edition, and then follow the steps on the page.

Note: Keep your invoice handy. Purchases made directly from Packt don't require one.

6

Building Reactive State Management Systems with RxJS

State management is hard, and for good reason. If we imagine the perfect state management library, the main features of that library would be scalability, predictability, performance, maintainability, developer experience, and flexibility. RxJS can help us with all of that. It can make our state more scalable by efficiently managing the complexity of data flows and user interactions throughout our app. We can model state changes as streams of events in a structured way, so it is easier to reason about state complexity. Also, RxJS enables us to express state changes declaratively and react to state changes in a natural way, where changes are propagated automatically throughout the system as they occur, which can lead to more efficient state updates, performance-wise. All of this makes state changes more predictable and testable, as well as easier to debug.

In this chapter, we're going to cover some of the most advanced and sophisticated ways of managing RxJS state:

- Building custom client-side state management
- Using NgRx for state management in Angular
- TanStack Query, meet RxJS – building your own TanStack query with Angular and RxJS

Technical requirements

To follow along with this chapter, you'll need the following:

- Angular v19+
- RxJS v7
- Node.js v22+
- npm v11+ or pnpm v10+

The code for the recipes in this chapter can be found in the GitHub repository here: `https://github.com/PacktPublishing/RxJS-Cookbook-for-Reactive-Programming/tree/main/Chapter06`

Building custom client-side state management

Imagine the perfect state management we mentioned in the introduction. What features would that state manager have? It would likely combine the best features from the best-known existing libraries. We would expect features such as the following:

- **Global state access**: Effortless access to the state from any component
- **Predictable state updates**: Without unwanted side effects
- **Scalability**: Easily grow your app to an infinite number of new modules/features, managing data flow complexity with ease
- **Reactivity**: Carry out an automatic component state refresh whenever there is a state update
- **Granular control**: The ability to create slices of smaller, more manageable states, each responsible for a specific domain
- **Performance**: Targeted re-renders for efficient state updates, providing the best possible user experience
- **Handling errors and side effects**: Gracefully handling network requests and creating resilient error handling
- **Developer experience**: Clear and concise usage, easy mental model when thinking about state changes, and integrated debugging tools

We know that there are a lot of libraries that solve these problems, but to truly appreciate a library, let's try to create our very own minimum Redux-like state management from scratch and understand the underlying complexity behind a system like this.

This is how Redux data flow usually looks like:

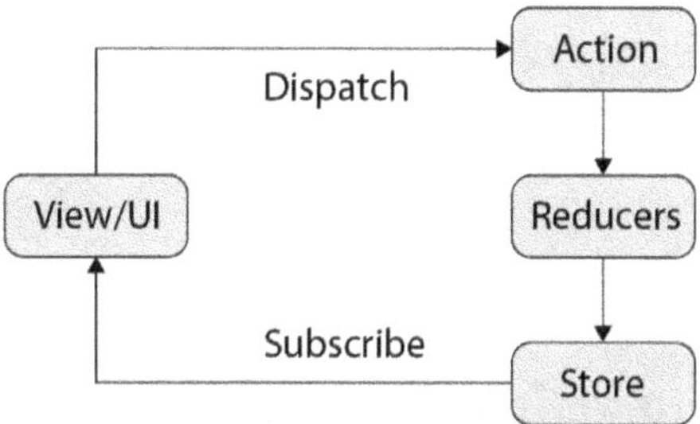

Figure 6.1: Redux mental model

How to do it...

In this example, we will build a small **Cooking Recipes** app, where we will load a list of recipes from the mocked data (using MockServiceWorker) and show them in the list. Also, we will have the ability to know which recipe is selected at the moment, and we will represent that in a separate state. For this recipe, we are not using any library for state management, but rather building our own custom one.

Step 1 — Defining the state

We'll start off by creating a recipes-store.service.ts file that will act as a state manager. First, we will put our state into a BehaviorSubject class. It can provide a solid foundation to build a simple, flexible, and reactive state. With BehaviorSubject, we can easily notify all subscribers about state changes by pushing new values, but also pulling the latest state value, since BehaviorSubject maintains and provides a current state value to all subscribers:

```typescript
import { BehaviorSubject } from "rxjs";

export class RecipesStoreService {
    private initialState: AppState = {
        recipesState: {
            recipes: [],
            selectedRecipe: null,
            error: null,
            loading: false,
        },
        ordersState: {
```

```
            orders: [],
        }
    };
    private state$ = new BehaviorSubject<AppState>(
        this.initialState
    );
}
```

Step 2 – Dispatching actions

Now we need to somehow provide the ability to dispatch an action that can change the state, in an immutable way. For this, we can use an **RxJS Subject** to establish one-way communication and broadcast events that happened within the system:

```
export class RecipesStoreService {
    public actions$ = new Subject<Action>();

    constructor() {
        this.actions$.pipe(
            withLatestFrom(this.state$),
            map(([action, state]) => rootReducer(
                                state, action))
        ).subscribe((state: AppState) => {
            this.state$.next(state);
        });
    }

    dispatch({ type, payload }: Action): void {
        this.actions$.next({
            type,
            payload
        });
    }
}
```

After dispatching an action, we will notify all the subscribers and start reacting to this new action, based on its type. In the following code, we combine the dispatched action with the `withLatestFrom` state that we have already defined in *Step 1* and apply a pure reducer function to make that state transition in an immutable way.

Let's say that in our `recipes.actions.ts`, we have action creators like so:

```ts
export interface Action<T = any> {
    type: string;
    payload?: T;
    error?: Error
}


export const LOAD_RECIPES = 'LOAD_RECIPES';
export const LOAD_RECIPES_SUCCESS = 'LOAD_RECIPES_SUCCESS';
export const LOAD_RECIPES_ERROR = 'LOAD_RECIPES_ERROR';

export const loadRecipesAction = (): Action => ({
    type: LOAD_RECIPES
});
export const loadRecipesActionSuccess = (payload:
    Recipe[]): Action => ({
        type: LOAD_RECIPES_SUCCESS,
        payload
});
export const loadRecipesActionError = (error: Error):
    Action => ({
        type: LOAD_RECIPES_ERROR,
        error
});
```

We will dispatch `loadRecipesAction` initially when the component mounts. As a result, a root reducer will react to a corresponding action and apply state transition changes. We define our on function as follows:

```ts
export function on(
    actionType: string,
    reducerFn: Reducer<AppState, Action>
) {
    return { actionType, reducerFn };
}
```

Step 3 – Applying the reducer function for state transitions

In our `recipes.reducer.ts` file, we'll create a reducer that will catch dispatched actions and make a state transition based on an action type and its payload:

```
function createReducer(
    ...ons: Record<string, any>[]
): Reducer<AppState, Action> {
    return function (state: AppState, action: Action) {
        for (let on of ons) {
            if (action.type === on.actionType) {
                return on.reducerFn(state, action);
            }
        }

        return state;
    };
}


export const recipesReducer = createReducer(
    on(LOAD_RECIPES, (state: AppState) => Object.assign(
        {},
        structuredClone(state),
        { loading: true }
    ))),
    on(LOAD_RECIPES_SUCCESS, (
        state: AppState,
        { payload }: Action
    ) => Object.assign(
        {},
        structuredClone(state),
        { recipes: payload ?? [], loading: false }
    ))),
    on(LOAD_RECIPES_ERROR, (
        state: AppState,
        { payload }: Action) => Object.assign(
```

```
        {},
        structuredClone(state),
        { error: payload, loading: false }
    }))),
)
```

We have created a reducer function by going through all possible actions, filtering out the action that actually happened, and applying a reducer function *on* the action that was dispatched.

For now, there is a way for us to dispatch a synchronous action and transition state, but what about handling a network request that `loadRecipesAction` should trigger?

Step 4 – Handling side effects

Back in our `RecipeStoreService` class, we will add a simple method that will handle effect creation and map it to the corresponding action that needs to happen after the effect is triggered:

```
createEffect(handler: () => Observable<Action>) {
    return handler().pipe(
        map(({ type, payload, error }) => this.dispatch({
            type,
            payload: payload ?? error
        })),
    );
}
```

Now we are ready to handle side effect in `RecipeService`, which is responsible for communication with the backend:

```
export class RecipesService {
    loadRecipes$ = this.recipeStore.createEffect(() => {
        return this.recipeStore.actions$
        .pipe(
            ofType(LOAD_RECIPES),
            exhaustMap(() => this.getRecipes().pipe(
                map(res => loadRecipesActionSuccess(res)),
            catchError((error: Error) =>
            // gracefully error exit and continue stream
                of(loadRecipesActionError(
```

```
                    error.message ?? error
              ))
            )
        ))
      );
    });


    getRecipes(): Observable<Recipe[]> {
        return this.http.get<Recipe[]>('/api/recipes');
    }


    loadRecipes(): void {
        this.recipeStore.dispatch(loadRecipesAction());
    }
}
```

In the preceding code, we have a small utility function, ofType, similar to NgRx, which will filter incoming actions, and handle a side effect for a specific action:

```
export function ofType(type: string) {
    return (source: Observable<Action>) => source.pipe(
        filter(action => action.type === type)
    );
}
```

What might be of interest here is the usage of the RxJS exhaustMap operator, which can help us with the following:

- Preventing redundant actions
- Rate limiting – new request won't be initiated until the previous one finishes
- Sequential requests – if you have a series of operations that need to be performed in sequence, and each operation depends on the result of the previous one, exhaustMap can ensure that each operation completes before the next one starts

exhaustMap versus switchMap

When handling concurrent requests in our effect, we can achieve almost the same result with the switchMap operator. The only difference is that if the same request is triggered before an ongoing request has finished, it will cancel the previous one and start the new request. On the other hand, exhaustMap will wait for the first request to resolve, and it will ignore new incoming requests. The approach we choose here might vary between different product use cases or personal preference.

Great, now our reducer will pick up the LOAD_RECIPES_SUCCESS action, extract the response data payload, and update the state. In case of an error, the LOAD_RECIPES_ERROR action will be dispatched, and the state will be updated with the error message.

Step 5 – Slicing the state

Now that we can dispatch an action, transition to the desired state, and handle side effects, we can subscribe to the slice of the store inside of our component and display data from the backend. Inside our recipes-store.service.ts, we will create a selector, with the ability to derive a specific piece of data from the app state:

```
selectState$(
    selector?: (state: AppState) => Partial<AppState>,
    cachedValues = 1
): Observable<Partial<AppState>> {
    return this.state$.asObservable().pipe(
        map((selector || ((state) => state))),
        shareReplay(cachedValues),
    );
}
```

What might be interesting here is the usage of the shareReplay operator, which is especially useful in scenarios where we want to multicast the same cached value to multiple subscribers. What this means in our case is that whenever we call the same selector in any different part of the application, those late-state subscribers would catch up on the previously emitted values. This way, we optimize app performance by returning the latest cached value immediately, without the need to calculate this slice of the same state again.

How shareReplay works under the hood

Under the hood, this operator leverages `ReplaySubject`, and in that way manages to multicast emitted values from the source Observable to the multiple subscribers. By default, `shareReplay` will cache the number of passed buffer values forever. Even when the number of subscribers drops to 0, it will not unsubscribe from `ReplaySubject`. If we are not careful, this might cause memory leaks in our application, but we might want to do this in cases when we want to avoid expensive computations for Observables that are frequently used, such as state selectors. If we want to have programmatic control over this behavior, `shareReplay` provides a configuration object that can be passed as an argument. Also, if would like unsubscriptions to be automatically handled by RxJS, we might consider using the `share` operator.

Finally, in our `recipes-list.component.ts` component, we can subscribe to a specific slice of a state:

```
export class RecipesListComponent {
    recipes: Recipe[] = [];

    constructor(
        private recipeStore: RecipesStoreService,
        private  recipesService: RecipesService
    ) { }

    ngOnInit() {
        this.recipesService.loadRecipes();
        this.recipeStore.selectState$((
            state: Partial<AppState>
        ) => state.recipesState?.recipes).subscribe(
            (recipes: Partial<AppState>) => {
                this.recipes = recipes as Recipe[];
            }
        );
    }
}
```

And voilà!

Figure 6.2: Cooking Recipes app

Now, if we open our app in a browser, we can see the list of cooking recipes that represent the client state.

Step 6 — Creating composable reducers

Often, we want to combine multiple reducers and compose them in a declarative, functional way. For these purposes, we will create a custom function that will combine the state and actions of two different reducers:

```
function combineReducers<S, A extends Action>(
    reducers: { [K in keyof S]: Reducer<S[K], A> }
): Reducer<S, A> {
    return (state: S | undefined, action: A): S => {
        if (! state) return {} as S;

        const newState = { ...state } as S;
```

```
        for (let key in reducers) {
            newState[key] = reducers[key](state[key],
                                             action);
        }

        return newState;
    };
}
```

Now, our `rootReducer` looks as follows:

```
export const rootReducer = combineReducers({
    recipesState: recipesReducer,
    ordersState: recipeOrderReducer
});
```

Step 7 - Creating meta-reducers

Developer experience is one of the most essential considerations when using state management libraries. It is important that we detect bugs quickly and effectively react to state changes. For these purposes, we will create a custom logging meta-reducer:

```
export function logMetaReducer(
    target: Function,
    context: any
) {
    return function (...args: any[]) {
        const [,{ type, payload }] = args;
        console.log(`%cCalling Action: ${type}\n`,
                    'color: #d30b8e', payload);
        const result = target.apply(context, args);
        console.log(`%cAction ${type} state:\n`,
                    'color: #ffc26e', result);
        return result;
    };
}
```

To apply a meta-reducer to each reducer, we will wrap it around `rootReducer`, so it becomes the following:

```
export const rootReducer = logMetaReducer(combineReducers({
    recipesState: recipesReducer,
    ordersState: recipeOrderReducer
}), this);
```

In our console, we can see our meta-reducer in action and observe all dispatched actions and state transitions!

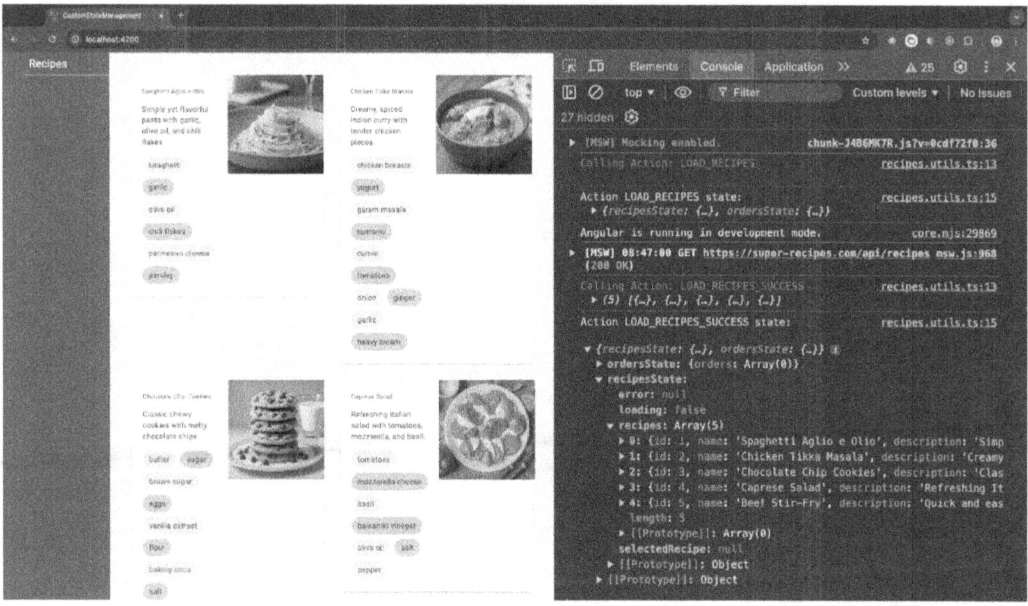

Figure 6.3: Meta-reducer logger

See also

- MSW: `https://mswjs.io/`
- The `shareReplay` operator: `https://rxjs.dev/api/index/function/shareReplay`
- The `share` operator: `https://rxjs.dev/api/index/function/share`
- The `exhaustMap` operator: `https://rxjs.dev/api/operators/exhaustMap`
- The `switchMap` operator: `https://rxjs.dev/api/operators/switchMap`
- The `structuredClone` global browser function: `https://developer.mozilla.org/en-US/docs/Web/API/structuredClone`

Using NgRx for state management in Angular

NgRx is a framework for building reactive applications with Angular, inspired by Redux. The following diagram from the NgRx docs provides a more visual overview of the key components of NgRx:

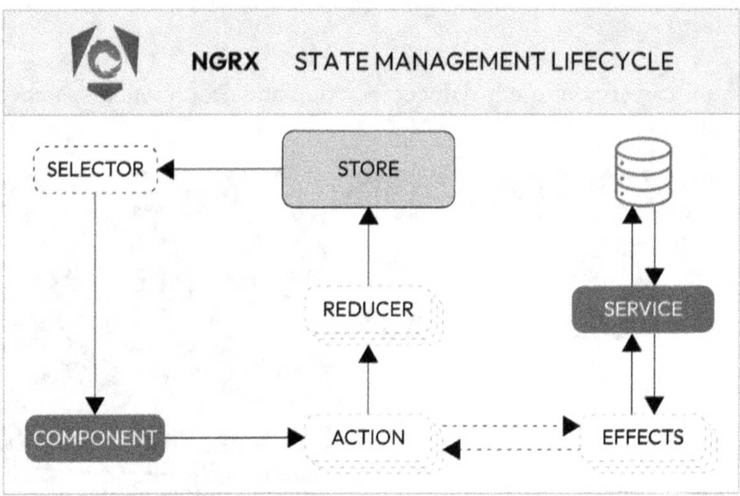

Figure 6.4: NgRx overview

With NgRx, we can do the following:

- Define the global and local stores
- Write side effects for handling async operations
- Dispatch actions
- Define reducers as pure functions for predictable state changes
- Write selectors for more granular control over the state
- Carry out time-travel debugging
- Normalize entity data
- Integrate with Angular router state
- Create a reactive store with Signals support

Now that we have a high overview of NgRx, let's dive into a practical example of how we can deal with state management challenges.

> **Important note**
>
> 
> At the time of writing this recipe, the latest Angular and NgRx versions were v18. In the examples, we are using the standalone approach to writing components and providing services with `appConfig`. If you are using the older module approach, the code may vary a bit, but the main approach and concepts relating to state management should stay the same.

How to do it...

In this example, we will build a small Cooking Recipes app, where we will load a list of recipes from the mocked BE (using `MockServiceWorker`) and show them in the list. Also, we will have the ability to know which recipe is selected at the moment. The recipe is pretty much the same as the previous one, but this time, we are leveraging NgRx as a solution for state management, so we can compare the reduced code complexity and edge cases we have to pay attention to, once we have a full production-ready state management solution. Also, we will explore some of the additional features that NgRx offers us, to make our code even more scalable, robust, and up to the latest trends. In the end, we will connect our store to **Angular Router**, so we are aware of all navigations and router states.

Step 1 – Configuring a NgRx store

In our global config, `app.config.ts`, first we need to provide a store from NgRx so that the store is available globally throughout our application:

```
import { RootStoreConfig } from '@ngrx/store';

export const appConfig: ApplicationConfig = {
    providers: [
        provideStore(reducers as RootStoreConfig<AppState,
                                        Action>)
    ]
}
```

`AppState` is an interface where we will define the structure of our global state:

```
export interface RecipesState {
    recipes: Recipe[];
    selectedRecipe: Recipe | null;
    error: Error | null;
    loading: boolean;
}

export interface AppState {
    recipesState: RecipesState;
}
```

In our `recipes.reducers.ts`, we can now define our feature reducer, which will control how the state would transition depending on dispatched actions:

```
import { map, catchError, of, exhaustMap } from "rxjs";
import { Actions, createEffect, ofType } from "@ngrx/effects";

export const initialState: State = {
    recipes: [],
    selectedRecipe: null,
    error: null,
    loading: false,
}

export const recipeReducer = createReducer(
    initialState,
    on(RecipesActions.loadRecipesAction, state => ({
        ...state,
        loading: true,
    })),
    on(RecipesActions.loadRecipesActionSuccess, (state, { recipes }) => ({
        ...state,
        recipes,
        loading: false,
    })),
```

```
    );

    export const recipesFeature = createFeature({
        name: 'recipesState',
        reducer: recipeReducer,
    });
```

In the preceding code, we defined the initial app state, created `recipeReducer`, which will handle state transitions, and in the end, connected our reducer to the feature state. Also, we can notice that if we dispatch `loadRecipesActions`, we will change the loading state to show the loader, and once the request has completed, we will set `loading` back to `false` to hide the spinner and set the received data as the response. A list of actions that we can dispatch is declared in `recipes.actions.ts`, and it looks like this:

```
    import { createAction, props } from "@ngrx/store";

    export const loadRecipesAction = createAction('[Recipes] Load Recipes');
    export const loadRecipesActionSuccess = createAction(
        '[Recipes] Load Recipes Success', props<{ recipes: Recipe[] }>()
    );
    export const loadRecipesActionError = createAction(
        '[Recipes] Load Recipes Error', props<{ error: string }>()
    );
```

Now we are ready to dispatch actions from our components. In `RecipeListComponent`, after injecting the store from @ngrx/store components, we can just call the action that will start fetching recipes:

```
    this.store.dispatch(loadRecipesAction());
```

Step 2 – Handling side effects

Sending an HTTP request and loading data is an external interaction or side effect, so we must define that as an async action. In our `recipes.effects.ts`, we have the following:

```
    import { map, catchError, of, exhaustMap } from "rxjs";
    import { Actions, createEffect, ofType } from "@ngrx/effects";

    export class RecipesEffects {
        loadRecipes$ = createEffect(() =>
```

```
    this.actions$.pipe(
      ofType(loadRecipesAction),
      exhaustMap(() => this.recipesService.getRecipes$().pipe(
          map(recipes => loadRecipeActionSuccess({
          recipes
        })),
          catchError((error: Error) =>
            of(loadRecipeActionError({
              error: error.message
          }))
          )
      ))
    )
  );
}
```

In this effect, we may observe that when an action of a certain type happens, we can trigger a corresponding side effect. NgRx has a built-in action filter with the `ofType` operator that matches actions being triggered and reacting upon them. So, when `loadRecipesAction` happens, we call our BE service and react to success and error cases. Like in the preceding recipe, note the use of the RxJS `exhaustMap` operator.

Step 3 – Defining selectors

NgRx offers us a really nice ability for granular control over the state by defining selectors that can create slices of our state. You can think of a selector as a query for a specific part of the state that you want to display within your components. There are multiple benefits of this approach:

- **Readability and maintainability**: We can extract logic for extracting the slices of state we need outside of a component

- **Memoization**: All selectors are cached by default, so we can have performance improvements, especially with complex state structures

- **Composability**: Selectors can be combined to have even more granular control

- **Testability**: Since selectors are pure functions and have no side effects, they can easily be tested
- **Type safety**: This helps us with intelligent code completion and early error detection, improving the overall developer experience

In our `recipes.selector.ts`, we have a slice of a state called `selectRecipesState`. This means that we can create a **feature selector** for that piece of state and create composable selectors for sub-pieces of feature state:

```
import { createFeatureSelector } from '@ngrx/store';
import * as fromRecipes from './recipes.reducer';


export const selectRecipesState =
    createFeatureSelector<fromRecipes.State>('recipesState');
export const selectRecipesWithSelectedRecipes =
    createSelector(
        selectRecipesState,
        (state: fromRecipes.State>) => state.selectedRecipe
    );
```

At this point, we have already managed to reproduce the same behavior from our previous recipe. Talking about reduced complexity, right?

Now, let's explore additional features of NgRx, and additionally improve our Cooking Recipes app.

Step 4 – Extending app state with NgRx Router State

With **Router State**, we can seamlessly integrate Angular's router with our app state to have all the benefits we already have (such as time-travel debugging, selectors, and improved testability) also for routing and navigation events. First, in our store config, we provide the Router store and add `routerReducer` to be part of `AppState`:

```
import { RootStoreConfig } from '@ngrx/store';
import { provideRouterStore, routerReducer } from '@ngrx/router-store';


export const appConfig: ApplicationConfig = {
    providers: [
        provideStore(reducers, {
            router: routerReducer
```

```
        } as RootStoreConfig<AppState, Action>),
        provideRouterStore()
    ]

}
```

Back in `reducers/index.ts`, we will add a router state to be part of `AppState`:

```
import * as fromRouter from '@ngrx/router-store';


export interface AppState {
    recipesState: RecipesState;
    router: fromRouter.RouterReducerState;
}
```

A nice addition to this is the **router selectors**, which we can use right out of the box:

```
export const {
    selectCurrentRoute, // select the current route
    selectFragment, // select the current route fragment
    selectQueryParams, // select the current route query params
    selectQueryParam, // factory function to select a query param
    selectRouteParams, // select the current route params
    selectRouteParam, // factory function to select a route param
    selectRouteData, // select the current route data
    selectRouteDataParam, // factory function to select a route data param
    selectUrl, // select the current url
    selectTitle, // select the title if available
} = getRouterSelectors();


export const selectRecipesWithCurrentRoute = createSelector(
    selectRecipesState,
    selectCurrentRoute,
    (recipesState, routerState) => ({
        recipesState,
        routerState
    })
);
```

Now, in our `recipes-list.component.ts`, we can subscribe to this slice of state:

```
import { select } from '@ngrx/store';
this.store.pipe(select(
    fromRecipes.selectRecipesWithCurrentRoute
)).subscribe(({ recipesState: { recipes } }) => {
    this.recipes = recipes;
});
```

Also, if we open NgRx Dev Tools, we can see router events being dispatched while we are navigating around the app.

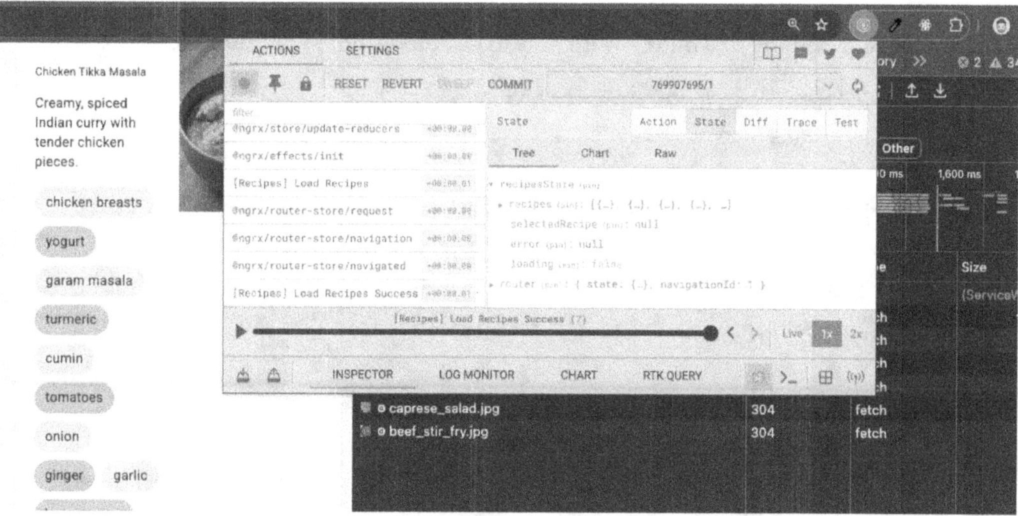

Figure 6.5: NgRx Store DevTools

Step 5 — Creating meta-reducers

Sometimes, we want to intercept the action before it modifies a state and do some work in between. Some of the use cases might be logging for debugging purposes, state persistence to local storage, and performance monitoring. In our example, we have implemented a simple logging system. First, we define a meta-reducer as part of the store config:

```
import { RootStoreConfig } from '@ngrx/store';
import { provideRouterStore, routerReducer } from '@ngrx/router-store';
import { metaReducers } from './reducers/recipes.meta-reducer';
```

```
export const appConfig: ApplicationConfig = {
    providers: [
        provideStore(reducers, {
            metaReducers,
            router: routerReducer
        } as RootStoreConfig<AppState, Action>),
    ]
}
```

Now, in our `recipes.meta-reducer.ts`, we can implement our custom debug function that will act as middleware between an action and a reducer.

Note that we are running this middleware only in dev mode, not in production:

```
import { isDevMode } from '@angular/core';
import { ActionReducer, MetaReducer } from '@ngrx/store';


export function debug<T>(reducer: ActionReducer<T>): ActionReducer<T> {
    return function (state, action) {
        console.log(`%cState:\n`, 'color: #ffc26e', state);
        console.log(`%cCalling Action: ${action.type}\n`,
                                    'color: #d30b8e');
        return reducer(state, action);
    };
}
export const metaReducers: MetaReducer<AppState>[] =
    isDevMode() ? [debug] : [];
```

After applying `metaReducer` in the app config, we may observe in the browser console all actions being dispatched with the payload and current state.

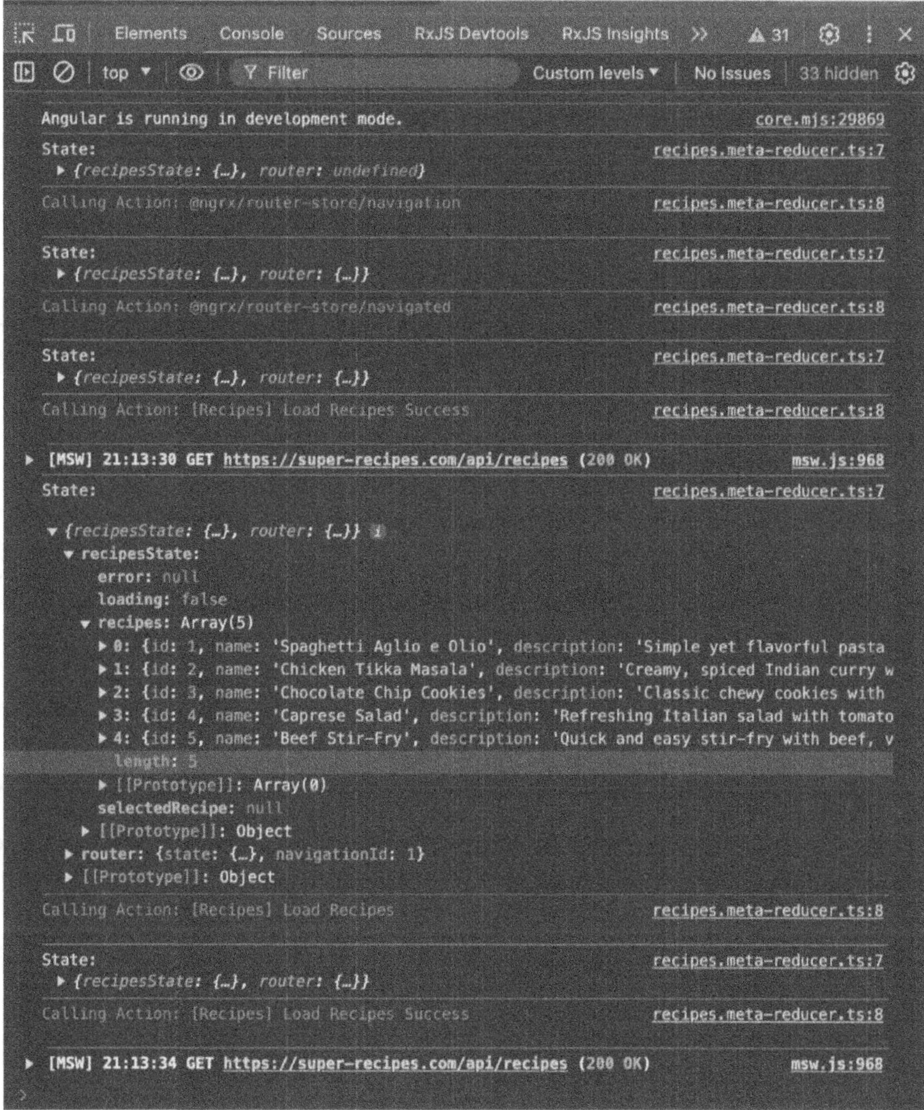

Figure 6.6: Logging the meta-reducer

See also

- NgRx docs: https://ngrx.io/docs

- Redux DevTools: https://chromewebstore.google.com/detail/redux-devtools/lmh
  kpmbekcpmknklioeibfkpmmfibljd?pli=1

TanStack Query, meet RxJS — building your own TanStack query with Angular and RxJS

TanStack Query has taken over our community by storm as a go-to async state management library, and for good reason. There are many benefits to using TanStack Query, such as the following:

- Declarative data fetching
- Automatic caching and re-fetching
- Robust error-handling mechanisms – gracefully manage failures and automatically retry failed requests
- Automatic garbage collection
- Excellent developer experience – dedicated Dev Tools that make it easier to debug and inspect your queries

One thing that we may notice from the first usage when working with TanStack Query is that it only supports promises and not Observables. But asynchronous programming and handling side effects are where RxJS can really excel. So, let's build our very own custom, minimalistic version of TanStack Query, but this time with the help of RxJS for managing async data flow.

How to do it...

In this example, we will build a small Cooking Recipes app in Angular, where we will load a list of recipes from the mocked BE (using MSW) and show them in the list. The way we are going to manage the state is by replicating a small set of features of TanStack Query, and we will call it `RxJS-Query`.

The features we will replicate are the following:

- Declarative queries
- Automatic caching by query keys
- Smart background re-fetches – on window focus, network regain, or query key change
- The **Stale-while-revalidate** caching strategy
- Composable query keys
- Request cancelation
- Deduplication of request
- Retry mechanism on request failures

- Garbage collection

- Small dev tools component to visualize cache store

Step 1 – Setting up declarative queries

If we look at TanStack's documentation in Angular, we can see what one query would look like.
Let's try to replicate the same dev experience and behavior. In our `RecipesListComponent`, we'll
write our first query that will retrieve the list of recipes using the `recipes` query key:

```
export class RecipesListComponent {
    recipes$: Observable<QueryState<Recipe[]>>

    constructor(
        private queryClient: QueryClientService,
        private recipesService: RecipesService
    ) {}

    ngOnInit(): void {
        this.queryClient.injectQuery(
            ['recipes'],
            () => this.recipesService.getRecipes$(),
            { staleTime: 1000 * 5 }
        );
    }
}
```

Step 2 – Caching queries with Map

Now we'll check out `QueryClientService` and the implementation behind the `injectQuery`
function:

```
export class QueryClientService {
    private cache = new Map<
        string,
        { state$: BehaviorSubject<any>; lastFetched: number }
    >();
    private query<T>(
        key: string[],
        queryFn: () => Observable<T>,
        options: QueryOptions,
```

```typescript
): Observable<QueryState<T>> {
    const compositeKey = JSON.stringify(key);
    let cachedValue = this.cache.get(compositeKey);
    const { staleTime = 0, retryNo = 3, gcTime = 30000 } = options;
    let { state$ } = cachedValue || {};


    if (!state$) {
        // start a new state stream
    }


    return state$.asObservable();
}


public injectQuery<T>(
    queryKey: string[],
    queryFn: () => Observable<T>,
    queryOptions: QueryOptions,
): Observable<QueryState<T>> {
    return this.query<T>(queryKey, queryFn, queryOptions);
}


}
```

Let's break down this example and what we have so far:

1. First, we will create a **Map** cache, which will store our queries and Observable streams by an array of query keys (or one big composable key). Each time we call a query function, first we will check whether there is a cache value already there, and if it is, then we will simply return an Observable value from the cache.

2. Now, let's check what happens if there is no previous cached value, and we need to trigger a new request (the code inside the `!state$` if block):

```typescript
state$ = new BehaviorSubject<QueryState<T>>({
    isLoading: true,
    isFetching: true,
});
this.cache.set(
    compositeKey,
    { state$, lastFetched: 0 }
```

```
    );

    return state$.pipe(
        filter((state: QueryState<T>) => state.isFetching),
        switchMap((val) =>
            merge(
                of(val),
                queryFn().pipe(
                    retry(retryNo),
                    map((data) => {
                        this.cache.set(compositeKey, {
                            state$,
                            lastFetched: Date.now() + staleTime,
                        });

                        return {
                            data,
                            isFetching: false,
                            isLoading: false
                        };
                    }),
                )
            ),
        ),
        shareReplay(1),
    );
```

Let's look at what we did here:

1. First, we set a new state with initial loading values. If you were wondering why we
   need both the isLoading and isFetching states, it's because we need isLoading
   to represent when the data is loading for the first time, and we need to display a
   spinner in the UI. We use isFetching when we do have data, but we are doing
   smart background re-fetches to revalidate stale data.

2. Then, we set the cache immediately, and not when the request has finished. By
   doing so, we deduplicate multiple of the same requests (if multiple components
   are calling the same query). Also, the switchMap operator will cancel the previous
   request if there is a new inbound request.

3. Then, we merge the loading state with queryFn, in order not to lose the previous loading state to show in the UI and to run in parallel queryFn, which sends the request. After the request has been completed, we will extract the response data payload, update the cache with values, and set staleTime (how long we consider data to be fresh from that point on).

4. In the end, we cache all previous values with the shareReplay operator.

Step 3 – Caching with the stale-while-revalidate mechanism

This is a popular caching mechanism that is used by **TanStack Query**, inspired by **HTTP Cache-Control Header**.

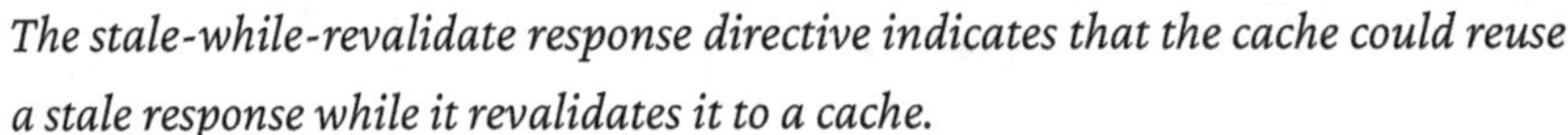

> *The stale-while-revalidate response directive indicates that the cache could reuse a stale response while it revalidates it to a cache.*
>
> *— MDN docs*

This means that whenever we request data by a query key, first we would check whether that data is fresh, and if it is, we would return data immediately. But if it is *stale*, we would still display the data, and do a background update to fetch fresh data, without disrupting the current user flow. Once the background revalidation completes and fresh data is available, **TanStack Query** seamlessly updates the UI to reflect the latest information. Key benefits of this approach are the following:

- **Improved perceived performance**: Users experience faster initial load times because they receive cached data immediately
- **Reduced Server load**: Fewer unnecessary requests are made to the server since cached data is utilized
- **Always up-to-date data**: The background revalidation ensures that the displayed data is eventually updated without requiring user interaction

In our example, we are going to achieve the same effect by defining staleTime in a number of milliseconds as QueryOption:

```
type QueryOptions = {
    refetchOnWindowFocus?: boolean;
    refetchOnReconnect?: boolean;
```

```
  staleTime?: number;
  retryNo?: number;
  gcTime?: number;
  // ... other options
};
```

Now, our condition for returning the state value from the Map cache might be the following:

```
if (!state$ || Date.now() > cachedValue.lastFetched)
```

Step 4 — Background updates

TanStack Query does smart background re-fetches based on certain triggers:

- Window focus
- Network regain after lost connection
- Component mount
- Change of a query key

If there is a query key change, then we will simply treat that as a new entry and store it under the new key in our Map cache. Component mount is also straightforward; once the component is mounted, we will call the query function. But the missing parts are the first two triggers. Let's react to those events in an RxJS way:

```
private queryTriggers(
    key: string[],
    { refetchOnWindowFocus = true, refetchOnReconnect = true }:
QueryOptions,
): void {
    const focus$ = refetchOnWindowFocus
        ? fromEvent(window, 'focus')
        : from([]);
    const networkReconnect$ = refetchOnReconnect
        ? fromEvent(window, 'online')
        : from([]);

    merge(focus$, networkReconnect$).subscribe(
        () => this.refetch(key));
}
```

We are using the RxJS `fromEvent` operator to create a stream of events; specifically, whenever we focus inside of our app or regain network, a new event will be emitted, and we will be notified about that. Once that happens, we call our RxJS-Query to do a background re-fetch and get us fresh data. Also, we could opt out of that default behavior by passing the `refetchOnWindowFocus` and `refetchOnReconnect` parameters:

```
public refetch(key: string[]): void {
    const compositeKey = JSON.stringify(key);
    const cachedValue = this.cache.get(compositeKey);
    let { state$, lastFetched } = cachedValue;

    if (state$ && Date.now() > lastFetched) {
        state$.next({ ...state$.value, isFetching: true });
    }
}
```

Since our state is `BehaviourSubject`, we can trigger a new HTTP request by calling the next method and setting a new fetching state to true.

Step 5 – Automatic garbage collection

Based on `gcTime`, defined as part of `QueryOptions`, we can automatically track a query by key and remove it from memory, to prevent memory leaks. `gcTime` can be infinite by default (we presume that we're going to need all data that has been fetched), but if we choose that we want to have a smaller time frame to store the data under a query key, we can do so as well. Once we define that time as, let's say, 30 seconds, we can have a function in charge of removing the cached query:

```
public removeQuery(key: string[]): void {
    const compositeKey = JSON.stringify(key);
    const cachedValue = this.cache.get(compositeKey);
    let { state$ } = cachedValue;

    if (state$) {
        this.cache.delete(compositeKey);
    }
}
```

The way we can call this function after that `gcTime` period is by leveraging the power of **RxJS schedulers**.

What is a scheduler?

An RxJS scheduler can help us with controlling the timing and execution of asynchronous operations within streams. They provide fine-grained control over concurrency and resource management, by letting us define an execution context in which an Observable can notify Observers.

In our example, at the end of our state stream, we can use the `finalize` operator and call `asyncScheduler` (time-based scheduler):

```
finalize(() =>
    asyncScheduler.schedule(
        () => this.removeQuery(key),
        gcTime
    ),
)
```

Now that we have covered the main features of our RxJS Query, take a glance at the full example in its full power here: `https://github.com/PacktPublishing/RxJS-Cookbook-for-Reactive-Programming/tree/main/Chapter06/rxjs-query`.

After this solid foundation, we could easily replicate the rest of TanStack Query's functionality and scale our RxJS Query, such as with mutations, optimistic updates, parallel requests, dependent requests, pagination support, or offline support.

See also

- TanStack's documentation: `https://tanstack.com/query/latest/docs/framework/angular/overview`

- merge: `https://rxjs.dev/api/index/function/merge`

- The `catchError` operator: `https://rxjs.dev/api/operators/catchError`

- The `shareReplay` operator: `https://rxjs.dev/api/index/function/shareReplay`

- HTTP Cache-Control Header: `https://developer.mozilla.org/en-US/docs/Web/HTTP/Headers/Cache-Control`

- The `fromEvent` operator: `https://rxjs.dev/api/index/function/fromEvent`

- RxJS schedulers: `https://rxjs.dev/guide/scheduler`

7

Building Progressive Web Apps with RxJS

Progressive Web Apps (PWAs) are web applications that use modern web capabilities to deliver a native app experience to users. They combine the best of web and mobile apps, providing a seamless, reliable, and engaging user experience across different devices. What makes PWAs special are features such as push notifications, offline access, background data sync, native app experiences, and so on.

In this chapter, we will implement some of the core PWA features by covering the following recipes:

- Delivering real-time food order updates with RxJS push notifications
- Implementing reactive background data sync
- Building offline-ready applications seamlessly with RxDB

Technical requirements

To follow along in this chapter, you'll need the following:

- Angular v19+
- RxJS v7
- Node.js v22+ and npm v11+
- RxDB

- NestJS v11+
- Dexie.js

The code for the recipes in this chapter is placed in the GitHub repository here: `https://github.com/PacktPublishing/RxJS-Cookbook-for-Reactive-Programming/tree/main/Chapter07`.

To convert an Angular application to a PWA, we can run one simple command that will add all the necessary configurations and a basic service worker to our project:

```
ng add @angular/pwa
```

Since service workers are one of the requirements for an app to be a PWA and enabled only in production mode, we must build our app and serve it locally to observe each recipe in action. In each recipe, we will use the simple `http-server` library to host the client app locally and observe the offline mode in the browser by running the following command in the terminal:

```
npm run build && http-server ${build-location} -c-1 -o
```

Delivering real-time food order updates with RxJS push notifications

Push notifications have become an important aspect of how users interact with our web and mobile applications. With push notifications, we can get timely updates and important reminders and alerts, drive user interaction, and increase conversions.

How to do it...

In order to deliver timely food order push notifications to our clients, we will combine RxJS power both in the Angular client app and in the NestJS backend app. In this recipe, we need a backend app as well because we need to deliver push notifications in a secure, authenticated way. The common practice in the industry to achieve a web server identifying itself to the push service is by leveraging **Voluntary Application Server Identification (VAPID)** keys.

Step 1 – Generating VAPID keys

Since VAPID keys act as a digital signature for push notifications, first, we need to generate a pair of public and private VAPID keys. The way we can do that is by installing the `web-push` library globally on our system, and calling the `generate-vapid-keys` command in the terminal:

```
npm install web-push -g
web-push generate-vapid-keys -json
```

After that, we can pick the results from the console and use the keys on the backend side (or load them from environment variables or a secure secret manager):

```
const vapidKeys = {
    publicKey: '//your public key',
    privateKey: '//your private key',
};
const options = {
    vapidDetails: {
        subject: 'mailto:example_email@example.com',
        publicKey: vapidKeys.publicKey,
        privateKey: vapidKeys.privateKey,
    },
};
```

Step 2 – Setting up a public key endpoint

Since we want to keep public and private keys on the server side, we will have an endpoint to get a public key. Now, the client app can send a request and get a public key, which we will need for sending push notifications to that client:

```
@Get('/api/publicKey')
getPublicKey() {
    return { publicKey: vapidKeys.publicKey };
}
```

Step 3 – Requesting push notification subscription

After the client gets a public key, we can request user permission to allow notifications in our browser. Angular's SwPush module takes away all the complexity behind interacting with the browser's **Push API**, by exposing the requestSubscription() method:

```
import { SwPush } from '@angular/service-worker';

interface PublicKeyResponse {
    publicKey: string;
}

@Injectable({ providedIn: 'root' })
export class PushNotificationService {
    constructor(private swPush: SwPush, private http: HttpClient) {}
```

```
subscribeToNotifications() {
    this.http.get<PublicKeyResponse>(
        'http://localhost:3000/api/publicKey').pipe(
            switchMap((res: PublicKeyResponse) => {
                return this.swPush.requestSubscription({
                    serverPublicKey: res.publicKey
                });
            }),
        catchError(err => {
            console.error(
            'Could not subscribe to notifications', err);
            return EMPTY;
        })
    )
    .subscribe();
    }
}
```

After calling `requestSubscription()`, we will notice in our browser that we are asking the user to allow push notifications:

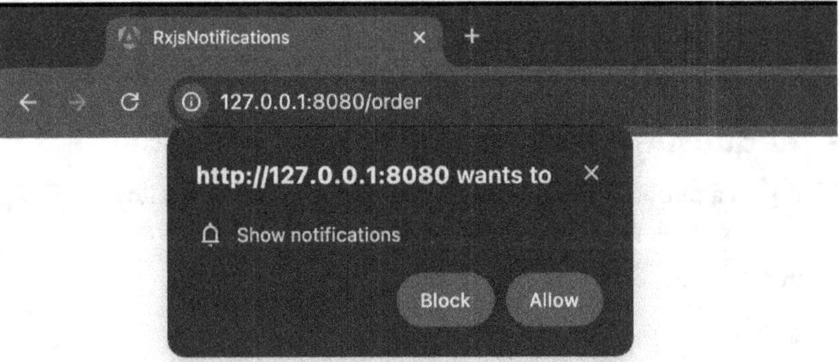

Figure 7.1: Notification user permission

Step 4 — Sending reactive push notifications from the API

At this point, we have user permission to show notifications in the browser. Now, we are ready to send push notifications from the server. First, we define a notification payload object that we are about to send to the client at a certain interval:

```
export const orderNotification = {
    [OrderStatus.ACCEPTED]: {
        "notification": {
            "title": "Order Accepted",
            "body": "Your order has been accepted and is
                     being prepared.",
            "icon": "http://localhost:3000/assets/burger.jpg",
        }
    },
    [OrderStatus.COURIER_ON_THE_WAY]: {
        "notification": {
            "title": "Courier on the way",
            "body": "Your order is out for delivery. Track
                     your order in real-time.",
            "actions": [{"action": "location",
                         "title": "Check Location"}],
            "data": {"onActionClick": {
                "default": {"operation": "openWindow",
                            "url": "http://127.0.0.1:8080/
                    geolocation?lat=12.9716&long=77.5946"},
                "rate": {"operation": "openWindow",
                         "url": "http://127.0.0.1:8080/
                    geolocation?lat=12.9716&long=77.5946"}
                }
            }
        }
    },
}
```

In this object, we will define what information each notification will have, and what user actions will offer. We can notice that when a food order is being accepted, we will have a notification title, body, and an icon. When the courier is on the way, we will have an action button, which will lead to the PWA geolocation page to see the current location of our food delivery.

In our backend endpoint that should deliver the notifications, we can define the RxJS stream that is calling the `sendNotifications()` method from the webpush package:

```
@Post('/api/subscriptions')
async addSubscription(@Body()sub:NotificationSubscription){
    return of(orderNotification[OrderStatus.ACCEPTED])
    .pipe(switchMap((notification) =>
        webpush.sendNotification(sub, JSON.stringify(
                            notification), options)),
        delayWhen(() => this.
                foodOrderService.processOrder()),
        switchMap(() => webpush.sendNotification(sub,
                JSON.stringify(orderNotification[
                OrderStatus.COURIER_ON_THE_WAY]),
                options)),
        delay(4000),
        switchMap(() => webpush.sendNotification(sub,
                JSON.stringify(orderNotification[
                OrderStatus.DELIVERED]), options)),
    );
}
```

Step 5 — Reacting to incoming push notifications

Finally, now that we have a backend endpoint that is sending us timely notifications, we can call that endpoint from a client app and subscribe to the incoming push notification:

```
subscribeToNotifications() {
    this.http.get<PublicKeyResponse>(
        '/api/publicKey').pipe(
    switchMap((res: PublicKeyResponse) => {
        return this.swPush.requestSubscription({
            serverPublicKey: res.publicKey
        });
    }),
```

```
    switchMap((sub: PushSubscription) =>
        this.http.post('/api/subscriptions', sub)),
        catchError(err => {
            console.error('Could not subscribe to
                            notifications', err);
            return EMPTY;
        })
    )
    .subscribe();
}
```

When we open our browser, we can observe incoming push notifications:

Figure 7.2: Food order push notifications

See also

- Angular University's complete guide on push notifications: `https://blog.angular-university.io/angular-push-notifications/`

- Angular documentation on push notifications: `https://angular.dev/ecosystem/service-workers/push-notifications`

- The `SwPush` class documentation: `https://angular.dev/api/service-worker/SwPush`

- Firebase cloud messaging: `https://firebase.google.com/docs/cloud-messaging`

Implementing reactive background data sync

Background data sync in PWAs allows our application to synchronize data in the background, even when the app is not actively being used. This ensures that the app's data is always up to date and provides a seamless user experience. This feature comes in handy, especially in offline use cases, since it will keep data fresh and we can have access to fresh data in offline mode.

How to do it...

In this recipe, we will simulate the PWA's background sync of data by leveraging Angular's interceptors and Dexie.js, a small wrapper around the browser's `IndexedDB` database.

Step 1 – Intercepting the recipe request

In `services/recipes.service.ts`, we have a simple HTTP request to our server:

```
getRecipes() {
    return this.http.get('/api/recipes');}
```

The way we can intercept each recipe request is by using Angular's interceptors. In `interceptors/background-sync.interceptor.ts`, we have generated a starting point for our background sync:

```
import { HttpInterceptorFn } from '@angular/common/http';
export const backgroundSyncInterceptor: HttpInterceptorFn =
    (req, next) => {
        return next(req);
};
```

Step 2 – Establishing background sync with API

Whenever there is an ongoing recipe request, we can set up a timer that will periodically send a request in the background to check whether there are any data updates. By doing so every five seconds, we will make sure that we have the latest fresh data in our web app:

```
import { HttpInterceptorFn } from '@angular/common/http';
import { exhaustMap, tap, timer } from 'rxjs';

export const backgroundSyncInterceptor: HttpInterceptorFn =
    (req, next) => {
        if (req.url.includes('/recipes')) {
            console.log(
                'Background sync request detected. Retrying
                 request...');
            return timer(0, 5000).pipe(
                take(5),
                exhaustMap(() => next(req)),
            );
```

```
        }
    return next(req);
};
```

Step 3 — Setting up Dexie.js

One of the main features of PWAs is the ability to work offline. The perfect time to prepare for offline conditions is when we are actually online. What we want here is to store the latest fresh data on the client, so that we have access to the latest possible data, even when we go offline. We will use the Dexie.js library to store data in IndexedDB after each background sync:

```
import Dexie from 'dexie';

export interface Recipe {
    id?: number;
    lastUpdated: number;
    data: {
        title: string;
        ingredients: string[];
        instructions: string;
    };
}


export class RecipesDB extends Dexie {
    recipes: Dexie.Table<Recipe, number>;

    constructor() {
        super('RecipesDB');
        this.version(1).stores({
            recipes: '++id'
        });
        this.recipes = this.table('recipes');
    }
}


export const db = new RecipesDB();
```

Let's explore this code:

1. By calling the parent Dexie constructor, we create the `RecipesDB` database.

2. We specify the database schema version and store the `recipes` table with an auto-incrementing primary key.

3. We reference the `recipes` table from `RecipesDB`.

Step 4 – Storing sync data in IndexedDB

Once we have the IndexedDB setup done, we can store data whenever we have fresh data gathered from a background sync:

```
return timer(2000, 5000).pipe(
    take(5),
    exhaustMap(() => next(req)),
    switchMap((response) => {
        if (response instanceof HttpResponse) {
            return response.body as RecipeResponse[];
        }

        return EMPTY;
    }),
    concatMap(async ({ id, ...data }: RecipeResponse) => {console.log(id);
        const existingRecipe = await db.recipes.get(id);
        const isRecipeStale = existingRecipe &&
        existingRecipe.lastUpdated < data.timestamp;

        if (!existingRecipe) {
            console.log(`Adding recipe with id ${
                id} in IndexedDB.`);
            return db.recipes.add({ id, data,
                lastUpdated: data.timestamp });
        }

        if (isRecipeStale) {
            console.log(`Updating recipe with id ${
                id} in IndexedDB.`);
```

```
                    return db.recipes.update(id, { data,
                        lastUpdated: data.timestamp });


                }
            console.log(`Recipe with id ${
                id} already exists in IndexedDB.`);
            return EMPTY;
        }),
        catchError((error) => {
            console.error('Error while syncing data:', error);
            return EMPTY;
        })
    );
```

When we get a backend response, we will check whether the specific food recipe already exists in
IndexedDB. If not, we can add that recipe to the database. However, if it does exist, then we are
going to check whether the recipe data is stale so that we know whether we need to update that
recipe. Finally, if the recipe exists in the database and the data is fresh, we will gracefully exit and
continue the stream since no changes need to be made in the database.

When we open our browser and inspect DevTools, we can check out the results:

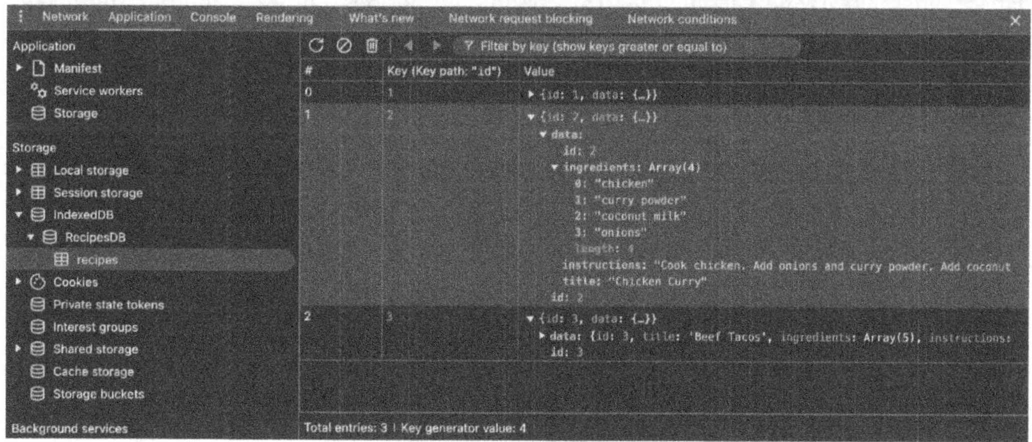

Figure 7.3: Recipes IndexedDB

Now that we have data stored in IndexedDB, we can create reactive queries on our IndexedDB database. In app.component.rs, we can create a reactive query and display recipes data in the UI:

```
import { liveQuery } from 'dexie';
recipes$ = liveQuery(() => db.recipes.toArray());
```

Finally, when we run the application build and open our browser in offline mode, we will still see the recipes data retrieved from IndexedDB.

Building offline-ready applications seamlessly with RxDB

RxDB is a powerful reactive NoSQL database. What makes RxDB so powerful is its ability to create efficient real-time apps, its offline-first approach, automatic background data updates, and many more.

Since it's built on top of RxJS, RxDB is reactive by default. We can write reactive database queries that will update automatically whenever the underlying data changes. RxDB provides Observables that act as change streams, allowing us to listen to any data modifications such as document insertions, updates, and deletes.

By combining RxJS with its change streams, RxDB enables you to build applications that react to data changes in real time, keeping the UI always in sync. Besides offline capabilities, this makes RxDB a perfect fit to build a PWA.

Getting ready

Since RxDB provides a wide range of possibilities, its documentation is a great learning resource for exploring all features. You can check it out here if your needs go beyond building a PWA: https://rxdb.info/quickstart.html.

How to do it...

In this recipe, we will keep the scope to how to set up RxDB and leverage RxJS as much as we can. We will build a small offline-first cooking app that keeps data in sync.

Step 1 – Defining the recipe schema

With RxDB, we can create a schema of a database object. This might be important because the schema can be used with RxDB to validate recipe objects, ensuring they have the correct structure and required properties before being stored or processed in the database:

```
export const recipeSchema = {
    title: 'recipe schema',
    description: 'describes a simple recipe',
    primaryKey: 'id',
    type: 'object',
    version: 0,
    properties: {
        id: {
            type: 'string',
        },
        title: {
            type: 'string',
            primary: true,
        },
        ingredients: {
            type: 'array',
            items: {
                type: 'string',
            },
        },
        instructions: {
            type: 'string',
        },
    },
    required: ['title', 'ingredients', 'instructions'],
};
```

When we break down this schema, we might notice key parts:

- **Schema metadata** provides information about the schema, including its title, description, primary key, type, and version
- The `properties` definition specifies the structure and types of the properties in the recipe object
- The `required` property lists the properties that are mandatory for a valid recipe object

Step 2 – Creating RxDatabase

When we have our recipe schema in place, we can create a food recipes client database. In `services/rxdb.service.ts`, we will have the following code:

```
import { RxDatabase, createRxDatabase } from 'rxdb';
import { getRxStorageDexie } from 'rxdb/plugins/storage-dexie';

async initDatabase(): Promise<RxDatabase> {
    const db = await createRxDatabase({
        name: 'recipesdatabase',
        storage: getRxStorageDexie()
    });

    await recipesDatabase.addCollections({
        recipes: {
            schema: recipeSchema
        }
    });
    return db;
}
```

First, we call the `createRxDatabase` method where we pass the database name and storage. We use the Dexie.js plugin, which is a wrapper around the browser's `IndexedDB` database.

After the database creation, we add a `recipes` collection with data schema. Now, we are ready to store recipe data in `IndexedDB`.

Step 3 – Subscribing to ChangeEvent

After the database and collection creation, we can perform CRUD operations on the recipe entity:

```
db.recipes.insert({
    id: crypto.randomUUID(),
    title: 'Spaghetti Carbonara',
    ingredients: ['spaghetti', 'eggs', 'bacon', 'parmesan
                  cheese'],
    instructions: 'Cook spaghetti. Fry bacon. Mix eggs and
                   cheese. Combine all ingredients.'
});
```

After inserting data into the RxDB collection, we can subscribe to `ChangeEvent` and track all changes in our client database:

```
db.$.subscribe((changeEvent:
    ChangeStreamEvent<RxDocument) => {
        console.dir(changeEvent)
});
```

Also, in `rxdb.service.ts`, we can create an RxJS stream whenever we want to add a new recipe and call the RxDB `insert()` method:

```
export class RxDBService {
    db$: Observable<RxDatabase> = from(this.initDatabase())
    .pipe(
        catchError((error) => {
            console.error('Error initializing database:',
                          error);
            return EMPTY;
        }),    retry(3),
        shareReplay({ bufferSize: 1, refCount: true })
    );
    addRecipe$ = new Subject<Recipe>();

    constructor() {
        this.addRecipe$
        .pipe(
```

```
                withLatestFrom(this.db$),
                switchMap(([recipe, db]) =>
                    db.collections['recipes'].insert(recipe)),
            catchError((error) => {
                console.error('Error inserting recipe:', error);
                return EMPTY;
            })
        )
        .subscribe();
    }
    addRecipe(data: Recipe): void {
        this.addRecipe$.next(data);
    }
    }
}
```

Since the recipe title is the database's primary key, we will get an error if we add the recipe with the same title.

Step 4 – Searching for a recipe with RxQuery

To create a query with **RxQuery**, first, we need to include the RxQuery builder plugin in our app's `main.ts` file:

```
import { RxDBQueryBuilderPlugin } from 'rxdb/plugins/query-builder';
addRxPlugin(RxDBQueryBuilderPlugin);
```

After that, back in `rxdb.service.ts`, we can call the `find()` method on a collection and pass a variety of selectors with **Query Builder** to search for the desired recipe by title:

```
recipes$ = new BehaviorSubject<Recipe[]>([]);
findRecipe$ = new Subject<string>();

constructor() {
    this.findRecipe$
    .pipe(
    withLatestFrom(this.db$),
    switchMap(
```

```
              ([recipeTitle, db]) =>
                  db.collections['recipes'].find().where(
                      'title').eq(recipeTitle).$
              ),
              map((recipes: RxDocument[]) => recipes.map((r) =>
                  r.toJSON()))
          )
          .subscribe((recipes) => this.recipes$.next(recipes as
                                              Recipe[]));
  }
  findRecipe(recipeTitle: string): void {
      this.findRecipe$.next(recipeTitle);
  }
}
```

Here, we can notice that we have searched the `recipes` collection to find a recipe whose title is an exact match with the desired recipe. After that, with $, we can observe query results and update the UI accordingly.

There's more...

Here are a few points to note:

- **Database migrations**: As your application grows and your data schema evolves, RxDB provides tools to manage these changes gracefully. You can define migration strategies that automatically update your existing data to match the new schema, preventing data loss and ensuring a smooth transition for your users. This also extends to the underlying storage engine. If you need to switch from one storage type to another, RxDB allows you to migrate all your data without any hiccups.

- **Real-time replication**: RxDB allows your application to seamlessly synchronize data with various backends such as GraphQL, CouchDB, and even other RxDB instances, making real-time collaboration a breeze. It achieves this through a simple, yet powerful replication protocol that ensures data consistency across all connected clients. Even better, RxDB excels in offline scenarios. Your app can continue to modify data while offline, and RxDB will automatically synchronize those changes with the server once a connection is re-established.

- **Conflict resolution**: RxDB acts as a safety net for your data when multiple users or offline devices make changes to the same information. This ensures that your data stays consistent even with many simultaneous edits, preventing data loss and confusion.

- **Backup mechanism**: In case of unexpected problems or data migrations, it can be a safety net. RxDB makes this process easy by writing the backup to the computer's filesystem in a format that's easy to understand and use. This gives us peace of mind knowing that valuable data is secure and can be recovered if needed, like having an extra copy of important files.

See also

- RxDB as a database for PWAs: `https://rxdb.info/articles/progressive-web-app-database.html`

- RxDB as offline first: `https://rxdb.info/offline-first.html`

- RxQuery: `https://rxdb.info/rx-query.html`

- RxDB conflict resolution: `https://rxdb.info/transactions-conflicts-revisions.html#conflicts`

8

Building Offline-First Applications with RxJS

We live in an increasingly connected world, and because of this, it's easy to overlook the significance of offline functionality. However, the reality is that internet connectivity isn't always guaranteed. Whether it's due to limited network coverage, or simply being in a remote location, there are countless scenarios where users might find themselves without an internet connection. This is where offline-first web apps come into play.

Offline-first web apps are designed to function seamlessly, even when users are offline. They prioritize providing core functionality and data access without relying on a constant internet connection. This approach has numerous benefits:

- **Enhanced user experience**: By ensuring that users can interact with an app regardless of network availability, offline-first apps deliver a smoother and more consistent experience. This eliminates the frustration of waiting for content to load or being unable to perform basic tasks when offline.

- **Increased accessibility**: Offline capabilities make web apps more inclusive, especially in areas with unreliable or limited internet access. This expands the potential user base and ensures that everyone can benefit from the app's features.

- **Improved performance**: Offline-first apps often load faster and respond more quickly, as they leverage cached data and resources. This leads to a more efficient and enjoyable user experience.

- **Reduced data costs**: For users with metered or expensive data plans, offline functionality can help minimize data usage. This is particularly valuable in regions where data costs are high.

- **Data synchronization**: Offline-first apps typically implement mechanisms to synchronize data with servers when connectivity is restored. This ensures that user data remains up to date and consistent across devices.

In order to deal with the complexity of designing offline web apps, we can use different offline strategies, carefully tailored for specific use cases:

Strategy	Use Cases
Cache-First	*Visuals that rarely change*: Website logos, icons, background images, and so on *App shell*: The basic framework of a single-page application for instant loading *Offline-accessible content*: Documentation, help files, user manuals *Infrequently updated product images*: E-commerce product photos that remain static for a while
Network-First	*Time-sensitive news articles*: Breaking news, live updates, current events *Real-time social media feeds*: Posts, comments, and interactions requiring immediate updates *Constantly changing financial data*: Stock prices, currency rates, market information, game leaderboards *Dynamic user-generated content*: New comments, forum posts, user reviews *Productivity and collaboration tools*: Shared documents, project management boards, and communication platforms where real-time updates are essential for effective teamwork

Strategy	Use Cases
Stale-While-Revalidate	*E-commerce product pages*: Show a cached version first, then update price and availability *Blog posts with occasional edits*: Display the cached post while fetching potential updates *Dashboards with live data*: Show cached metrics initially, then refresh with live server data *Content with moderate update frequency*: Articles that might get minor edits or updates
Cache-Network-Race	*Websites with mixed content*: Static elements (header, footer) alongside dynamic content (articles, comments). *Applications with real-time features*: Display cached data instantly while fetching live updates *Situations prioritizing speed above all*: When the fastest possible response is crucial, regardless of initial content freshness
Optimistic Update	*Interactive forms and input fields*: Provide immediate feedback by updating the UI before server confirmation (e.g., adding a comment, sending a message) *Simple actions with high user expectations for speed*: Liking a post, adding an item to a cart, favoring an item

Table 9.1: Offline strategies

In this chapter, we will cover the following recipes:

- Implementing seamless RxJS offline-first apps using a Cache-First strategy
- Prioritizing fresh data with RxJS network-first strategy
- Optimizing data freshness and performance with Stale-While-Revalidate Strategy
- Racing Cache and Network strategy
- Implementing the optimistic update pattern

Technical requirements

To complete this chapter, you'll need:

- Angular v19+
- Angular Material
- RxJS v7
- Node.js v22+
- npm v11+ or pnpm v10+

The code for recipes in this chapter is placed in the GitHub repository at `https://github.com/PacktPublishing/RxJS-Cookbook-for-Reactive-Programming/tree/main/Chapter08`.

To make Angular applications work offline, we can run one simple command, which will add all the necessary configurations and a basic service worker to our project:

```
ng add @angular/pwa
```

Since service workers are enabled only in production mode, to observe each recipe in action, we must build our app and serve it locally. In each recipe, we will use the simple **http-server** library to host the client app locally and observe offline mode in the browser by running the following command in the terminal:

```
npm run build && http-server ${build-location} -c-1 -o
```

What is in common for all the recipes in this chapter is that whenever we have a step called *Going offline*, it is a necessary step to do in order to check offline behavior.

Also, what is in common for all strategies in this chapter (except the optimistic update pattern) is that we will need to generate an Angular interceptor. All of our logic to simulate offline mode will be in a file `offline.interceptor.ts`.

In Angular, we can simply use the following command to generate our request interceptor:

```
ng generate interceptor interceptors/offline
```

Implementing seamless RxJS offline-first apps using a Cache-First strategy

In this recipe, we're going to explore how to implement an offline strategy where we first check whether we have data inside the cache, then we fall back to the network.

How to do it...

We are going to leverage Angular's **interceptors** and simulate the same behavior as if we were implementing the **Cache-First offline strategy** inside a service worker.

Step 1 – Extracting data from the Cache API

Usually, on the modern web, we store data for the offline mode inside a browser's **Cache API**. When we use offline mode, the **Cache-first strategy** says:

1. First, try to get the data from the Cache API.

2. If there is data in the cache, return it immediately to the interceptor as a response.

3. If the data is not matched by the request's URL key, then we proceed to the network and check whether we are back online.

The implementation of a strategy like this would be as follows:

```
export const offlineInterceptor: HttpInterceptorFn = (req:
    HttpRequest<unknown>, next: HttpHandlerFn) => {
    return openCache$.pipe(
        switchMap((cache: Cache) =>
            from(cache.match(req.url))),
        switchMap((cacheResponse: Response | undefined) => {
            if (cacheResponse) {
                return from(cacheResponse.json());
            }

            return continueRequest$;
        }),
        map((response: unknown) => {
            return new HttpResponse({
                status: 200,
                body: response
            })
        })
    );
}
```

Step 2 – Falling back to the network

When we have network access, everything runs smoothly because our data is just one HTTP network request away. But we must not take this for granted, and this is a perfect time to prepare for offline events by caching the latest fresh data:

```
const openCache$ = from(caches.open('my-app-cache'));
const continueRequest$ = next(req).pipe(
    withLatestFrom(openCache$),
    map(([response, cache]) => {
if (response instanceof HttpResponse) {
        cache.put(req.url, new Response(JSON.stringify(response.body)));
        return response.body;
    }

    return EMPTY;
}),
    // exponential backoff if request fails (check Chapter01)
);
```

Let's break down what we are doing here:

1. First, we create an Observable stream out of values returned from cache storage with the `my-app-cache` key. Then, we combine that stream with the intercepted request `continueRequest$`.

2. Then, we check whether we are online.

3. If that is the case, once we get the response from the network, we will open our cache storage and put the latest fresh values there by the key to the corresponding request URL.

Now, we are ready for offline mode!

Step 3 – Going offline

First, we would serve the application from a local server:

```
npm run build && http-server ./dist/rxjs-offline-cache-first/browser -c-1
-o
```

Now, if we open a browser and Dev Tools, we can start playing around:

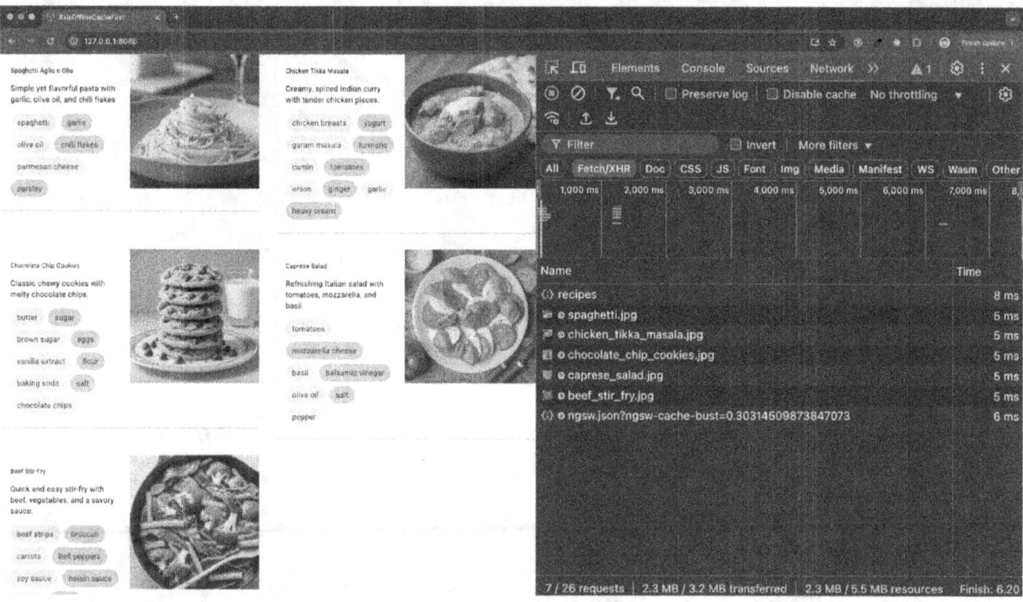

Figure 8.1: Online request

On the **Network** tab, we can observe that there is an ongoing network request when we are online, which is expected. What we also might notice is that on the **Application** tab, the cache storage is visually represented. We can also see our cache entry, my-app-cache:

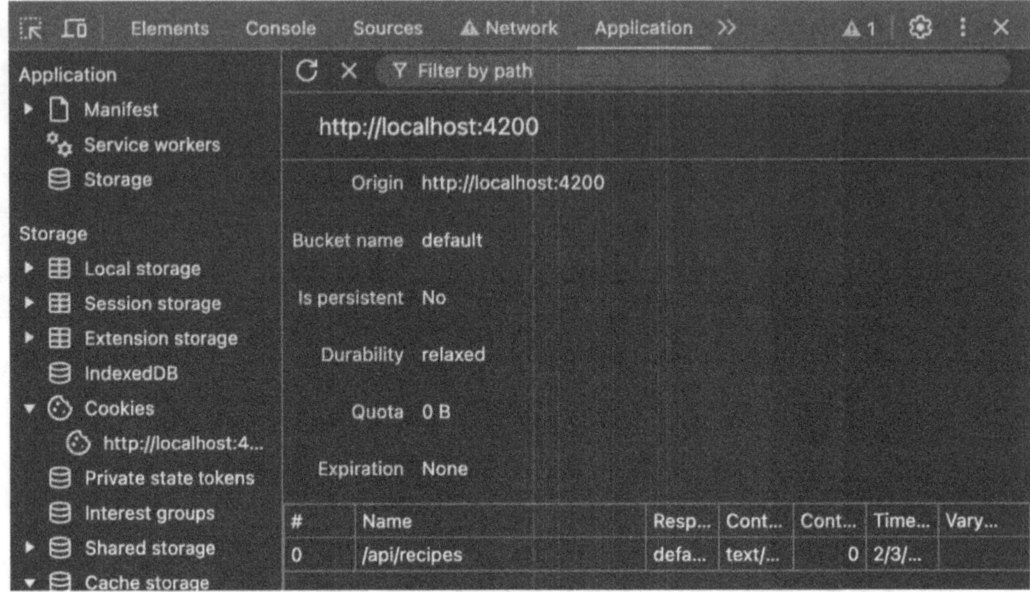

Figure 8.2: Cache storage

Finally, if we go into offline mode, we will see that there is no ongoing or failing network request, but the data is still there, and the whole app works as when it was back online.

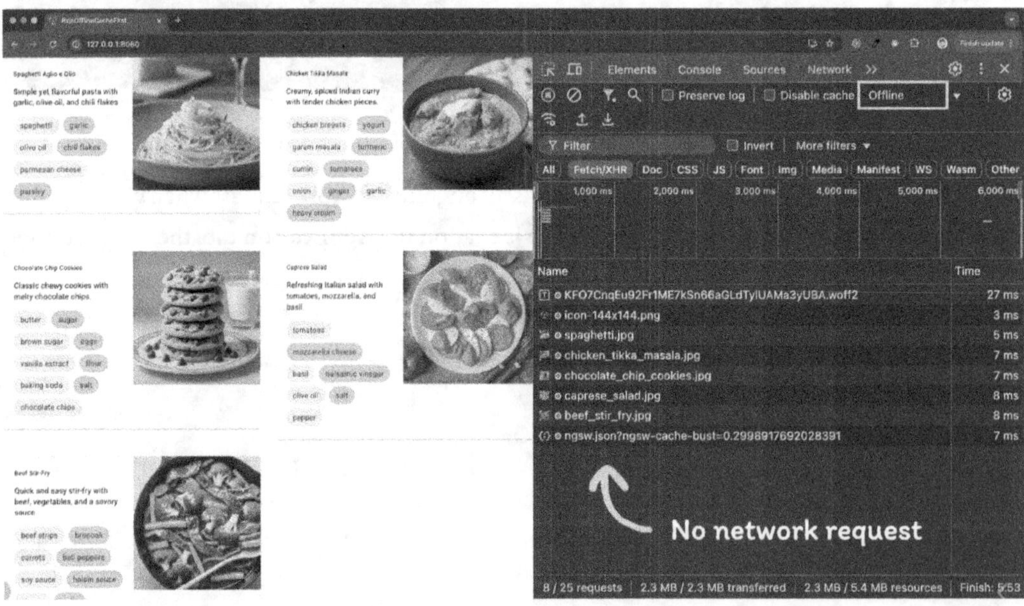

Figure 8.3: Cache-first offline mode

Prioritizing fresh data with RxJS network-first strategy

In this recipe, we're going to follow the opposite approach to the preceding recipe. Here, we're going to send a network request first, and if we are offline and the request fails, then we'll fall back to the cache. In this way, we can always have the latest fresh values in our cache, even when we go offline.

How to do it...

We are going to leverage Angular's interceptors and simulate the same behavior as if we were implementing a **network-first offline strategy** inside a service worker.

Step 1 – Sending a network request when online

When we have our interceptor ready, we can intercept each HTTP request, update the cache storage to keep the data fresh in the cache, and continue with the request:

```
const openCache$ = from(caches.open('my-app-cache'));
const continueRequest$ = next(req);

return continueRequest$.pipe(
  withLatestFrom(openCache$),
  map(([response, cache]) => {
    if (response instanceof HttpResponse) {
      cache.put(
        req.url,
        new Response(JSON.stringify(response.body)));
    }

    return response;
  }),
  catchError(() => cacheFallback(req, openCache$))
);
```

Let's break down what we are doing here:

1. First, we create an Observable stream out of the values returned from the cache storage with the `my-app-cache` key. Then, we combine that stream with the intercepted request, `continueRequest$`.

2. We send the request, and once we get the response from the network, we will open our
    cache storage and put the latest fresh values there by the key to the corresponding request
    URL.

3. When we go offline, the request will fail, and then we will fall back to the cache.

Step 2 – Falling back to the cache

If there is a network error, we will catch that error and implement `cacheFallback`:

```
const cacheFallback = (
  req: HttpRequest<unknown>,
  openCache$: Observable<Cache>
) => {
  return openCache$.pipe(
    switchMap((cache: Cache) =>
      from(cache.match(req.url))),
    switchMap((cacheResponse: Response | undefined) => {
      if (cacheResponse) {
        return from(cacheResponse.json());
      }

      return EMPTY;
    }),
    map((response: unknown) => {
      return new HttpResponse({
        status: 200,
        body: response
      })
    })
  );
}
```

When we experience the offline mode and network request fails, we do the following:

1. First, we open Cache API.

2. Then we check if there is a `match` in the cache with the current request URL.

3. If there is a match, we return cached data as a response.

4. If there is no match from the cache, we gracefully exit the stream.

Step 3 – Going offline

First, we would serve application from a local server:

```
npm run build && http-server ./dist/rxjs-offline-network-first/browser
-c-1 -o
```

Now, if we open a browser and Dev Tools, we can start playing around:

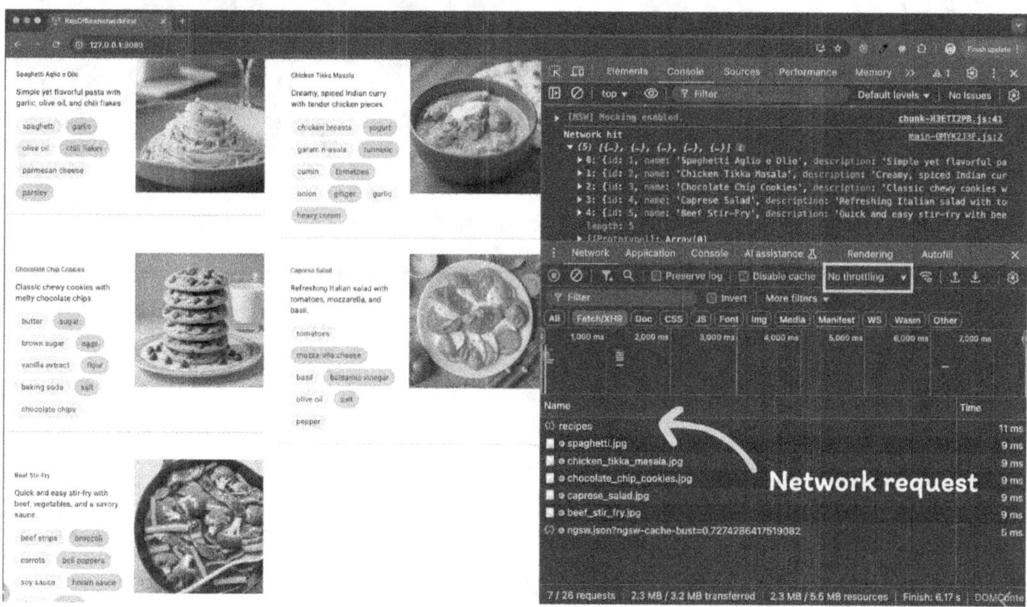

Figure 8.4: Online mode

When we are online, we can see that the network request is being sent. The network response will refresh our cache data so that we can have the latest possible values once we go offline.

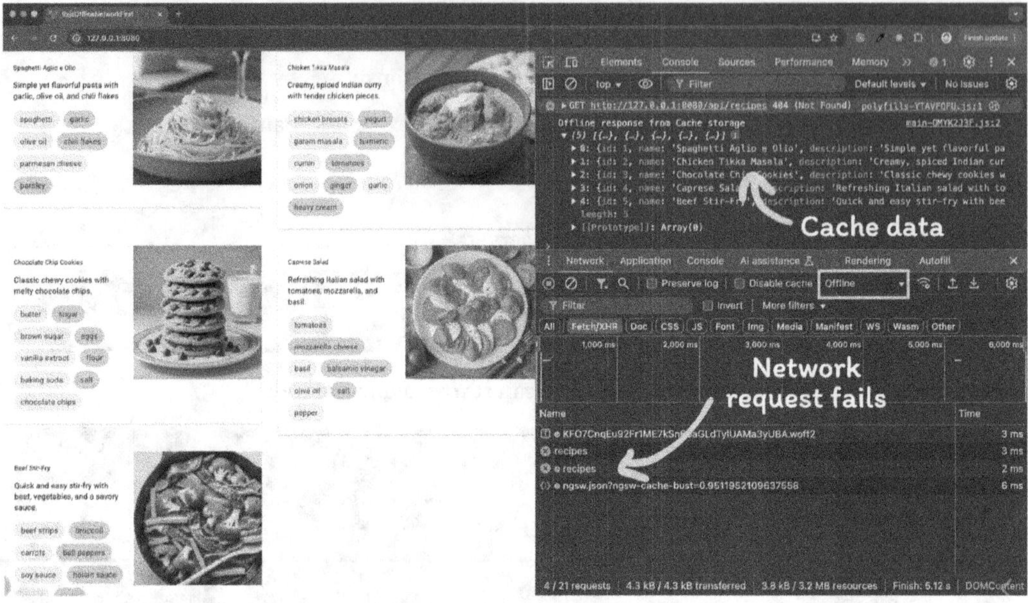

Figure 8.5: Network-first offline mode

Once we go offline, we can see that the network request fails, but since we have a cache fallback, everything works as expected, and we show the latest data from the cache.

An obvious drawback of this approach might be use cases where the network is slow. We would wait for the slow network response, although we might have data from the cache ready to be shown in the UI. The next two strategies aim to resolve that challenge.

Optimizing data freshness and performance with the Stale-While-Revalidate strategy

Stale-While-Revalidate is a common strategy when we want to always show some data to the user, even if the data might be out of date. After that, we send the network request in the background and refresh the data afterward. This can also help us if we go offline since we can show the old data first, then retry and check in the background if we are back online.

How to do it...

We are going to leverage Angular's interceptors and simulate the same behavior as if we were implementing the Stale-While-Revalidate offline strategy inside a service worker. The strategy here is to create two streams that will emit values in order, first for the cache data, and the second for the network response data.

Step 1 – Extracting data from the cache

Now that our interceptor is ready, we can intercept each HTTP request, and show cached data while we are offline:

```
const openCache$ = from(caches.open('my-app-cache'));
const dataFromCache$ = openCache$.pipe(
  switchMap((cache: Cache) => from(cache.match(req.url))),
  switchMap((cacheResponse: Response | undefined) => {
    if (cacheResponse) {
      return from(cacheResponse.json());
    }

    return EMPTY;
  }),
  map((response: unknown) => new HttpResponse({
    body: response
  })),
);
```

Let's break down what we are doing here:

1. First, we open the cache, `my-app-cache`, and create an Observable stream from it.

2. Then, we check whether there is a match in the cache with the current request URL.

3. If there is cache data, we return it as a response.

4. If there is no cache data, we gracefully complete the stream without the result.

Step 2 – Checking for the fresh data in the background

When we complete the stream from the cache storage, we will send the network request to check
for fresh data:

```
const continueRequest$ = next(req).pipe(
  withLatestFrom(openCache$),
  map(([response, cache]) => {
    if (response instanceof HttpResponse) {
      cache.put(
        req.url,
        new Response(JSON.stringify(response.body))
      );
    }

    return response;
  }),
  // exponential backoff if request fails (check Chapter01)
);
```

Now, we can use the RxJS concat operator to control the sequence of events for the Stale-While-
Revalidate offline strategy:

```
return concat(
  dataFromCache$,
  continueRequest$
);
```

This means that if we experience offline conditions, first we show the cache data to the user, and
after we do that, we send a request in the background to check whether we are back online and
refresh the data.

Step 3 – Going offline

First, we will serve application from a local server:

```
npm run build && http-server ./dist/rxjs-offline-stale-while-revalidate/
browser -c-1 -o
```

If we open a browser and Dev Tools, we can see this strategy in action:

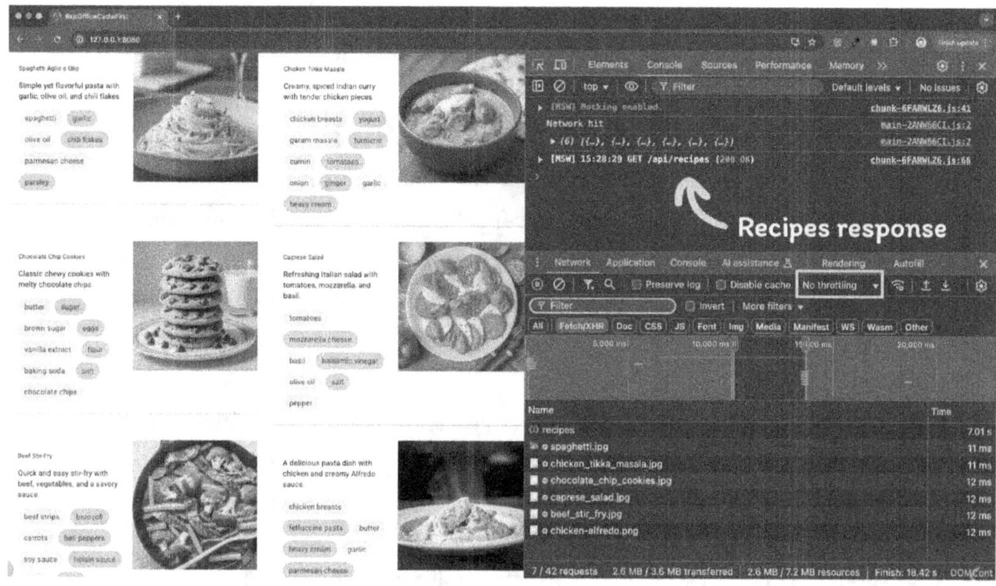

Figure 8.6: Online request

On the **Network** tab, we can see that there is an ongoing network request when we are online, which is expected. This is when we prepare for offline conditions and fill in our cache with the latest data:

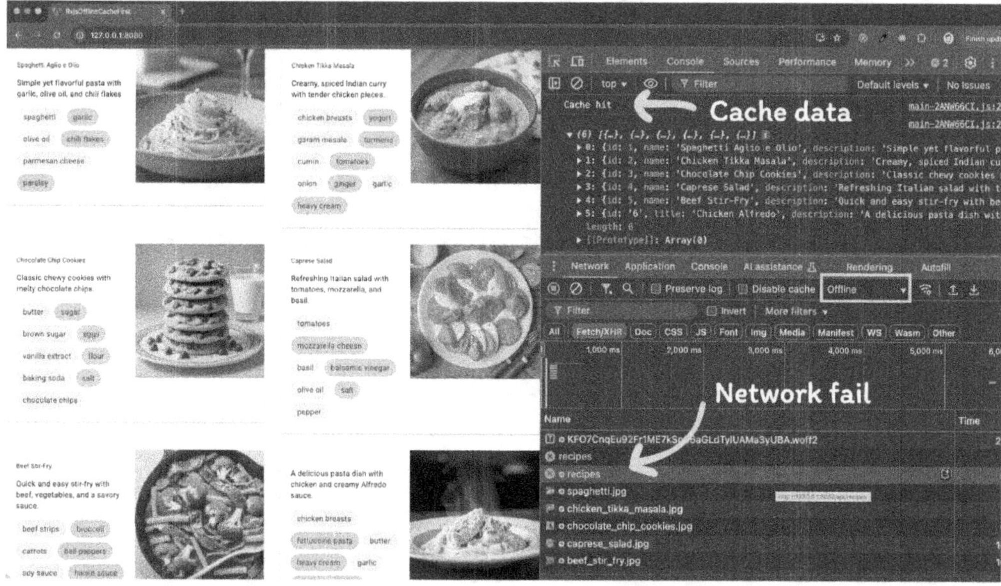

Figure 8.7: Stale-While-Revalidate offline mode

Once we go into the offline mode, we can observe the **Stale-While-Revalidate** strategy in action. We show cache data immediately, but we are checking in the background if we are back online. Once we are back online, we are going to see fresh data from the server.

Racing Cache and Network strategy

We can think of this strategy as **the winner takes all**. We try to get the data from the cache and from the network at the same time, and whoever is faster, we show their response. The strategy aims to display data as quickly as possible, prioritizing the first available source. This strategy ensures that users see content quickly, even if they are offline or have a slow network connection.

How to do it...

We are going to leverage Angular's interceptors and simulate the same behavior as if we were implementing **Racing Cache and Network offline strategy** inside of a service worker.

Step 1 – Extracting data from the cache

First, we are going to define a stream for extracting data from the cache:

```
let dataFromCache$: Observable<HttpEvent<unknown>>;


const openCache$ = from(caches.open('my-app-cache'));
dataFromCache$ = openCache$.pipe(
  switchMap((cache: Cache) => from(cache.match(req.url))),
  switchMap((cacheResponse: Response | undefined) => {
    if (cacheResponse) {
      return from(cacheResponse.json());
    }

    return NEVER;
  }),
  map((response: unknown) => {
    return new HttpResponse({
      status: 200,
      body: response
    })
  })
);
```

Let's break down what we are doing here:

1. First, we open the cache, `my-app-cache`, and create an Observable stream from it.

2. Then, we check whether there is a match in the cache with the current request URL.

3. If there is a match, we return cached data as a response.

4. If there is cache data, we return it as a response.

5. If there is no cache data, we simply continue the stream without emitting any value (without completion of the stream). We can achieve this effect by using `NEVER` operator that keeps the observable open indefinitely without emitting values. This is intended to prevent premature stream completion when no cache is available.

Step 2 – Sending a network request

This is sending" the way we can define a network request stream:

```
let continueRequestWithCacheSave$: Observable<HttpEvent<unknown>>;

continueRequestWithCacheSave$ = next(req).pipe(
  withLatestFrom(openCache$),
  map(([response, cache]) => {
    if (response instanceof HttpResponse) {
      cache.put(
        req.url,
        new Response(JSON.stringify(response.body)));
    }

    return response;
  }),
  catchError(() => dataFromCache$),
);
```

Let's break down what we are doing here:

1. We create an Observable stream of our interceptor's next function and combine it with a promise that we get as a result of opening cache storage.

2. We send the request, and once we get the response from the network, we open our **Cache** storage and put the latest fresh values there by the key to the corresponding request URL.

3. If the request fails when we go offline, we will refer to the cached value.

Step 3 — Network & cache race

Now once we have defined both streams, we are ready for the race. To achieve that effect, we can leverage RxJS `raceWith` operator. This means that if we return the following stream:

```
return dataFromCache$.pipe(
  raceWith(continueRequestWithCacheSave$),
);
```

We would end up with a response from whoever wins the race. Since we have a two-second delay inside of our MSW network handler, it is obvious that the cache will win in every case except initially, when there is no cache data. We can test this and play around with it by putting a delay of more than two seconds at the beginning of `dataFromCache$` stream.

Step 4 — Going offline

First, we serve the application from a local server:

```
npm run build && http-server ./dist/rxjs-offline-race-network-cache/
browser -c-1 -o
```

If we open a browser and Dev Tools, we can start the race:

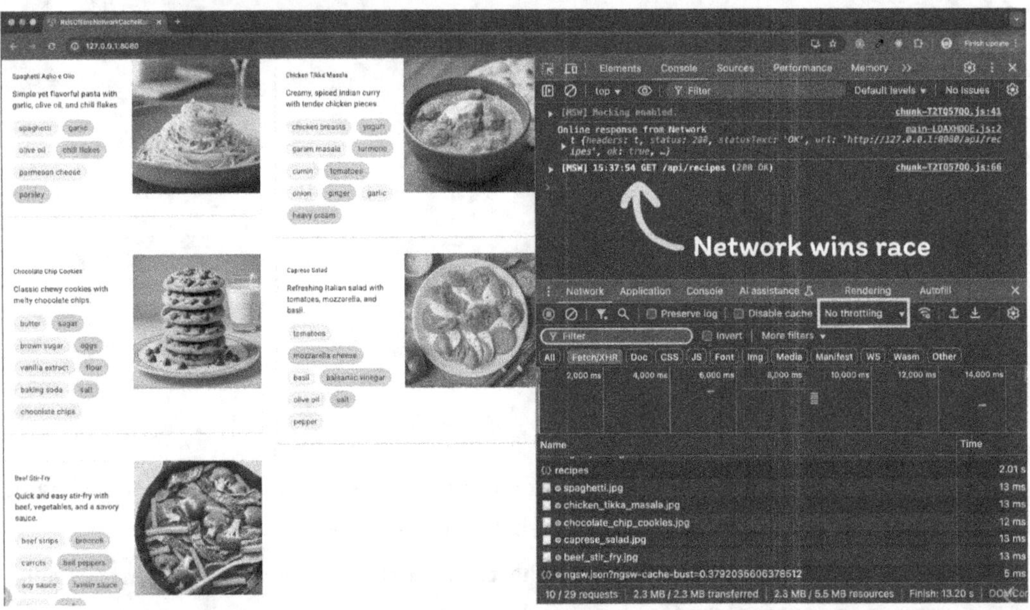

Figure 8.8: Network wins

Initially, we can see that network request wins, since we had nothing in the cache storage. But if we refresh the page and look at Dev Tools, we can see that reading from the cache is faster than a network request, so this time, the cache wins:

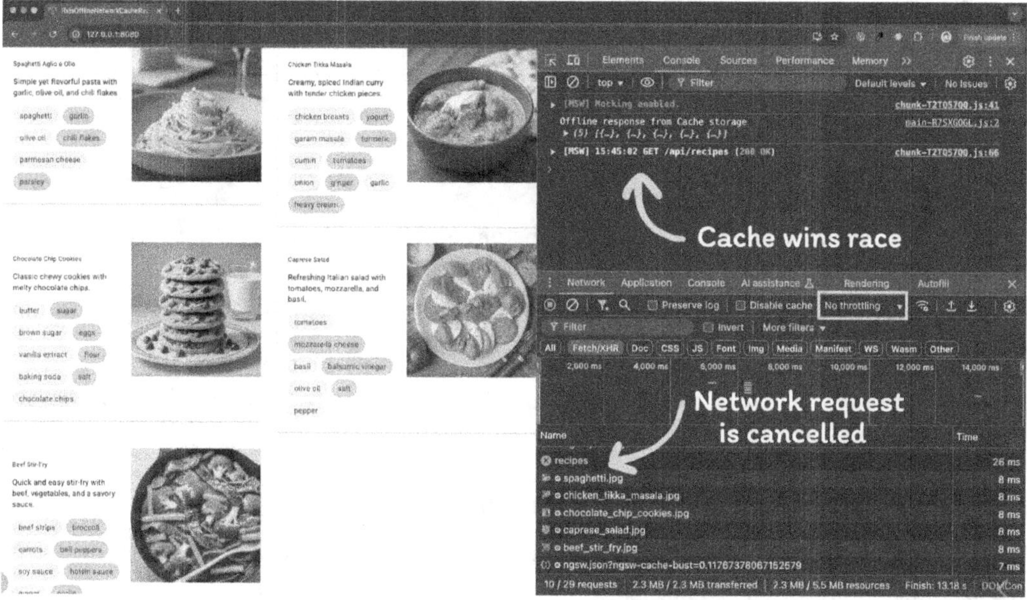

Figure 8.9: Racing the cache and the network in offline mode

Finally, if we go into offline mode, we can see the **Racing Cache and Network** strategy in action. First, we will try to send the request, see that the request is failing, and then go to the cache.

See also

- Http-server library: `https://github.com/http-party/http-server#readme`
- Big thank you to Jake Archibald for the inspiration for this chapter with his blog **Offline Cookbook**: `https://jakearchibald.com/2014/offline-cookbook/`
- MDN Cache API docs: `https://developer.mozilla.org/en-US/docs/Web/API/Cache`
- Angular Service Worker guide: `https://angular.dev/ecosystem/service-workers/getting-started`

Implementing the optimistic update pattern

The **optimistic update pattern** is a user interface design strategy that enhances user experience by immediately reflecting changes made by the user, even before those changes are confirmed by the server. This approach creates a sense of responsiveness and fluidity, reducing the perception of lag and improving overall user satisfaction. This pattern can come in handy, especially in situations when we go offline.

How to do it...

In this recipe, we are going to implement a custom operator called `optimisticUpdate`, which will handle a `POST` request in a way that we immediately show the result to the user, then in the background continue with the network request. If we are offline and the request fails, we will do a retry after a certain period of time. If the request fails the second time, then we will provide a rollback option, which in most cases would be that we remove the item from the list that we added optimistically.

Step 1 – Creating a custom operator

In our `operators/optimistic-update.operator.ts` file, we will place our custom RxJS operator for handling optimistic `POST` requests:

```typescript
import { Observable, concat, of, throwError } from 'rxjs';
import { catchError, ignoreElements, retry } from 'rxjs/operators';

export function optimisticUpdate<T, E = any>(
  originalValue: T,
  rollback: (value: T, error: E) => void,
  retryConfig: { count: number, delay: number } =
    { count: 1, delay: 3000 }
): (source: Observable<T>) => Observable<T> {
  return (source: Observable<T>) => {
    return concat(
      of(originalValue),
      source.pipe(
        ignoreElements(),
        retry(retryConfig),
        catchError((error) => {
          rollback(originalValue, error);
          return throwError(() => error);
```

```
        })
      )
    );
  };
}
```

Let's break down what we are doing here:

1. First, as operator arguments, we provide a recipe object that we are about to send to the backend, and a rollback function (what should we do if the request fails).

2. Then, with the concat operator, we combine two streams that should execute in order, one stream being the optimistic original value of the original object value we are about to post, the other stream being the actual request to the backend.

3. We immediately return the original value of the original object value as the first emitted value and show that recipe in the UI optimistically.

4. After that, we start dealing with the ongoing request. In case of request failure, we define the retry mechanism by desire: in this case, we will have one retry within three seconds.

5. If we are offline, and the request fails, then we catch that error and provide a rollback option.

Step 2 – Applying the optimistic update operator

In `recipes.service.ts`, we have the `postRecipe` method for posting one new recipe:

```
public recipes$ = new Subject<Recipe | Error>();


postRecipe(): void {
  this.http.post<Recipe>('/api/recipes', this.recipe).pipe(
    optimisticUpdate(
      this.recipe,
      (originalItem: Recipe, error: Error) => {
        // Rollback UI changes here
        this.recipes$.next(error);
      }
    ),
    filter((recipe) => !!recipe)
  ).subscribe(
    (recipe: Recipe) => this.recipes$.next(recipe)
  );
}
```

Here, we can see that in case of a `postRecipe` method call, we immediately put the new potential recipe value inside of a `Subject`. If there's an error, we have a rollback option to show the error message, instead of a recipe.

Step 3 — Going offline

First, we would serve application from a local server:

```
npm run build && http-server ./dist/rxjs-optimistic-update/browser -c-1 -o
```

If we open a browser and Dev Tools, we can start playing around with this strategy. We immediately see the new recipe in the list, although we are offline:

Figure 8.10: Optimistic update

After three seconds and a retry, the request still fails, so we remove the recipe item from the list:

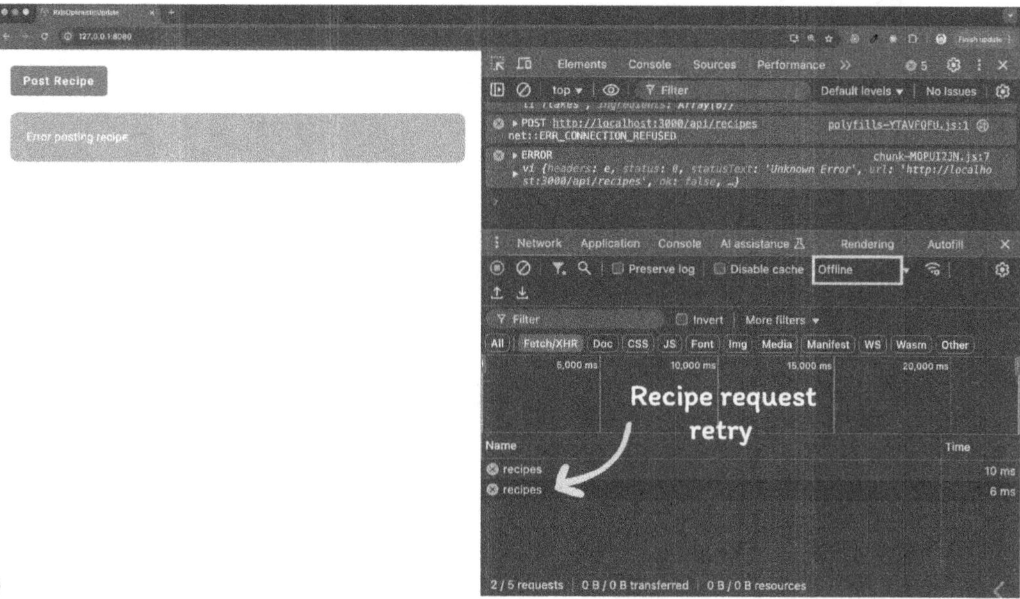

Figure 8.11: Optimistic update rollback

Learn more on Discord

To join the Discord community for this book – where you can share feedback, ask questions to the author, and learn about new releases – follow the QR code below:

```
https://packt.link/RxJSCookbook
```

Going Real-Time with RxJS

We live in a world of technology, where we want to always feel connected, and where information changes quickly. That is why it is an important requirement for modern web apps to provide us with dynamic and engaging experiences, without the need for manual browser refresh. Instant live sports event updates, smooth chat experiences, online multiplayer games, and tools where we can collaborate easily: these are all examples of real-time web apps.

One of the main technologies we can use to achieve real-time magic is WebSocket. WebSocket is a powerful technology that enables real-time, two-way communication between a web browser and a server. This persistent connection allows for instant data transfer, making it ideal for applications that require live updates and interactions. In this chapter, we will see in action WebSocket's efficiency, low latency, and full-duplex communication capabilities, which make it a powerful tool.

But what about developer experience when building these kinds of user experiences? That is where RxJS fits in, to orchestrate real-time data effectively, in an elegant, asynchronous, and reactive way.

In this chapter, we will cover the following recipes:

- Implementing real-time data visualization charts
- Crafting a modern chat application
- Playing real-time multiplayer Tic-Tac-Toe

Technical requirements

To follow along with this chapter, you'll need:

- RxJS v7
- Angular v19+
- NestJS v11+
- Node.js v22+
- npm v11+ or pnpm v10+

The code for the recipes in this chapter can be found in the GitHub repository here: `https://github.com/PacktPublishing/RxJS-Cookbook-for-Reactive-Programming/tree/main/Chapter09`.

Implementing real-time data visualization charts

We are living in a world of data, and by visualizing data within our system and enabling interaction and exploration, we enable our users to get a deeper understanding of complex datasets. One of the ways we can achieve this is by using charts. Charts can empower users to uncover hidden patterns and insights within their data.

How to do it...

In this recipe, we will visualize food recipe orders over a period of a year, by subscribing to the WebSocket connection, and observe live changes as data arrives.

Step 1 – Connecting to RxJS WebSocket

In our `RecipesService` class, we will establish a connection to WebSocket and open a topic for orders data that we can subscribe to:

```
import { webSocket, WebSocketSubject } from 'rxjs/webSocket';

export class RecipesService {
  private socket$!: WebSocketSubject<Message>;
  public orders$!: Observable<Message>;

  constructor() {}

  connect() {
    if (!this.socket$ || this.socket$.closed) {
```

```
        this.socket$ = webSocket<Message>({
          url: environment.wsEndpoint,
          deserializer: (e) => JSON.parse(e.data) as Message,
        });
        this.orders$ = this.socket$.multiplex(
          () => ({ subscribe: 'orders' }),
          () => ({ unsubscribe: 'orders' }),
          (message) => message.type === 'orders'
        );
      }
    }
  }
```

Step 2 – Reconnecting to WebSocket after losing connection

After we have successfully established the connection with WebSocket, we must take into consideration scenarios where we lose connection or there is a server issue. This might be critical in real-time applications to maintain data flow reliability and build resilient WebSocket connections.

In operators/retry-connection.ts, we have defined a custom RxJS operator to handle resiliency scenarios for us:

```
import { catchError, Observable, of, OperatorFunction, retry, timer } from
'rxjs';


type TRetryOptions = {
    count: number;
    delayTime: number;
}


type TMessage = {
    type: string;
    payload?: unknown;
}


export function retryConnection<T>({ count, delayTime }: TRetryOptions):
OperatorFunction<T, T | TMessage> {
  return (source: Observable<T>) =>
    source.pipe(
```

```
    retry({
      count,
      delay: (err, retryAttempt) => {
          console.error('Socket connection failed:', err);
          return timer(retryAttempt * delayTime);
      },
    }),
    catchError((err: Error) => {
      console.error('Socket connection failed:', err);
      return of({ type: 'error', payload: err } as TMessage);
    })
  );
}
```

Now we can pipe into the orders$ WebSocket stream and apply the retryConnection operator:

```
this.orders$ = this.socket$.multiplex(
  () => ({ subscribe: 'orders' }), // Subscription message
  () => ({ unsubscribe: 'orders' }), // Unsubscription message
  (message) => message.type === 'orders' // Filter function
).pipe(
  retryConnection<Message>({
    count: 5,
    delayTime: 1000,
  }),
);
```

This will ensure users experience uninterrupted real-time updates.

Step 3 — Subscribing to socket data and visualizing data

Back in our component recipes-chart.component.ts, with the help of the ApexCharts library, we have already set up the component and configuration for 12 data slots for each month of the year. Now, all that is left to be done is to provide the data to the component by subscribing to the orders$ Observable from our service:

```
@ViewChild(ChartComponent, { static: false }) chart!: ChartComponent;


ngOnInit() {
  this.recipesService.connect();
```

```
}

ngAfterViewInit(): void {
  this.recipesService.orders$.subscribe((message: Message) => {
    this.orders = [...this.orders, ...message.payload];
    this.chart.updateSeries([{
      name: 'Orders',
      data: this.orders,
    }]);
  });
}
ngOnDestroy() {
  this.recipesService.close();
}
```

Finally, if we open our browser, we can observe all data as it arrives over a socket.

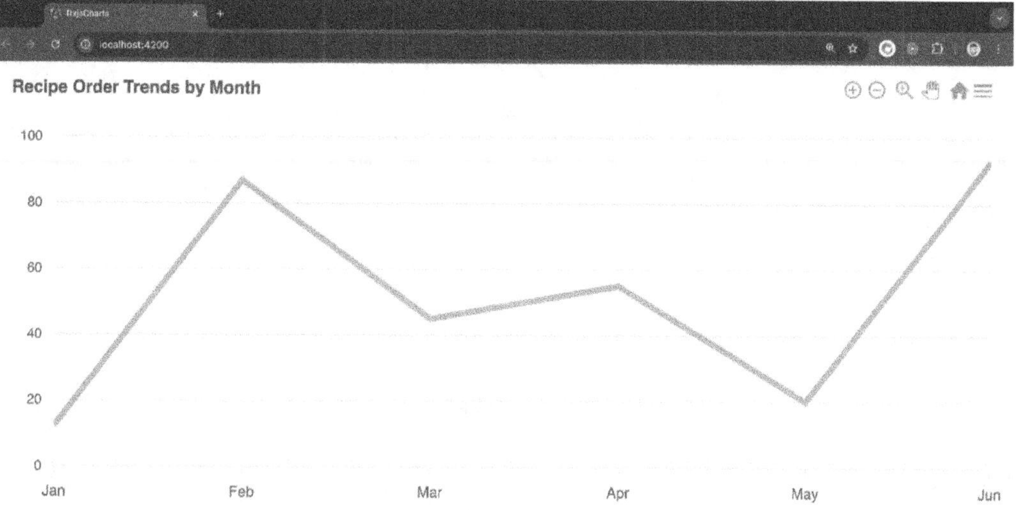

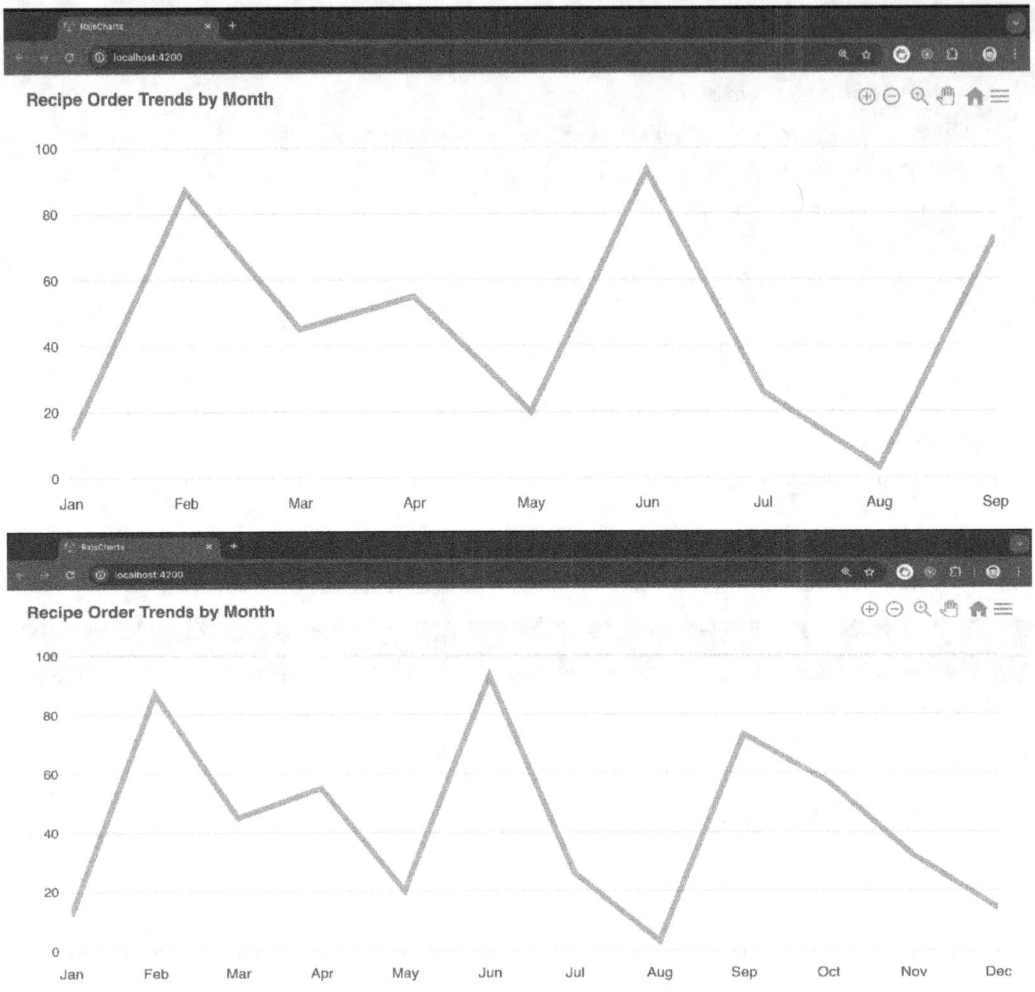

Figure 9.1: Real-time RxJS chart

See also...

- The `ApexCharts` library: `https://apexcharts.com/`
- The `WebSocket` function: `https://rxjs.dev/api/webSocket/webSocket`

Crafting a modern chat application

Chat applications are essential in today's world to stay connected with your work colleagues, friends, and family. They have revolutionized how people connect, fostering personal relationships and facilitating efficient collaboration in professional settings. But carefully crafting such real-time apps can be challenging, with a lot of things to consider, like on-time message delivery, reliability, handling chat events like reply, sending voice messages and images, etc.

How to do it...

In this recipe, we're going to build a minimalistic clone of the Instagram chat app. We will be able to communicate with our friends using this chat, check if our friends are typing, and check friends' online status. We are going to use Angular and NestJS to handle all WebSocket events, since both frameworks have first-class support with RxJS. We will use NestJS to handle server-side handling of WebSocket communication, and, of course, Angular for the client side.

Step 1 – Creating a NestJS WebSocket gateway

In our server app, we are going to leverage the NestJS WebSocket gateway feature to create a real-time chat connection. NestJS provides support for two WebSocket platforms out of the box: socket. io and ws. Since RxJS WebSocket is built upon the ws module, we're going to use that one as well. We will install dependencies for the ws platform:

```
npm i --save @nestjs/websockets @nestjs/platform-ws
```

After installation, we can use the WebSocket adapter on application startup:

```
import { WsAdapter } from '@nestjs/platform-ws';

async function bootstrap() {
    const app = await NestFactory.create(AppModule);
    app.useWebSocketAdapter(new WsAdapter(app));
    await app.listen(3000);
}
bootstrap();
```

Now, we are ready to create our WebSocket gateway. When we go to `chat.gateway.ts`, we can see how to handle new, incoming connections:

```
import {
  ConnectedSocket,
  OnGatewayConnection,
  OnGatewayDisconnect,
  WebSocketGateway,
  WebSocketServer
} from '@nestjs/websockets';
import * as WebSocket from 'ws';

@WebSocketGateway(8080)
export class ChatGateway implements OnGatewayConnection,
OnGatewayDisconnect {
  @WebSocketServer()
  server: WebSocket.Server;
  constructor(
    private chatConnectionService: ChatConnectionService,
    private chatService: ChatService,
  ) {}

  handleConnection(@ConnectedSocket() client: WebSocket): void {
    this.chatConnectionService.handleClientConnection(client);
  }
}
```

We are using the `@WebSocketGateway` decorator to say that class `ChatGateway` will handle WebSocket connections on port 8080. The `ChatGateway` class also implements the `OnGatewayConnection` interface, which provides a lifecycle hook that allows us to execute code whenever a new client connects to our WebSocket server. With the `@ConnectedSocket` decorator, we get access to the client socket.

In `chat-conection.service.ts`, we will handle new client connections and disconnections from WebSocket:

```
import { Injectable, OnModuleInit } from '@nestjs/common';
import { BehaviorSubject, tap } from 'rxjs';
import * as WebSocket from 'ws';
```

```
import { Message } from '../chat.type';

@Injectable()
export class ChatConnectionService implements OnModuleInit {
  private clients$ = new BehaviorSubject<WebSocket[]>([]);
  private clientOneId = 'b9ec382c-a624-40ba-9865-a81be0d390a8';
  private clientTwoId = 'e1426280-0169-4647-b7d1-5e061a23a0d8';

  handleClientConnection(client: WebSocket): void {
    const clients = this.clients$.getValue();

    if (clients.length >= 2) {
      // only 2 people in chat
      client.close();
      return;
    }

    client.id = !clients.map((c: WebSocket) => c.id).includes(
      this.clientOneId)
      ? this.clientOneId
      : this.clientTwoId;
    this.clients$.next([...clients, client]);
  }

  handleDisconnect(client: WebSocket): void {
    const clients = this.clients$.getValue();
    this.clients$.next(clients.filter((c: WebSocket) =>
      c.id !== client.id));
  }


}
```

In the `clients$` BehaviorSubject, we keep track of all client connections to WebSocket. Whenever there is a new connection, we will check if we already have two chat participants. Otherwise, we will assign a new random ID to each new client, since the ws module doesn't have a native way to track client IDs.

Now we can subscribe and react to new connection events:

```
onModuleInit() {
  this.clients$
    .pipe(
      tap((clients: WebSocket[]) => {
        clients.forEach((client) => {
          client.send(
            JSON.stringify({
              event: 'connect',
              data: {
                clientId: client.id,
                otherClientId:
                  client.id === this.clientOneId
                    ? this.clientTwoId
                    : this.clientOneId,
              },
            }),
          );
        });
      }),
    )
    .subscribe();
}
```

In this way, we can broadcast a new event connect to all clients, with messages containing information about the connection.

Step 2 — Connecting to RxJS WebSocket from the frontend app

In our Angular app, we will have a ChatService to handle our WebSocket connection logic:

```
import { Injectable } from '@angular/core';
import { Observable } from 'rxjs';
import { webSocket, WebSocketSubject } from 'rxjs/webSocket';


export interface IWsMessage<T> {
  event: string;
  data?: T;
```

```
}

@Injectable({
  providedIn: 'root'
})
export class ChatService {
  private socket$: WebSocketSubject<Message>;
  public clientId$!: Observable<Message>;

  constructor() {
    this.connect();
  }
  connect() {
    if (!this.socket$ || this.socket$.closed) {
      this.socket$ = webSocket<IWsMessage<IMessage>>({
        url: 'ws://localhost:8080',
        deserializer: (e) => JSON.parse(e.data) as IWsMessage<IMessage>,
      });
      this.clientConnection$ = this.socket$.multiplex(
        () => ({ subscribe: 'connect' }),
        () => ({ unsubscribe: 'connect' }),
        (message) => message.event === 'connect'
      );
    }
}
```

Initially, we will establish a WebSocket connection and subscribe to the connect topic. After a
successful connection, here we would get all relevant events regarding ongoing client connections.

Step 3 – Handling chat topic messages

When we type something in the input chat field and click the send button, we call the service
method sendChatMessage:

```
sendChatMessage(message: string, clientId: string) {
this.socket$.next({
  event: 'message',
  data: {
    topic: 'chat',
    message,
```

```
      clientId
  }});
}
```

By doing so, we are sending a message event to our WebSocket for processing. Back in our back-end chat.gateway.ts, we can subscribe to the message event by defining a new event handler:

```
import {
  MessageBody,
  SubscribeMessage,
} from '@nestjs/websockets';

@WebSocketGateway(8080, { pingTimeout: 2000 })
export class ChatGateway implements OnGatewayConnection,
OnGatewayDisconnect {
  @SubscribeMessage('message')
  handleMessage(
    @MessageBody() data: { topic: string; message: string;
      clientId: string },
  ): void {
    const { topic, message, clientId } = data;

    this.chatService.sendTopicMessage(topic, {
      id: crypto.randomUUID(),
      message,
      clientId,
      timestamp: new Date(),
    });
  }
}
```

With the @MessageBody decorator, we extract the data we have sent over the socket from the client, in our case, the chat topic key.

Whenever there is a new message, we want to send that message to the chat topic. It is time to create a reactive stream of incoming messages assigned to that topic in chat.service.ts:

```
private topics: {
  [topicKey: string]: ReplaySubject<Message | { typing: string } | any>;
} = {
```

```typescript
    chat: new ReplaySubject(100),
  };


  onModuleInit() {
    const chatTopic$ = this.topics['chat'].pipe(
      shareReplay({ bufferSize: 1, refCount: true }),
    );

    const messages$ = chatTopic$.pipe(
      filter((data: WsMessage<string>) => 'message' in data),
      scan((acc, message) => [...acc, message], []),
      map((messages) => ({ event: 'chat', data: messages })),
    );

    messages$.subscribe(
      (response: { event: string; data: Message[] }) => {
        this.chatConnectionService.broadcastMessage(response);
      },
    );
  }


  sendTopicMessage(topic: string, message: Message | ChatEvent): void {
    if (this.topics[topic]) {
      this.topics[topic].next(message);
    }
  }
}
```

The perfect way to have a chat history is by leveraging RxJS's `ReplaySubject`, since every new connection can see all previous events. Also, we can leverage the `shareReplay` operator to multicast chat history to all connected clients. Now we can broadcast incoming messages to all clients and show them to all chat participants.

Back in our frontend app, in `chat.service.ts`, we can multiplex RxJS WebSocket to subscribe to our chat topic:

```typescript
public chat$!: Observable<Message>;
  this.chat$ = this.socket$.multiplex(
    () => ({ subscribe: 'chat' }),
    () => ({ unsubscribe: 'chat' }),
```

```
    (message) => message.event === 'chat'
  );
getChatSocket$(): Observable<Message> {
  return this.chat$;
}
```

Finally, in our component chat.component.ts, we can subscribe to the message history:

```
messages: Array<Message> = [];


ngOnInit(): void {
  this.chatService
    .getChatSocket$()
    .subscribe(({ data }: WsMessage) => {
      this.messages = data;
    );
  }
}
```

We can then open two client browsers next to each other and start chatting:

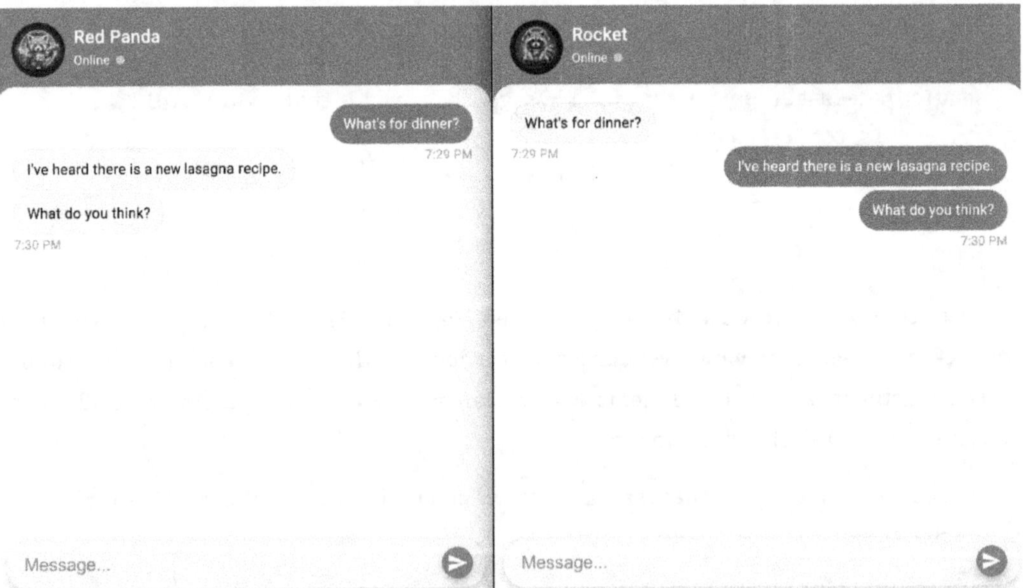

Figure 9.2: Reactive chat messages

Step 4 – Handling the event when a user is typing

Whenever a user is typing something in the chat, if there is something in the input, we can emit the typing event from the frontend app:

```
sendIsTyping(clientId: string, isTyping: boolean = true) {
  this.socket$.next({ event: 'typing', data: { topic: 'chat', clientId,
    isTyping } });
}
```

Now we need to handle this event from the backend:

```
@SubscribeMessage('typing')
handleTyping(
  @MessageBody() data: { topic: string; clientId: string;
    isTyping: boolean },
): void {
  const { topic, isTyping, clientId } = data;

  this.chatService.sendTopicMessage(topic, {
    clientId,
    isTyping,
  });
}
```

Since we are sending new data to the same topic we have set up in *step 3*, our chat.service.ts lifecycle hook finally looks like this:

```
onModuleInit() {
  const chatTopic$ = this.topics['chat'].pipe(
    shareReplay({ bufferSize: 1, refCount: true }),
  );

  const messages$ = chatTopic$.pipe(
    filter((data: WsMessage<string>) => 'message' in data),
    scan((acc, message) => [...acc, message], []),
    map((messages) => ({ event: 'chat', data: messages })),
  );

  const typing$ = chatTopic$.pipe(
```

```
      filter((data: ChatEvent) => 'isTyping' in data),
      distinctUntilKeyChanged('isTyping'),
      map(({ clientId, isTyping }: ChatEvent) => ({
        event: 'chat',
        data: { clientId, isTyping },
      })),
    );

  merge(messages$, typing$).subscribe(
    (response: { event: string; data: Message[] }) => {
      this.latestMessages$.next(response.data);
        this.chatConnectionService.broadcastMessage(response);
    },
    );
  }
```

What is different from what we had in *step 3* is that we are merging the typing$ stream with chat
messages. Now we have information when the other client has started typing, and we can have
that information show on the frontend:

```
isTyping = false;

ngOnInit(): void {
  this.chatService.getChatSocket$().pipe(
    filter(({ data }: IWsMessage<IChatEvent | IMessage[]>) => (
    data as IChatEvent).clientId !== this.clientId),
  ).subscribe(({ data }) => {
    if ('isTyping' in data) {
      this.isTyping = data.isTyping;

      return;
    }

    this.messages = data as IMessage[];
  });

}
```

Now, when we open two browsers side by side and start typing in one application, the other client will see that the first client has started typing.

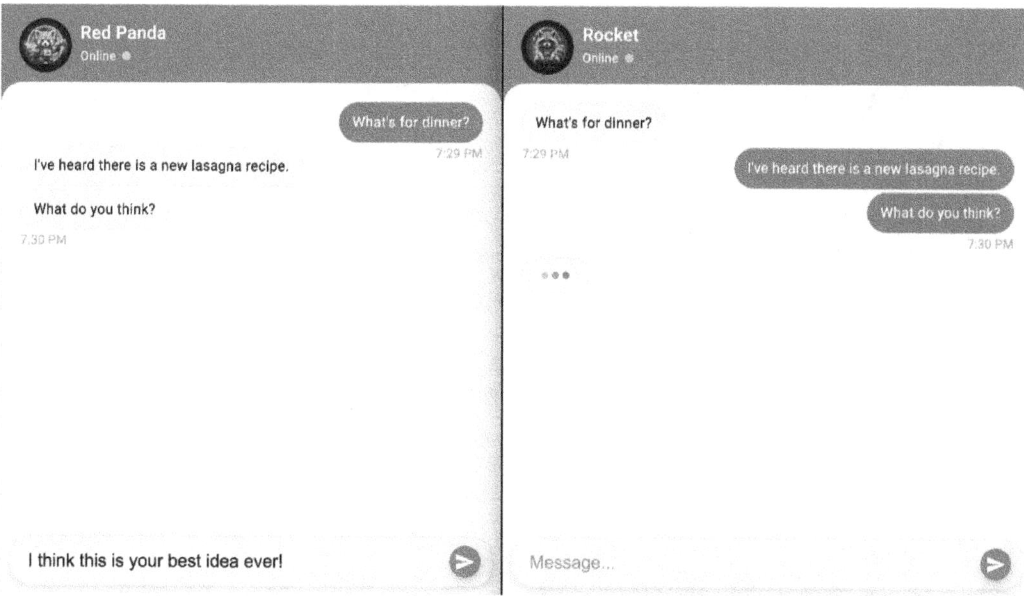

Figure 9.3: User is typing event

Step 7 – Handling client disconnection

You have probably noticed the green online indicator next to each chat participant. But what if one of them leaves the chat? Then, we would expect that indicator to change to offline, right?

To achieve this effect, we can leverage the `OnGatewayDisconnect` lifecycle hook from NestJS:

```
handleDisconnect(@ConnectedSocket() client: WebSocket): void {
  this.chatConnectionService.handleDisconnect(client);
}
```

Whenever a client disconnects from a socket, we can call the `handleDisconnect()` method from `chat-connection.service.ts`:

```
handleDisconnect(client: WebSocket): void {
  const clients = this.clients$.getValue();
  this.clients$.next(clients.filter((c: WebSocket) => c.id !== client.
id));
}
```

Here, we simply filter out the disconnected client and notify the `clients$ ReplaySubject` about this change. Now, we can extend the message that we are broadcasting with the `isOnline` property:

```
client.send(
  JSON.stringify({
    event: 'connect',
    data: {
      clientId: client.id,
      otherClientId:
        client.id === this.clientOneId
          ? this.clientTwoId
          : this.clientOneId,
        isOnline: clients.length === 2,
    },
  }),
);
```

We can easily test this behavior by closing the window of one of the clients.

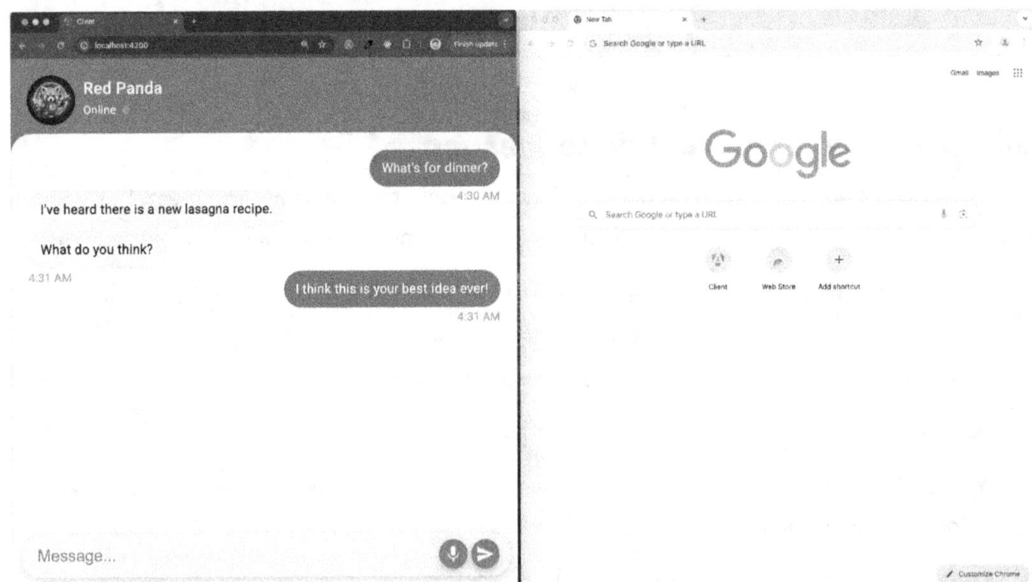

Figure 9.4: Online indicator

Step 8 – Handling WebSocket disconnection

There is one more use case that is critical in real-time applications to maintain data flow reliability, and that is the case when WebSocket connection is temporarily unavailable.

In this step, we are going to introduce an error-handling mechanism to queue messages during connection outages and attempt to resend them once the connection is re-established. We will use an RxJS ReplaySubject to store messages and replay historical messages once we establish a connection again.

Back in our chat.service.ts, we are going to extend the sendChatMessage() method to handle the case when the socket is closed:

```
private socketOfflineMessages$ = new
ReplaySubject<IWsMessage<IMessage>>(100);

sendChatMessage(message: string, clientId: string) {
  if (this.socket$.closed) {
    this.socketOfflineMessages$.next({ event: 'message',
      data: { topic: 'chat', message, clientId }});
    this.connect();

    return;
  }

  this.socket$.next({ event: 'message', data: { topic: 'chat', message,
                  clientId }});
}
```

Now that we have messages stored in socketOfflineMessages$, we can observe when we establish a WebSocket connection again in the connect() method:

```
this.socket$ = webSocket<IWsMessage<IMessage>>({
  url: 'ws://localhost:8080',
  deserializer: (e) => JSON.parse(e.data) as IWsMessage<IMessage>,
  openObserver: {
    next: () => {
      this.socketOfflineMessages$.subscribe(
        (message: IWsMessage<IMessage>) => {this.socket$.next(message);
      });
```

```
      },
    },
  });
```

We can notice that the RxJS webSocket function accepts openObserver as part of a configuration object, which we can leverage to resend all messages while the server is down.

For more information about WebSocket reconnection strategies, take a look at the *Implementing real- time data visualization charts* recipe.

Step 9 — Sending voice messages

In the client app chat.service.ts, we will add a separate method, sendVoiceMethod(), which will be called once we press the mic button in the UI:

```
const constraints = { audio: true };
const audioChunks: BlobPart[] = [];
const micRecording$ = from(navigator.mediaDevices.
getUserMedia(constraints));
const audioChunkEvent$ = micRecording$.pipe(
  switchMap((stream: MediaStream) => {
    const mediaRecorder = new MediaRecorder(stream);
    mediaRecorder.start();
    setTimeout(() => {
      mediaRecorder.stop();
    }, 5000); // Record for 5 seconds

    return merge(
      fromEvent(mediaRecorder, 'dataavailable'),
      fromEvent(mediaRecorder, 'stop'),
    );
  })
);
```

Here, we can observe that we are using the MediaDevices Web API by requesting permission to use the microphone on our device and creating the Observable stream micRecording$. Once we allow microphone permission in our browser, we can create a new MediaRecorder, start recording, and stop the recording after 5 seconds.

Now once we have `MediaRecorder` available, we can create event streams from the `dataavailable` and stop events:

```
return audioChunkEvent$.pipe(
  map((audioEvent: BlobEvent | Event) => {
    if ('data' in audioEvent) {
      audioChunks.push(audioEvent.data);

      return EMPTY;
    }

    const audioBlob = new Blob(audioChunks, { type: 'audio/wav' });
    const reader = new FileReader();
    reader.readAsDataURL(audioBlob);
    return fromEvent<BlobEvent>(reader, 'loadend');
  }),
  switchAll(),
  tap((progressEvent: Event) =>
    this.sendVoiceMessageToServer(progressEvent, clientId)),
  catchError((error: Error) => {
    console.error('Error accessing media devices.', error);

    return EMPTY;
  })
).subscribe();
```

If the `dataavailable` event happens, we will update new audio chunks. If the recording stops, we will gather the reordered audio by creating a new file blob out of the recorded content, encoding the result into Base64 format as a data URL, and returning the `loadend` stream event down the Observable pipeline.

Now, at the end of the stream, we have the result available as a data URL that we can send as a voice message through our chat topic to the WebSocket gateway:

```
sendVoiceMessageToServer(progressEvent: Event, clientId: string) {
  if (!progressEvent) return;
  const reader = progressEvent.target as FileReader;
  const base64AudioMessage = reader.result as string;
```

```
  this.socket$.next({ event: 'message', data: { topic: 'chat', clientId,
message: base64AudioMessage } });
}
```

Our backend will store the voice message in the same `ReplaySubject` as the rest of the messages, which means that we would get new WebSocket messages the same way as before, with just a little modification in the chat messages subscription:

```
this.chatService.getChatSocket$().pipe(
  filter(({ data }: IWsMessage<IChatEvent | IMessage[]>) =>
      (data as IChatEvent).clientId !== this.clientId),
).subscribe(({ data }) => {
  if ('isTyping' in data) {
    this.isTyping = data.isTyping;

    return;
  }

  this.messages = data.map((chatMessage: IMessage) => {
    if (chatMessage.message.startsWith('data:audio')) {
      return { ...chatMessage, isVoice: true };
    }

    return chatMessage;
  });
});
```

Here, we will check whether the message starts with `data:audio`, which indicates that we are dealing with a data URL or voice message. Now, we can differentiate between a regular message and voice message, and in the case of a voice message, pass the source to the HTML audio element.

Finally, when we open our browser, we can record a voice message to our friend:

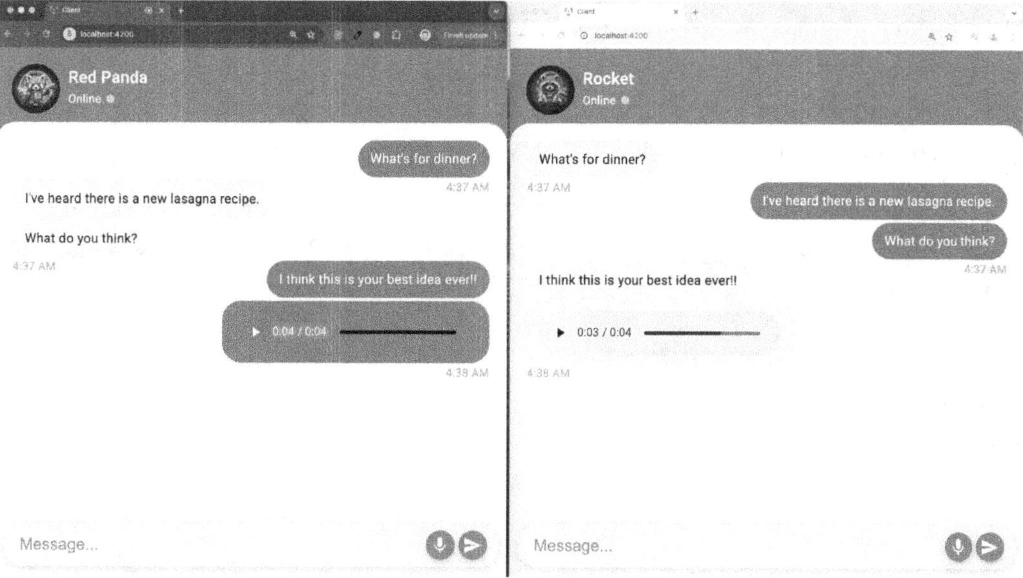

Figure 9.5: Voice message

See also...

- NestJS gateways: `https://docs.nestjs.com/websockets/gateways`

- RxJS **webSocket** function: `https://rxjs.dev/api/webSocket/webSocket`

- MDN **MediaRecorder** Web API: `https://developer.mozilla.org/en-US/docs/Web/API/MediaRecorder`

- MDN data URLs: `https://developer.mozilla.org/en-US/docs/Web/URI/Schemes/data`

- MDN HTML audio element: `https://developer.mozilla.org/en-US/docs/Web/HTML/Element/audio`

Playing real-time multiplayer Tic-Tac-Toe

Tic-Tac-Toe must be one of the most well-known games in the world. It seems like a simple game to learn, but don't let that fool you. It's a game of wit and strategy. In this recipe, we will re-create Tic-Tac-Toe as a real-time multiplayer online game. Let the games begin!

How to do it...

To build this online game, we are going to use Angular and NestJS to handle all WebSocket events, since both frameworks have first-class support for RxJS. We will use NestJS to handle the server side of handling a player's moves, and Angular as a client app for showing the 3x3 grid for the game, handling user interaction, and sending WebSocket events to our API.

We will also need to follow the instructions for creating a NestJS WebSocket gateway and connecting to WebSocket from the client app described in *steps 1* and *2* of the *Crafting a modern chat application* recipe.

Step 1 – Handling multiplayer

Whenever we have a new WebSocket connection, it means that we have a new player joining the game. Since Tic-Tac-Toe can be played by only two players, we will limit the game to two players. If there are more connections, they will be in spectator mode:

```typescript
@WebSocketGateway(8080)
export class GameGateway implements OnGatewayConnection, OnModuleInit {
  private clients$ = new BehaviorSubject<WebSocket[]>([]);

  handleConnection(@ConnectedSocket() client: WebSocket): void {
    if (this.clients$.getValue().length >= 2) {
      client.send(
        JSON.stringify({ event: 'join', data: 'Game has already started.'
      }),
      );
      client.close();
      return;
    }

    const clients = this.clients$.getValue();
    const clientId = crypto.randomUUID();
    client.id = clientId;
    client.player = !clients.map(
      (c) => c.player).includes('X') ? 'X' : 'O';
    this.clients$.next([...clients, client]);
  }
}
```

In the case of spectators, we will just notify them that the game has started. Otherwise, we will assign X to the first player and O to the second one:

```
onModuleInit(): void {
  this.clients$
    .pipe(
      tap((clients) => {
        clients.forEach((client) => {
          client.send(
            JSON.stringify({
              event: 'join',
              data: {
                player: client.player,
                board: this.board,
                nextPlayer: this.currentPlayer,
              },
            }),
          );
        });
      }),
    )
    .subscribe();
}
```

Finally, it's game time! If we put two browser windows next to each other, we can see that both players have joined the match.

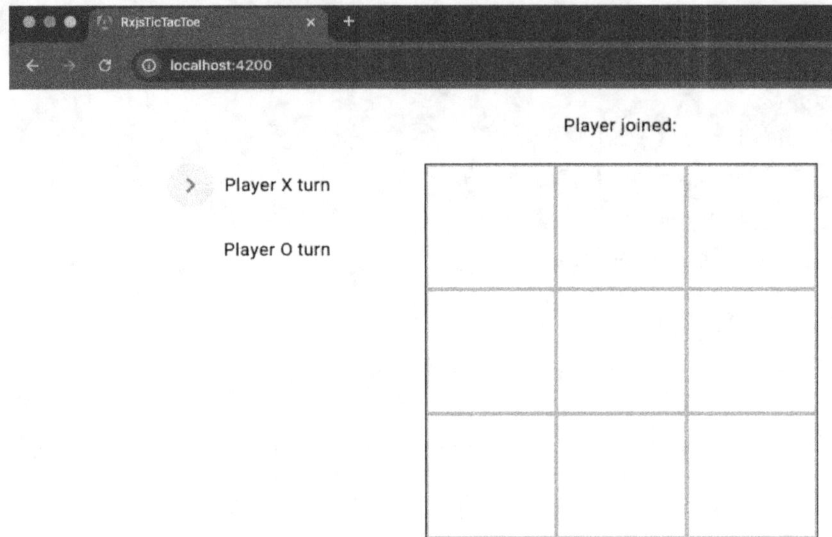

Figure 9.6: Players have joined

Step 2 — Playing a move

Once both players have joined, we can start playing the game! When we click on a board field, we will send an event to the WebSocket gateway. In the client app `game.service.ts`, we will define the `move()` method:

```
move(field: number, player: string, currentPlayerTurn: string): void {
  if (player !== currentPlayerTurn) {
    return;
  }


  this.send({ event: 'move', data: field });
}
```

We can notice that we are preventing the same player from playing twice in a row. If it's the correct player's turn to play, we will send the index of the clicked field on the board game.

In our `game.gateway.ts`, we will create an event handler for the move event:

```
@SubscribeMessage('move')
handleMove(@MessageBody() data: number): void {
```

```
    this.moves$.next(data);
  }
```

Whenever we have a new move from a player, our system will react by updating the board state and switching the player's turn:

```
const playerMoves$ = this.moves$.pipe(
  withLatestFrom(this.clients$),
  filter(([move]) => this.board[move] === null),
  map(([move, clients]) => {
    const nextPlayer = this.currentPlayer === 'X' ? 'O' : 'X';
    this.board[move] = this.currentPlayer;

    clients.forEach(client => {
      client.send(JSON.stringify({ event: 'boardUpdate',
        data: { move, currentPlayer: this.currentPlayer, nextPlayer } }));
    });

    this.currentPlayer = nextPlayer;

    return clients;
  }),
  shareReplay({ bufferSize: 1, refCount: true }),
).subscribe();
```

By sending the boardUpdate event, our frontend app can accept that event and react to the latest player move. We would send the information about the move field, which player played that move, and the next player's turn. Back in our client app game.service.ts:

```
public boardUpdate$!: Observable<WsMessage>;
  this.boardUpdate$ = this.socket$.multiplex(
    () => ({ subscribe: 'boardUpdate' }),
    () => ({ unsubscribe: 'boardUpdate' }),
    (message) => message.event === 'boardUpdate'
  );
getBoardUpdate$() {
  return this.boardUpdate$;
}
```

Now, we can subscribe to the latest board state in `game-board.component.ts` and update the UI:

```
currentPlayerTurn = 'X';
board = Array(9).fill(null);


constructor(private wsService: WebSocketService) { }


ngOnInit() {
  this.wsService.getBoardUpdate$().subscribe(({ data }: WsMessage) => {
    const { move, currentPlayer, nextPlayer } = data;
    this.board[move] = currentPlayer;
    this.currentPlayerTurn = nextPlayer;
  });


}
```

When we open two separate browser tabs and start playing moves, we can see real-time updates
in the UI:

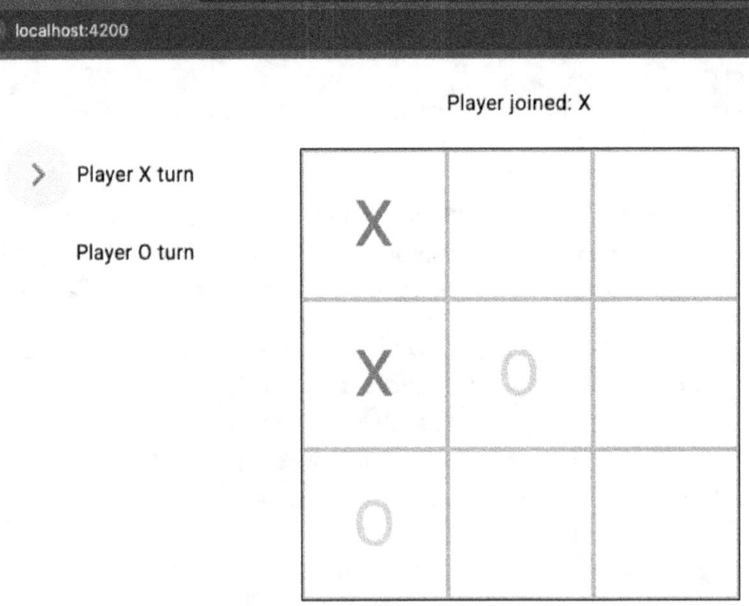

Figure 9.7: Player move

Step 3 – Checking the winner

At the end of each move, we can check whether the game is over. The game will be over in two scenarios – if we have a winner or if there is a draw:

```
playerMoves$.pipe(
  tap((clients) => this.handleCheckWinner()),
  tap((clients) => this.handleCheckDraw()),
  shareReplay({ bufferSize: 1, refCount: true }),
).subscribe();
private handleCheckWinner(clients: WebSocket[]): void {
  const winner = this.gameService.checkWinner(this.board);
  if (winner) {
    this.moves$.complete();

    clients.forEach((client) => {
      client.send(JSON.stringify({ event: 'winner', data: winner }));
    });

    this.resetGame();
  }
}
```

In the backend app `game.service.ts`, we have implemented these two checks:

```
checkWinner(): string | undefined {
  const winningScenarios = [
    [0, 1, 2], // Top row
    [3, 4, 5], // Middle row
    [6, 7, 8], // Bottom row
    [0, 3, 6], // Left column
    [1, 4, 7], // Middle column
    [2, 5, 8], // Right column
    [0, 4, 8], // Diagonal \
    [2, 4, 6] // Diagonal /
  ];

  for (const scenario of winningScenarios) {
    const [a, b, c] = scenario;
```

240   *Going Real-Time with RxJS*

```
    if (this.board[a] && this.board[a] === this.board[b]
    && this.board[a] === this.board[c]) {
      this.moves$.complete();

      return this.board[a];
    }
  }
}
```

The way we are doing this winner check is by having all winning scenarios upfront and simply
seeing whether the current state of the board matches one of the winning cases. Also, we are
completing player the moves$ subject to prevent memory leaks after ending the game.

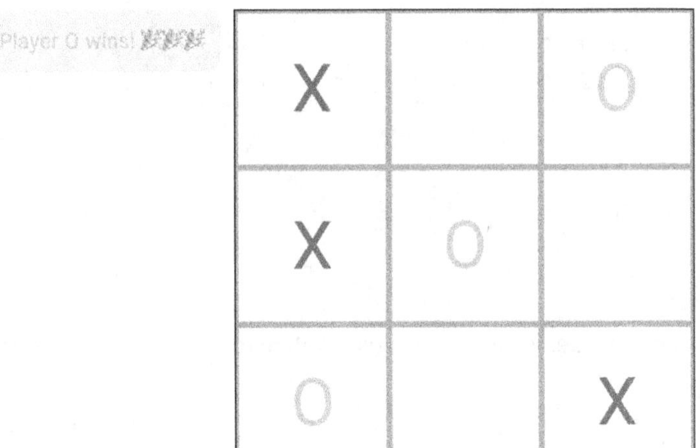

Figure 9.8: Player wins

In case of a draw, we can send all clients the draw event and show the restart game button. Back
in our game.service.ts, we can simply check for a draw:

```
checkDraw(board: Array<string>): boolean {
  return board.every(cell => cell !== null) && !this.checkWinner(board);
}
```

Once we open the UI, we can see the restart button, and we can start the game over:

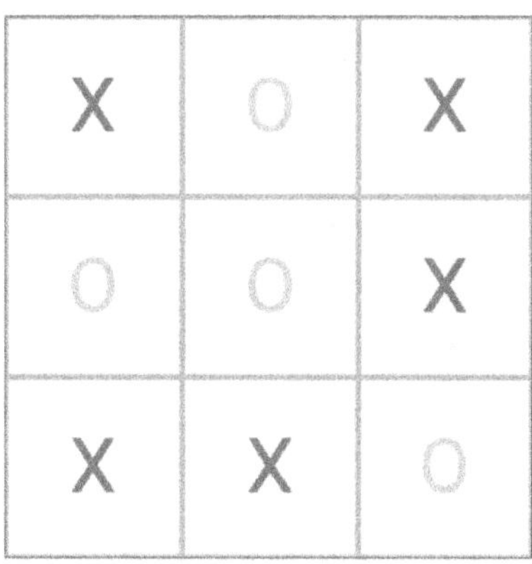

Figure 9.9: Draw game

See also...

- NestJS gateways: `https://docs.nestjs.com/websockets/gateways`
- RxJS **webSocket** function: `https://rxjs.dev/api/webSocket/webSocket`

Get This Book's PDF Version and Exclusive Extras

UNLOCK NOW

Scan the QR code (or go to `packtpub.com/unlock`). Search for this book by name, confirm the edition, and then follow the steps on the page.

Note: Keep your invoice handy. Purchases made directly from Packt don't require one.

10

Building Reactive NestJS Microservices with RxJS

With NestJS, we can build scalable, responsive, message-driven, and resilient server-side applications efficiently. Since NestJS has first-class support for RxJS, this can take our reactive game to a whole new level. RxJS can help us enhance responsiveness by handling large volumes of concurrent requests and gracefully handling failures and recovery mechanisms. It can also help us with handling asynchronous operations, which can be especially useful in an event-driven system.

In this chapter, we will cover the following recipes:

- Crafting resilient REST API microservices in NestJS
- Mastering reactive event streaming with Kafka
- Going real time with gRPC streaming in NestJS

Technical requirements

To follow along with this chapter, you'll need:

- RxJS v7
- NestJS v11+
- Kafka v2.13-3.8.0
- KafkaJS v2.2.4
- grpc-js v1.12.2
- Node.js v22+
- npm v11+ or pnpm v10+

The code for recipes in this chapter can be found in the GitHub repository here: `https://github.com/PacktPublishing/RxJS-Cookbook-for-Reactive-Programming/tree/main/Chapter10`.

Crafting resilient REST API microservices in NestJS

Resilient REST API microservices are essential for creating robust and dependable systems, since they are designed to handle unexpected traffic surges gracefully. They help prevent cascading failures by isolating problems, ensuring that if one service has an issue, it doesn't bring down the whole application. This isolation also contributes to high availability, as other services can continue operating even when one is down.

Getting ready

Check out *Chapter 1* for more HTTP communication strategies in RxJS.

How to do it...

In this recipe, we are going to have two NestJS microservices, namely `recipes-api` and `orders-api`, communicating with each other synchronously, and will delve deep into resiliency patterns. We are going to explore different techniques for how we can create REST APIs that are robust and reliable.

Step 1 – Establishing communication between services

Once we have both services running, we can easily establish communication between them over HTTP. From the `recipes-api` service, we will send a request to `orders-api` running on localhost on port 3000. Once we get the response from `orders-api`, we can simply extract data about the latest recipe orders from the response:

```
getOrders(): Observable<string> {
    return this.httpService.get<string>('/orders')
    .pipe(
        map(({ data }) => data),
    );
}
```

Step 2 – Applying an exponential backoff strategy

In our `recipes.service.ts`, we have a `getOrder()` method:

```
getOrder(): Observable<string> {
    return this.httpService.get<string>('http://localhost:3000/orders')
    .pipe(
        map(({ data }) => data),
            catchError(error => {
                return of(error);
        }),
        retry({
            count: 3,
            delay: (error, retryCount) => {
                console.log(
                    `Attempt ${retryCount}: Error occurred during network
                    request, retrying in ${Math.pow(2, retryCount)}
                    seconds...`
                );
            return timer(Math.pow(2, retryCount) * 1000);
            },
        }),
    );
}
```

If `orders-api` is unavailable, or there is a transient error, we will implement the exponential backoff strategy. The strategy says that we have a certain number of retries to the failed service, but the time between retry attempts gradually increases.

Step 3 – Implementing the bulkhead resiliency strategy

Bulkhead is a resiliency strategy where we isolate resources of one service and control concurrent requests for those resources. The benefit of this approach is that in case of an error, we prevent cascading errors so that other microservices continue working as expected without affecting the general stability of a system.

In *step 2*, we described how to handle an individual service method when handling HTTP communication. But what if we want to have the same resiliency strategy across the whole microservice?

In that case, we can leverage NestJS interceptors. In our `bulkhead.interceptor.ts`, we will implement the bulkhead resiliency strategy:

```typescript
@Injectable()
export class BulkheadInterceptor implements NestInterceptor {
    private readonly MAX_CONCURRENT_REQUESTS = 3;
    private activeRequests = 0;
    private requestQueue: (() => Observable<any>)[] = [];

    intercept<T>(context: ExecutionContext, next: CallHandler):
    Observable<T> {
        const request$ = next.handle().pipe(
            catchError((err) => of(err)),
            finalize(() => {
                this.activeRequests--;
                this.processQueue();
            }),
        );

        if (this.activeRequests < this.MAX_CONCURRENT_REQUESTS) {
            this.activeRequests++;

            return request$;
        }

        const queueRequest$: Observable<T> = new Observable((observer) => {});

        return queueRequest$;
    }
}
```

We can notice that if we have available resources, we will process the request immediately. Otherwise, if there are more ongoing requests to the microservice than allowed concurrency, we put those requests into a queue, and schedule processing of those requests when the service has more resources available:

```typescript
const queueRequest$: Observable<T> = new Observable((observer) => {
    this.requestQueue.push(() => {
        return next.handle().pipe(
```

```
                catchError((err) => {
                    observer.error(err);

                    return of(err);
                }),
                map((result) => {
                    observer.next(result);

                    return result;
                }),
            );
        });

    // try to process the queue right away
        this.processQueue();
    });


    return queueRequest$;
```

Finally, when we check the queue, we can put the first request that went into the queue and complete the request task:

```
private processQueue() {
    if (
        this.requestQueue.length > 0 &&
        this.activeRequests < this.MAX_CONCURRENT_REQUESTS
    ) {
        const task = this.requestQueue.shift()!;
        this.activeRequests++;

        task().subscribe({
            complete: () => {
                this.activeRequests--;
                this.processQueue();
            },
        });
    }
}
```

Another approach is to leverage the power of the RxJS mergeMap operator, which has built-in concurrency support. In that case, we could simply use this pattern, and our interceptor would look like this:

```
import { Observable, Subject, mergeMap } from 'rxjs';


@Injectable()
export class BulkheadInterceptor implements NestInterceptor {
    private readonly MAX_CONCURRENT_REQUESTS = 3;
    private requestQueue = new Subject<Observable<any>>();

    constructor() {
        this.requestQueue
        .pipe(mergeMap((task) => task, this.MAX_CONCURRENT_REQUESTS))
        .subscribe();
    }

    intercept(context: ExecutionContext, next: CallHandler):
    Observable<any> {
        this.requestQueue.next(next.handle());

        return this.requestQueue.asObservable();
    }
}
```

See also...

- Resiliency patterns on the NestJS blog: `https://medium.com/@ali-chishti/resiliencypatterns-nestjs-b39351f8dea8`
- Resiliency best practices: `https://dev.to/lucasnscr/resilience-and-best-patterns-4mo`

Mastering reactive event streaming with Kafka

Apache Kafka is a distributed event-streaming platform used by thousands of companies for high-performance pipelines of real-time data, delivered with low latency. Apache Kafka was originally developed at LinkedIn, and later became open source. What is so powerful about Kafka is that it is easily accessible and resilient to system crashes.

Kafka's real-time data processing makes it perfect for many use cases, like:

- **User activity tracking** – companies like Uber, Netflix, and Spotify use Kafka to monitor user interactions, clicks, and page views.

- **Event bus for microservices** – Kafka can act as a message queue and help multiple microservices communicate and stay synchronized.

- **Observability** – Kafka can be easily integrated with observability tools to track the health and performance of the system, as well as process and analyze error data. Cloudflare uses Kafka for analytics purposes.

- **Real-time apps** – Kafka can process payments, stock trades, geolocation, or any other data in real time. It can also easily be integrated with data analytic tools like Apache Spark.

- **IoT sensor data** – Kafka can be used to collect and analyze data from sensors in devices like smart home appliances.

Getting ready

To follow along with this recipe efficiently, we will cover some basic terms and definitions when it comes to Kafka.

- **Topic** – immutable log of events kept in order. A topic stores information by key, so we can access values by the key. Also, the timestamp and metadata are included.

- **Producer** – sources of data that are publishing/writing records of data to Kafka topics.

- **Consumer** – subscribes to the topic and processes data. Consumers can group and aggregate data.

- **Broker** – a Kafka server that hosts Kafka topics and handles data storage and message delivery.

- **Cluster** – a group of brokers working together to provide fault tolerance and scalability.

- **Partition** – topics are separated into divided partitions, ordered sequences of records that can be distributed across different brokers. This enables load balancing and fault tolerance.

- **ZooKeeper** – a centralized service that manages the coordination and state of the Kafka cluster. It helps with things like electing leaders for partitions and managing broker registrations.

Also, in Kafka's official documentation, there is a Quickstart on how to download and start a Kafka server locally `https://kafka.apache.org/quickstart`.

Now we are ready to tackle real-time data processing with KafkaJS.

How to do it...

In this recipe, we will create a reactive Kafka producer and consumer. We will leverage the power of RxJS to process the stream of data, and to craft a resiliency mechanism that will be useful in a distributed system.

Step 1 – Setting up the Kafka producer

In our `message-broker.service.ts`, we're going to start off by creating a Kafka instance and connecting our producer to the Kafka server:

```ts
private readonly kafka: Kafka;
private readonly producer: Producer;

constructor() {
    this.kafka = new Kafka({
        brokers: ['localhost:9092'],
        retry: {
            retries: 0
        }
    });
    this.producer = this.kafka.producer({
        allowAutoTopicCreation: true
    });
}
```

In the broker array, we list all Kafka brokers running in the background.

Kafka retry mechanism

You may notice that we have disabled Kafka's built-in retry mechanism. You might want to do this when there is a need for a custom backoff retry pattern. The reason we are doing it here is for learning purposes when implementing resilient Kafka connections with RxJS. More info about KafkaJS's default retry mechanism can be found in the documentation: `https://kafka.js.org/docs/retry-detailed`.

Also, we got access to the Kafka producer. Now, if we call the `connect()` method on a producer, we will be connected to the Kafka broker, and we can produce the first messages.

Step 2 — Setting up the Kafka consumer

In the constructor of `rxjs-message-consumer.ts`, we are going to carry out the process of Kafka instantiation, the same as we did with the producer:

```typescript
private readonly consumers: Consumer[] = [];
constructor() {
    this.kafka = new Kafka({
        brokers: ['localhost:9092'], // Replace with your Kafka broker
                                     //address
        retry: {
            retries: 0
        }
    });
}


async consume(topics: string[], config?: ConsumerConfig) {
    const consumer = this.kafka.consumer({ groupId: 'my-group' });
    await consumer.connect();
    await consumer.subscribe({ topics, fromBeginning: true });
    await consumer.run({
        eachMessage: async ({ topic, partition, message }) => {
            // consume messages
            console.log({
                topic,
                partition,
                offset: message.offset,
                value: message.value.toString()

            });

        },
    });
    this.consumers.push(consumer);
}


async onApplicationShutdown() {
```

```
await Promise.all(this.consumers.map(consumer => consumer.
    disconnect()));
}
```

Now, whenever we call a consumer method from different services, we are going to take several crucial steps:

1. Get access to a Kafka consumer, as per `groupId`.
2. Connect to the Kafka broker.
3. Subscribe to certain topics that we pass as part of the parameters.
4. Run our consumer and process messages in the `eachMessage` callback.
5. Push the current consumer to the list of consumers, to keep track of all of them.

Now that we have done the very basic setup of the Kafka message broker, we are ready to add a little bit of reactivity with the magic of RxJS!

Step 3 – Going reactive with the Kafka producer

Whenever we send an HTTP request to our NestJS API controller `AppController`, we will call a produce method from our `MessageBrokerService`:

```
public kafkaMessage$ = new ReplaySubject<KafkaMessage>();

async produce(topic: string, message: string) {
  this.kafkaMessage$.next({
    topic,
    compression: CompressionTypes.GZIP,
    messages: [{ value: message }],
  });
}
```

The request body payload that we are sending as each message would look something like this:

```
{
"message": "{ \"id\": 3, \"name\": \"Pasta alla Gricia\", \"description\":
\"A Roman pasta dish featuring guanciale (cured pork jowl), pecorino
romano cheese, and black pepper.\", \"ingredients\": [\"pasta (rigatoni or
bucatini)\", \"guanciale\", \"pecorino romano cheese\", \"black pepper\"]
}"
}
```

Now, when we have all incoming messages stored in an RxJS subject, we can send new messages to the Kafka broker, in a reactive way. In the service's `message-broker.ts` init lifecycle hook, we can subscribe to the new messages:

```
this.kafkaMessage$.pipe(
  concatMap((kafkaMessage) => from(this.producer.send(kafkaMessage))),
).subscribe();
```

Here, we are creating an Observable stream from the return value of the producer's send method. By utilizing the `concatMap` operator, we will not only send all incoming messages to the Kafka broker but also keep the order of messages.

This is a basic example of sending new messages to the Kafka broker, but with the producer connected. What about making a reactive producer that is resilient to connection errors?

Step 4 – Reacting to producer connection events

At the beginning of our producer service, we are going to simulate what would happen if our producer got disconnected:

```
public producerActiveState$ = new Subject<boolean>();


async onModuleInit() {
    setTimeout(() => {
        console.log('Disconnecting producer...');
        this.producer.disconnect();
    }, 40000);
    setTimeout(() => {
        console.log('Connecting producer...');
        this.producer.connect();
    }, 50000);

    this.handleBrokerConnection();
}
```

In a scenario like this, it is crucial that the producer stays resilient and keeps collecting incoming messages. Once it is connected back to the broker, the producer should send all messages and continue accepting the new ones.

In the `handleBrokerConnection` method, we have the following:

```
handleBrokerConnection(): void {
    const producerConnect$ = from(this.producer.connect()).pipe(
        retry({
            count: 3,
            delay: (error, retryCount) => {
                console.log(
                    `Attempt ${retryCount}: Error occurred during network
                    request, retrying in ${Math.pow(2, retryCount)}
                    seconds...`
                );
                return timer(Math.pow(2, retryCount) * 1000);
            },
        }),
        catchError(error => {
            console.error(`Error connecting to Kafka: ${error}`);
            this.producerActiveState$.next(false);
            return EMPTY;
        }),
    );
    producerConnect$.subscribe();
}
```

Here, we have a few things going on:

1. The `producerConnect$` stream is created from the `this.producer.connect()` Promise response.

2. In case of transient errors, we apply an exponential backoff reconnection strategy until our producer gets the connection back.

After we are successfully connected to the producer, we can listen to the producer's CONNECT and DISCONNECT events. When the connection status changes, we will keep track of the active state of a producer in a separate subject:

```
this.producer.on(this.producer.events.CONNECT, () => {
    this.producerActiveState$.next(true);
});
```

```
const producerDisconnect$ = fromEventPattern(
    (handler) => this.producer.on(this.producer.events.DISCONNECT
        handler),
);
```

Also, whenever there is a producer disconnection, we will switch to the producerConnect$ stream, as part of our reconnection strategy.

```
producerDisconnect$.pipe(
    switchMap(() => producerConnect$)
).subscribe(() => this.producerActiveState$.next(false));
```

Step 5 – Buffering messages when the producer is disconnected

Since we are already keeping track of the producer's active state, we can separate active and inactive states as follows:

```
const producerActive$ = this.producerActiveState$.asObservable().pipe(
    filter(activeState => activeState));
const producerInactive$ = this.producerActiveState$.asObservable().pipe(
    filter(activeState => !activeState));
```

Now the RxJS magic starts! Based on these states, we can decide what we want to do with the incoming messages:

```
const acceptIncomingMessages$ = this.kafkaMessage$.pipe(windowToggle(
    producerActive$, () => producerInactive$));
const bufferIncomingMessages$ = this.kafkaMessage$.pipe(bufferToggle(
    producerInactive$, () => producerActive$));
```

With the help of the windowToggle operator, we get fine-grained control over toggling between when we want to collect new stream events and when to stop. If the producer is disconnected, we will stop the regular emissions of the message. However, at that point, we want to collect all incoming messages in a buffer, in order not to lose them once the producer is reconnected. For those purposes, we can leverage the bufferToggle operator, which will keep track of all messages while we are in the producerInactive$ state. After that, we can merge those two streams and send messages to the broker in both cases:

```
merge(
    acceptIncomingMessages$,
    bufferIncomingMessages$
```

```
).pipe(
    mergeAll(),
    concatMap((kafkaMessage) => from(this.producer.send(kafkaMessage))),
    catchError(() => of('Error sending messages to Kafka!')),
).subscribe();
```

Step 6 — Handling backpressure on the producer

In cases where our API is overwhelmed with new incoming messages, our producer might not be able to send all messages one by one. This might lead to performance issues like latency, memory leaks in our API, or even server crashes. What might be handy in those situations is applying the backpressure pattern. There are two main backpressure strategies: lossy and lossless backpressure. Depending on the use case, we might choose which strategy to implement by using different RxJS operators.

- Lossy backpressure: `throttle`, `throttleTime`, `debounce`, `debounceTime`, `sample`, `sampleTime`, `skip`, `skipLast`, `skipUntil`, `skipWhile`
- Lossless backpressure: `delay`, `buffer`, `bufferCount`, `bufferTime`, `bufferToogle`, `bufferWhen`, `window`, `windowCount`, `windowTime`, `windowToggle`, `windowWhen`

The lossy backpressure strategy has a simpler form where the consumer starts dropping messages when overwhelmed. This strategy might be useful in situations where receiving the latest data is more important than processing every single message, e.g., real-time stock prices.

In our use case, we have decided that we will go with lossless backpressure, since we don't want to lose any messages:

```
merge(
    acceptIncomingMessages$,
    bufferIncomingMessages$
).pipe(
    mergeAll(),
    bufferTime(2000),
    filter(messages => messages.length > 0),
    concatMap((kafkaMessage) => from(this.producer.sendBatch(
        { topicMessages: kafkaMessage }
    ))),
    catchError(() => of('Error sending messages to Kafka!')),
).subscribe();
```

Note the few changes that we have applied to the stream:

1. We are using the `bufferTime` operator for lossless backpressure, and every two seconds, we are collecting all messages into a buffer.

2. We are filtering time frames without any messages, meaning empty buffers.

3. Instead of producing one message, we are going to send a batch of messages with the method `sendBatch()`.

Now, when we send a few HTTP requests, we can observe in the console that messages are successfully being sent to the Kafka broker and the consumer is being notified.

```
PROBLEMS    OUTPUT    DEBUG CONSOLE    TERMINAL    PORTS

up] Consumer has joined the group","groupId":"my-group","memberId":"kafkajs-319a0a40-1624-4088-a3
34-ce6dd9e62818","leaderId":"kafkajs-319a0a40-1624-4088-a334-ce6dd9e62818","isLeader":true,"membe
rAssignment":{"recipes-topic":[0]},"groupProtocol":"RoundRobinAssigner","duration":26262}
consumed message {
  topic: 'recipes-topic',
  partition: 0,
  offset: '13',
  value: '{ "id": 2, "name": "Cacio e Pepe", "description": "Another minimalist Roman pasta dish
with pecorino romano cheese and black pepper.", "ingredients": ["spaghetti", "pecorino romano che
ese", "black pepper"] }'
}
consumed message {
  topic: 'recipes-topic',
  partition: 0,
  offset: '14',
  value: '{ "id": 3, "name": "Pasta alla Gricia", "description": "A Roman pasta dish featuring gu
anciale (cured pork jowl), pecorino romano cheese, and black pepper.", "ingredients": ["pasta (ri
gatoni or bucatini)", "guanciale", "pecorino romano cheese", "black pepper"], "image": "/assets/i
mages/gricia.jpg" }'
}
```

Figure 10.1: Kafka messages

But as we can see now, we get messages asynchronously under the same topic. Wouldn't it be nice if could collect all of them under the same topic, and have an array of messages that we can process?

Step 7 — Going reactive with the Kafka consumer

In our consumer's `run()` method, we were previously logging the incoming messages. Now, let's process them in a reactive way:

```
private readonly messages$ = new Subject<KafkaMessage>();


await consumer.run({
    eachMessage: async ({ topic, partition, message }) => {
        const kafkaMessage = {
```

```
                topic,
                compression: CompressionTypes.GZIP,
                offset: message.offset,
                messages: [{ value: message.value.toString() }]
            };

            this.messages$.next(kafkaMessage);
        },
    });
```

Whenever there is a new message, our `messages$` subject will be notified about it. We can consume those messages reactively by doing the following:

```
consumeMessages(): void {
    this.messages$.asObservable().pipe(
        groupBy(person => person.topic, {
            connector: () => new ReplaySubject(100) }),
        concatMap(group$ => group$.pipe(
            scan((acc, cur) => ({
                topic: group$.key,
                messages: acc.messages ? cur.messages.concat(acc.messages)
:
                                         cur.messages,
            }), {} as KafkaConsumedMessage))
        ),
        catchError((error) => {
            console.log('Error consuming messages from Kafka!');

            return EMPTY;
        }),
    tap(console.log),
).subscribe();
```

Here, we can see that with the help of the groupBy operator, we can collect all messages under the same topic. After that, we use `concatMap` to have messages in order, while also transforming the inner stream to put all the messages into the same array with the `scan` operator. An alternative approach might be to use the `mergeScan` operator alongside the map operator.

When we send new POST requests to our API, we will see that messages are efficiently grouped into the array under the same topic and ready for processing.

```
PROBLEMS    OUTPUT    DEBUG CONSOLE    TERMINAL    PORTS

{
  topic: 'recipes-topic',
  messages: [
    {
      id: 3,
      name: 'Pasta alla Gricia',
      description: 'A Roman pasta dish featuring guanciale (cured pork jowl), pecorino romano che
ese, and black pepper.',
      ingredients: [Array],
      image: '/assets/images/gricia.jpg'
    },
    {
      id: 2,
      name: 'Cacio e Pepe',
      description: 'Another minimalist Roman pasta dish with pecorino romano cheese and black pep
per.',
      ingredients: [Array]
    }
  ]
}
```

Figure 10.2: Grouping Kafka messages

We might also notice the order of the messages, where the most recent ones are at the beginning of the array.

Step 8 – Handling backpressure on the consumer

As we have already done for the producer, we are going to apply lossless backpressure to the consumer part. At the beginning of the stream, we would add the `bufferTime` operator to handle lossless backpressure. Finally, our stream looks like this:

```
this.messages$.asObservable().pipe(
    bufferTime(1000),
    concatMap(messages => messages),
    groupBy(person => person.topic, {
        connector: () => new ReplaySubject(100) }),
    concatMap(group$ => group$.pipe(
        scan((acc, cur) => ({
            topic: group$.key,
            messages: acc.messages
            ? cur.messages.concat(acc.messages)
            : cur.messages,
```

```
        }), {} as KafkaConsumedMessage)
      )
    ),
    catchError((error) => {
        console.log('Error consuming messages from Kafka!');

        return EMPTY;
    }),
    tap(console.log),
  ).subscribe();
```

Step 9 — Implementing the dead-letter queue pattern

At this point, consumption of our messages can run smoothly. We can process messages or connect
our consumers to Apache Spark: anything we want. But what about the deserialization of the
messages over the Kafka event bus? What if there is an error in processing the message? For those
instances, we will send a message with an invalid format. We will use the same stringified request
payload as before; we're just going to delete one comma, so that parsing of this message fails.

In a real-life scenario, if the processing of a message fails, we want to keep track of all failed
processing events, send those events to the monitoring service, and schedule them to reinitiate
re-processing or additional checks.

For those purposes, we will implement the dead-letter queue pattern. This is a mechanism for
handling messages that failed to be processed by the consumer and sent to a separate topic. We
will extend the previous implementation of the consumer's run() method from *step 7*:

```
private readonly dlq$ = new ReplaySubject<KafkaMessage>();


await consumer.run({
    eachMessage: async ({ topic, partition, message }) => {
        const kafkaMessage = {
            topic,
            compression: CompressionTypes.GZIP,
            offset: message.offset,
            messages: [{ value: message.value.toString() }]
        };
        let parsedMessage = null;
        try {
```

```
                parsedMessage = this.deserializeMessage(kafkaMessage);
        } catch (error) {
            this.dlq$.next({
                topic: 'dlq',
                compression: CompressionTypes.GZIP,
                messages: [{ value: message.value.toString() }],
                error
            });
            return;
        }


        this.messages$.next(parsedMessage);
      },
  });
```

What the `deserializeMessage()` method will do is basically try to call `JSON.parse()` for every message. If deserialization fails, we will send that message to the dlq topic, with information about the message and the error that happened.

Whenever we have a new message sent to the dlq subject, we can react to that event by scheduling a new value emission:

```
async onModuleInit() {
    this.dlq$.pipe(
        delay(5000),
        // send DLQ error to monitoring service every night at 2am
        subscribeOn(asyncScheduler),
        materialize(),
        tap(console.log)
    ).subscribe();
}
```

Finally, when we try to send a message that contains the error for processing, we would see the following log in the console:

```
PROBLEMS    OUTPUT    DEBUG CONSOLE    TERMINAL    PORTS

tarted +2ms
{"level":"INFO","timestamp":"2024-10-20T21:50:17.016Z","logger":"kafkajs","message":"[Consumer] S
tarting","groupId":"my-group"}
{"level":"INFO","timestamp":"2024-10-20T21:50:43.552Z","logger":"kafkajs","message":"[ConsumerGro
up] Consumer has joined the group","groupId":"my-group","memberId":"kafkajs-b99d54d6-9096-420a-93
b9-13e4b9dd19ca","leaderId":"kafkajs-b99d54d6-9096-420a-93b9-13e4b9dd19ca","isLeader":true,"membe
rAssignment":{"recipes-topic":[0]},"groupProtocol":"RoundRobinAssigner","duration":26535}
Notification {
  kind: 'N',
  value: {
    topic: 'dlq',
    compression: 1,
    messages: [ [Object] ],
    error: Error: SyntaxError: Expected ',' or ']' after array element in JSON at position 260
        at RxjsKafkaConsumerService.deserializeMessage (/Users/secerzema/Desktop/packt-rxjs-cookb
ook/RxJS-Cookbook-for-Reactive-Developers/Chapter11/rxjs-kafka/reactive-kafka-broker/src/rxjs-kaf
ka-consumer/rxjs-kafka-consumer.service.ts:94:19)
        at Runner.eachMessage (/Users/secerzema/Desktop/packt-rxjs-cookbook/RxJS-Cookbook-for-Rea
ctive-Developers/Chapter11/rxjs-kafka/reactive-kafka-broker/src/rxjs-kafka-consumer/rxjs-kafka-co
nsumer.service.ts:67:42)
        at Runner.processEachMessage (/Users/secerzema/Desktop/packt-rxjs-cookbook/RxJS-Cookbook-
```

Figure 10.3: Dead-letter queue pattern

See also

- Apache Kafka in 6 minutes: `https://www.youtube.com/watch?v=Ch5VhJzaoaI`

- What is Kafka? by IBM: `https://www.youtube.com/watch?v=aj9CDZm0Glc`

- Kafka in 100 Seconds by Fireship: `https://www.youtube.com/watch?v=uvb00oaa3k8`

- System Design: Apache Kafka In 3 Minutes by ByteByteGo: `https://www.youtube.com/watch?v=HZklgPkboro`

- Kafka Deep Dive w/ a Ex-Meta Staff Engineer: `https://www.youtube.com/watch?v=DU8o-OTeoCc`

Going real time with gRPC streaming in NestJS

gRPC is an open-source remote procedure call framework, created by Google in 2016. Remote procedure call means that with the gRPC protocol, built upon HTTP/2, we can execute a method from another machine or computer, as if we were running it locally. The fact that it is using HTTP/2 instead of HTTP/1.1 makes a significant performance boost, since it allows multiple streams of messages over a single long-lived TCP connection, and provides support for features like multiplexing, headers compression, and bi-directional streaming. This leads to reduced latency when communicating between different services.

gRPC uses Protocol Buffers as a language-agnostic mechanism for serializing structured data, offering efficient and compact data encoding. Compared to JSON, as a standard way of exchanging data on the web, Protocol Buffers are much faster and easier to decode and store on a server. Also, gRPC can help us when building type-safe APIs that scale, since Protocol Buffers enforce type-checking, which leads to reduced errors and improved code quality.

Use cases where we can leverage gRPC protocol are communication between microservices, real-time applications like chat apps and video streaming, IoT applications, etc.

Getting ready

If you haven't used gRPC before, their official documentation might be a great starting point: `https://grpc.io/docs/what-is-grpc/introduction/`. Also, NestJS provides documentation on how to set up a gRPC microservice: `https://docs.nestjs.com/microservices/grpc`.

How to do it...

Ever wondered how food delivery apps like Wolt or Uber Eats give us real-time information about the location of a courier who is delivering our order? Well, now it's time to find out how that works under the hood. In this recipe, we are going to build a gRPC microservice in a NestJS server app that accepts the food order and, with a little bit of RxJS magic, streams to the client the results of different states of food preparation.

Step 1 – Defining a .proto file

A `.proto` file is like a blueprint that defines the structure of communication between a client and a server. By defining this Protocol Buffers structure in a `.proto/order.proto` file, we can serialize data in a more efficient way than JSON and send food order data over the network:

```
syntax = "proto3";
package order;

service FoodOrderService {
    rpc CreateOrder (stream OrderRequest)
    returns (stream OrderResponse);
}

message OrderRequest {
    string item = 1;
    int32 quantity = 2;
```

```
}

message OrderResponse {
    string id = 1;
    string item = 2;
    int32 quantity = 3;
    string status = 4;
}
```

Here's a quick breakdown of the `.proto` file definition:

1. We are using version 3 syntax for Protocol Buffers: `https://protobuf.dev/reference/ protobuf/proto3-spec/`.

2. The package helps us avoid naming conflicts between different Protocol Buffers files.

3. The service definition includes the service name, RPC method, and request and response types. The `CreateOrder` method handles a stream of `OrderRequest` messages and returns a stream of `OrderResponse` messages.

4. We define messages that we will send over the network. You can think of messages as **Data Transfer Objects (DTOs)** in the REST protocol. A message defines the structure of the data that is exchanged between the client and the server in a gRPC service.

Step 2 – Configuring a gRPC microservice

In our `main.ts` file, we will set up our food order microservice that communicates over the gRPC protocol:

```
import { MicroserviceOptions, Transport } from '@nestjs/microservices';
import { NestFactory } from '@nestjs/core';
import { join } from 'path';
import { ReflectionService } from '@grpc/reflection';
import { AppModule } from './app.module';

async function bootstrap() {
    const app = await NestFactory
    .createMicroservice<MicroserviceOptions>(
        AppModule,
        {
        transport: Transport.GRPC,
        options: {
```

```
                package: 'order',
                protoPath: join(__dirname, './proto/order.proto'),
                url: 'localhost:5000',
                onLoadPackageDefinition: (pkg, server) => {
                    new ReflectionService(pkg).addToServer(server);
                },
            },
        });
        await app.listen();
    }
    bootstrap();
```

Here, we define all the necessary options for effective gRPC communication, like transport, package name, path to `.proto` file, and server URL. Also, what you may notice is that we set up a gRPC server reflection. This allows clients to discover the available services and their methods on the server without needing the Protocol Buffers file. The benefit of this approach is easier developer experience; it is also easier to test and debug gRPC services.

Step 3 – Creating a gRPC controller

In our `order.controller.ts`, we can define the gRPC method, which will handle the creation of new food orders:

```
@Controller()
export class OrderController {
    constructor(private readonly orderService: OrderService) { }

    @GrpcStreamMethod('FoodOrderService', 'CreateOrder')
    createOrder(
        stream: Observable<OrderRequest>
    ): Observable<OrderResponse> {
        return stream.pipe(mergeMap((data: OrderRequest) =>
                        this.orderService.createOrder(data), 3));
    }
}
```

Here, we can notice a few important things:

1. With the @GrpcStreamMethod decorator, we can match the service and RPC method from our .proto file.

2. The controller accepts a new OrderRequest as an Observable stream, which means that we can pipe into that stream and leverage RxJS.

3. We can also return OrderResponse as an Observable stream.

4. With the power of the RxJS mergeMap operator, we can handle the concurrency of incoming requests. This means that no more than three orders can be processed at the same time, and other requests will be queued and processed when we have three or fewer ongoing requests.

Step 4 — Streaming food order reactive updates

In our order.service.ts, we will define a method, createOrder, that accepts new orders and returns the latest status of the specific order:

```ts
@Injectable()
export class OrderService {
    createOrder(orderRequest: OrderRequest): Observable<OrderResponse> {
        const id = crypto.randomUUID();
        const newOrder: OrderResponse = { orderRequest,
            status: OrderStatus.PENDING };
    }
    const currentOrder$ = new BehaviorSubject<OrderResponse>(newOrder);

    return currentOrder$.asObservable();
}
```

Once we accept a new order, we immediately change its status to PENDING and notify the client that the order is being processed. Over time, we will switch this status over the gRPC stream to other statuses, like ACCEPTED, PREPARING, COURIER_ON_THE_WAY, or CANCELLED.

Now, once we have gRPC streaming in place, we can use the power of RxJS to simulate reactive stream changes over time, update the order status, and notify the client about the changes:

```ts
const id = crypto.randomUUID();
const newOrder: OrderResponse = { orderRequest, id,
    status: OrderStatus.PENDING };
const orderStatus$ = new BehaviorSubject<OrderResponse>(newOrder);
```

```typescript
createOrder(orderRequest: OrderRequest): Observable<OrderResponse> {
    const id = crypto.randomUUID();
    const newOrder: OrderResponse = { ...orderRequest, id,
        status: OrderStatus.PENDING };
    const orderStatus$ = new BehaviorSubject<OrderResponse>(newOrder);

    of(newOrder)
    .pipe(
        delay(1000),
        map((order: OrderResponse) => {
            order.status = OrderStatus.ACCEPTED;
            orderStatus$.next(order);
            return order;
        }),
        delay(1000),
        map((order: OrderResponse) => {
            order.status = OrderStatus.PREPARING;
            orderStatus$.next(order);
            return order;
        }),
        delay(10000),
        map((order: OrderResponse) => {
            order.status = OrderStatus.DELIVERED;
            orderStatus$.next(order);
            return order;
        }),
        tap(() => orderStatus$.complete()),
        takeUntil(this.stop$),
    )
    .subscribe();

    return orderStatus$.asObservable();
    }
}
```

Here, we are simulating the food preparation process by simply delaying the notifications about the order status changes. At the end of a stream, we will complete the `orderStatus$` stream, because we want to notify the controller that the request has completed, and we can move on to the next concurrent requests.

Step 5 — Streaming a courier's geolocation updates

In between the `PREPARING` and `DELIVERED` statuses, we will have one more status, when the courier is delivering the food order from the venue to the customer. The way we can simulate this is simply by attaching geolocation coordinates at a certain interval:

```
switchMap((order: OrderResponse) => {
    order.status = OrderStatus.COURIER_ON_THE_WAY;

    return interval(2000).pipe(
        map(i => {
            const orderWithLocation = {
                order,
                location: { lat: 40.7128 + i * 0.1, lng: -74.0060 + i * 0.1
                }
            };
            this.orderStatus$.next(orderWithLocation);

            return orderWithLocation;
        }),
        startWith({ ...order, location: { lat: 40.7128, lng: -74.0060 } }),
        takeUntil(merge(timer(10001), this.stop$),
    );
}),
```

We can see that every two seconds, we will update the location of the courier and notify the gRPC client about the change. Also, since we have an inner Observable that we have created with the interval operator, we need to be careful about memory leaks. In cases where we need fine-grained control over when an Observable stream should end, we can use operators like `takeUntil`, which will automatically unsubscribe any observers on a given signal (in our case, emission from the timer operator after 10,001 milliseconds, or when we stop the service).

Finally, when we test our gRPC controller using an API testing tool like Postman, we can see how we are streaming data efficiently and giving clients timely notifications about changes within the system.

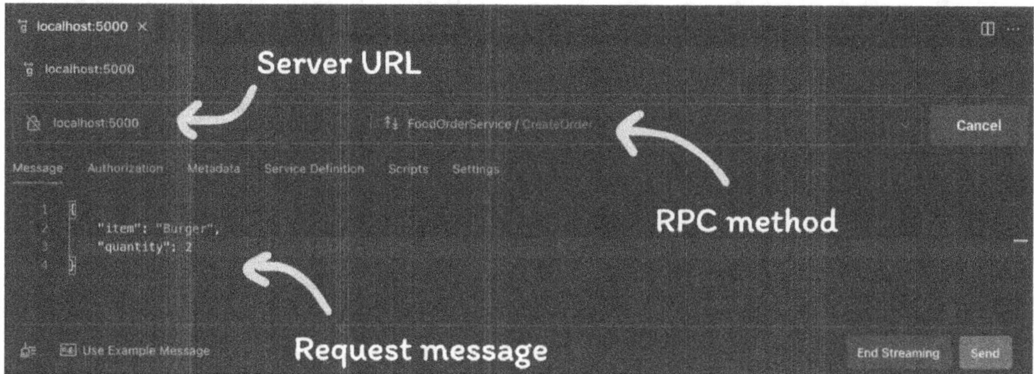

Figure 10.4: Postman gRPC request

After sending the request message, we can track our food orders in real time and know exactly when to expect our delicious meals.

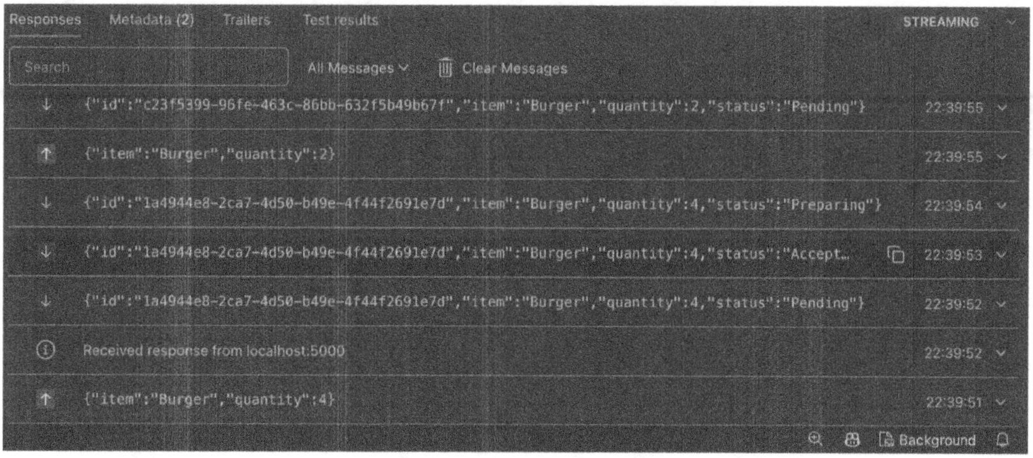

Figure 10.5: gRPC streaming

See also...

- *Getting started with gRPC* from Google: `https://www.youtube.com/watch?v=cSGBbwvW1y4`

- *What is RPC? gRPC Introduction.* from ByteByteGo: `https://www.youtube.com/watch?v=gnchfOojMk4`

- *How LinkedIn Improved Latency by 60%*: `https://www.linkedin.com/pulse/how-linkedin-improved-latency-60-deep-dive-power-google-syed-vln8c/`

- Why top companies are switching to gRPC: `https://www.youtube.com/shorts/t0ONFCY6NWI`

- Prime Reacts on gRPC: `https://www.youtube.com/watch?v=9IxE2UQqJCw`

- NestJS documentation on gRPC streaming: `https://docs.nestjs.com/microservices/grpc#grpc-streaming`

- Guide on how to use Postman to test gRPC endpoints: `https://learning.postman.com/docs/sending-requests/grpc/grpc-request-interface/`

- gRPC web: `https://github.com/grpc/grpc-web`

Learn more on Discord

To join the Discord community for this book – where you can share feedback, ask questions to the author, and learn about new releases – follow the QR code below:

`https://packt.link/RxJSCookbook`

11
Unlock Your Exclusive Benefits

Your copy of this book includes the following exclusive benefits:

- ⟳ Next-gen Packt Reader
- DRM-free PDF/ePub downloads

Follow the guide below to unlock them. The process takes only a few minutes and needs to be completed once.

Unlock this Book's Free Benefits in 3 Easy Steps

Step 1

Keep your purchase invoice ready for *Step 3*. If you have a physical copy, scan it using your phone and save it as a PDF, JPG, or PNG.

For more help on finding your invoice, visit `https://www.packtpub.com/unlock-benefits/help`.

Note: If you bought this book directly from Packt, no invoice is required. After *Step 2*, you can access your exclusive content right away.

Step 2

Scan the QR code or go to packtpub.com/unlock.

On the page that opens (similar to *Figure 11.1* on desktop), search for this book by name and select the correct edition.

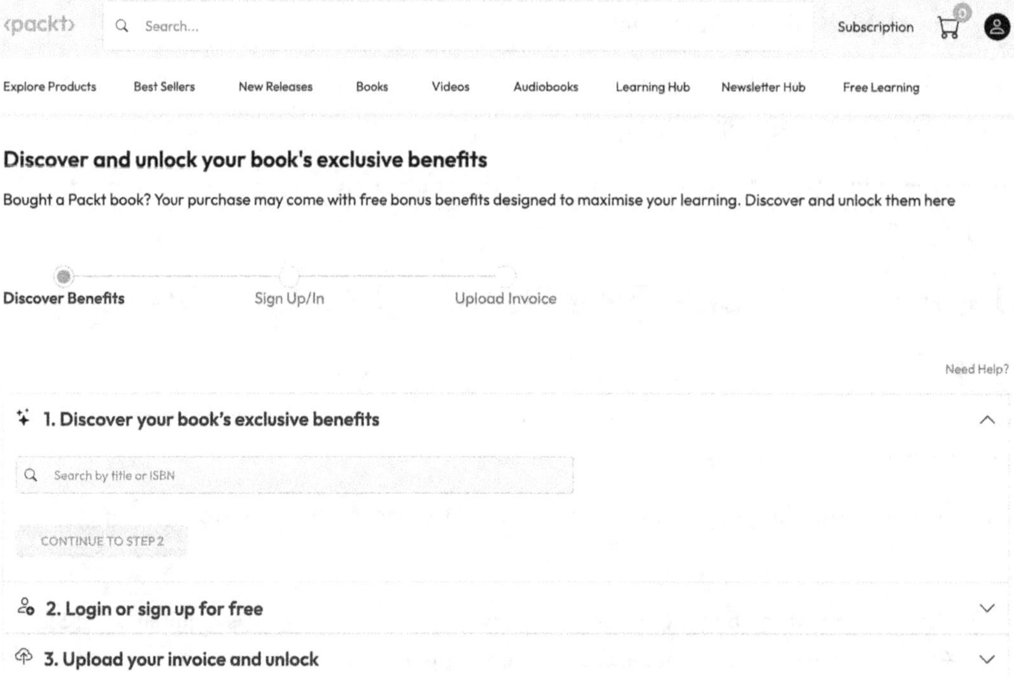

Figure 11.1: Packt unlock landing page on desktop

Step 3

After selecting your book, sign in to your Packt account or create one for free. Then upload your invoice (PDF, PNG, or JPG, up to 10 MB). Follow the on-screen instructions to finish the process.

Need help?

If you get stuck and need help, visit `https://www.packtpub.com/unlock-benefits/help` for a detailed FAQ on how to find your invoices and more. This QR code will take you to the help page.

Note: If you are still facing issues, reach out to `customercare@packt.com`.

Index

N

native HTMLAudioElement 61

NestJS
gRPC streaming 262, 263
REST API microservices, crafting 244

network errors
catching 14
circuit breaker pattern, using 18-21
exponential back off pattern, using 17
handling 14
retry pattern, using 15, 16

network-first offline strategy 195

network requests
concurrent requests, handling 12
handling 8
handling, in parallel 10
handling, in sequence 8, 9

NgRx 116, 150
actions, dispatching 120, 121
effect errors, testing 121
effects, testing 120, 121
integration test, setting up 119
mock actions, setting up 119
mock store, setting up 117
store selectors, testing 118
used, for testing complex
	state management 116

NgRx docs
reference link 159

NgRx effect testing
reference link 122

NgRx for state management
app state, extending with
	NgRx Router State 155-157
meta-reducers, creating 157, 158
NgRx store, configuring 151-153

selectors, defining 154, 155
side effects, handling 153, 154
using, in Angular 150, 151

NgRx Router State
used, for extending app state 155

NgRx testing selectors
reference link 122

NgRx testing strategies
reference link 122

O

observables 68

offline-first apps 187
benefits 187, 188
strategy 188, 189

offline-ready applications
building, with RxDB 180

offline-ready applications, RxDB
recipe schema, defining 181, 182
recipe, searching with RxQuery 184, 185
RxDatabase, creating 182
subscribing, to ChangeEvent 183, 184

operators 68

optimistic update pattern 206
custom operator, applying 207, 208
custom operator, creating 206, 207
implementing 206
offline mode 208, 209

P

particles.js library 84

partition 249

pattern matching 41

PerformanceObserver Web API
reference link 133

packtpub.com

Subscribe to our online digital library for full access to over 7,000 books and videos, as well as industry leading tools to help you plan your personal development and advance your career. For more information, please visit our website.

Why subscribe?

- Spend less time learning and more time coding with practical eBooks and Videos from over 4,000 industry professionals
- Improve your learning with Skill Plans built especially for you
- Get a free eBook or video every month
- Fully searchable for easy access to vital information
- Copy and paste, print, and bookmark content

At www.packt.com, you can also read a collection of free technical articles, sign up for a range of free newsletters, and receive exclusive discounts and offers on Packt books and eBooks.

Other Books You May Enjoy

If you enjoyed this book, you may be interested in these other books by Packt:

Reactive Patterns with RxJS and Angular Signals

Lamis Chebbi

ISBN: 978-1-83508-770-1

- Get to grips with RxJS core concepts such as Observables, subjects, and operators
- Use the marble diagram in reactive patterns
- Delve into stream manipulation, including transforming and combining them
- Understand memory leak problems using RxJS and best practices to avoid them
- Build reactive patterns using Angular Signals and RxJS
- Explore different testing strategies for RxJS apps
- Discover multicasting in RxJS and how it can resolve complex problems
- Build a complete Angular app reactively using the latest features of RxJS and Angular

Effective Angular

Roberto Heckers

ISBN: 978-1-80512-553-2

- Create Nx monorepos ready to handle hundreds of Angular applications
- Reduce complexity in Angular with the standalone API, inject function, control flow, and Signals
- Effectively manage application state using Signals, RxJS, and NgRx
- Build dynamic components with projection, TemplateRef, and defer blocks
- Perform end-to-end and unit testing in Angular with Cypress and Jest
- Optimize Angular performance, prevent bad practices, and automate deployments

Packt is searching for authors like you

If you're interested in becoming an author for Packt, please visit authors.packtpub.com and apply today. We have worked with thousands of developers and tech professionals, just like you, to help them share their insight with the global tech community. You can make a general application, apply for a specific hot topic that we are recruiting an author for, or submit your own idea.

Share your thoughts

Now you've finished *RxJS Cookbook for Reactive Programming*, we'd love to hear your thoughts! Scan the QR code below to go straight to the Amazon review page for this book and share your feedback or leave a review on the site that you purchased it from.

https://packt.link/r/178862405X

Your review is important to us and the tech community and will help us make sure we're delivering excellent quality content.